Christopher J. Carlin

Collected Papers

III

PHAENOMENOLOGICA

COLLECTION FONDÉE PAR H. L. VAN BREDA ET PUBLIÉE SOUS
LE PATRONAGE DES CENTRES D'ARCHIVES-HUSSERL

22

ALFRED SCHUTZ

Collected Papers

III

ALFRED SCHUTZ

Collected Papers

III

Studies in Phenomenological Philosophy

EDITED BY
I. SCHUTZ

WITH AN INTRODUCTION BY
ARON GURWITSCH

MARTINUS NIJHOFF / THE HAGUE

Photomechanical reprint, 1975

PRINTED IN THE NETHERLANDS

ISBN 90 247 5090 3

CONTENTS

EDITOR'S NOTE

The COLLECTED PAPERS contained in this third and final volume: STUDIES IN PHENOMENOLOGICAL PHILOSOPHY were originally published between the years 1953–1958 with the exception of the paper: "William James's Concept of the Stream of Thought Phenomenologically Interpreted," which was published in 1941.

I wish to express my deep indebtedness and my warm thanks to H. L. Van Breda, Rudolf Böhm, Arvid Brodersen, Dorion Cairns, Arthur Goddard, Aron Gurwitsch, Robert Jordan, Frederick Kersten, Thomas Luckmann, Maurice and Lois Natanson and Jacques Taminiaux who all have helped in the preparation of the three volumes of the COLLECTED PAPERS and without whose invaluable assistance and cooperation this task never could have been accomplished.

The papers were originally published in the following form: "William James's Concept of the Stream of Thought Phenomenologically Interpreted," *Philosophy and Phenomenological Research* (hereafter referred to as PPR), Vol. I, June 1941; "Edmund Husserl's Ideas, Volume II," PPR, Vol. XIII, March 1953; "Phenomenology and the Foundations of the Social Sciences (Ideas, Volume III by Edmund Husserl)," PPR, Vol. XIII, June 1953; "The Problem of Transcendental Intersubjectivity in Husserl" was published in German as "Das Problem der transzendentalen Intersubjektivität bei Husserl," *Philosophische Rundschau*, Vol. V, 1957 (note: The discussion by Eugen Fink and the reply by Alfred Schutz are not included in the German paper; however, there is also a French translation, by Maurice de Gandillac, which does include that discussion as well as the comments of other discussants: "Le Problème de l'intersubjectivité transcendentale chez Husserl," in *Husserl* (Cahiers de Royaumont, Philosophie No. III), Paris: Les Éditions de Minuit, 1959); "Type and Eidos in Husserl's Late Philosophy," PPR, Vol. XX, December 1959; "Max Scheler's Philosophy," in *Les Philosophes célèbres*, edited by Maurice Merleau-Ponty, Paris: Lucien Mazenod, 1956 (in French translation); "Max Scheler on Epistemology and Ethics," *Review of Metaphysics*, Vol. XI, December 1957 and March 1958 (note: Section D on "Scheler's Criticism of Kant's Philosophy," which was originally intended to be part of the essay, has been added); "Some Structures of the Life-World," translated from the German by Aron Gurwitsch, appears in print for the first time; Professor Gurwitsch's Introduction first appeared under the title "The Common-Sense World as Social Reality – A Discourse on Alfred Schutz," *Social Research*, Vol. XXIX, Spring 1962. Grateful acknowledgment is made to the publishers and editors of these journals and books for permission to republish these papers.

I wish to add a special word of thanks to Lester Embree for preparing the Index and to Mr. G. H. Priem of Martinus Nijhoff for his help and cooperation.

Ilse Schutz

PREFACE

Alfred Schutz devoted his life to a clarification of the foundations of the social sciences. His first formulation of the pertinent problems is contained in DER SINNHAFTE AUFBAU DER SOZIALEN WELT, EINE EINLEITUNG IN DIE VERSTEHENDE SOZIOLOGIE, now available in a second unrevised German edition with an English translation in preparation. Since 1932, the date of this work, Alfred Schutz pursued painstaking and detailed investigations of issues which arose in connection with his early endeavors. These investigations were originally published as a series of essays and monographs over a period of about twenty years and are now assembled in the COLLECTED PAPERS of which this is the third and final volume. They form a unitary whole insofar as a common core of problems and theoretical ideas is presented from varying perspectives. Together DER SINNHAFTE AUFBAU DER SOZIALEN WELT and the three volumes of COLLECTED PAPERS set forth a comprehensive and consistent theory of the world of everyday life as the reality with which the social sciences are essentially concerned.

Alfred Schutz was preparing a systematic presentation of his theory and of the results of his investigations into the structures of the world of everyday life when death overtook him. The manuscript containing the final statement of his philosophical and sociological thinking was not completely ready for publication at the time of his death. It is now being brought into book form by Professor Thomas Luckmann, one of his former students. The book will first be published in German under the title: DIE STRUKTUREN DER LEBENSWELT. A translation into English is planned.

Alfred Schutz's philosophical and sociological work is being continued by his colleagues and students. His influence is growing steadily. At no time during his life was his work as well known and as widely discussed as it is at present. The consistency of his thought becomes more apparent with each publication of his writings. The reader will find in DIE STRUKTUREN DER LEBENS-WELT the unified presentation of Alfred Schutz's theory of the world of everyday life.

Aron Gurwitsch

INTRODUCTION

by

Aron Gurwitsch

In these pages I propose to concentrate on a certain group of problems that not only were of primary importance in Alfred Schutz's thinking but also hold a central position in contemporary philosophical thought, especially in the work of Edmund Husserl and later authors who belong to what may be called the phenomenological movement in a broad sense of the term. These problems concern the world of common sense, the world of daily life – *Lebenswelt,* as Husserl calls it – and our experience of that world. In pointing out the originality of Schutz's contributions in this area of thought I hope also to indicate, though perhaps in a rather sketchy way, his position within contemporary philosophical thought.

I

Since Schutz repeatedly refers to Husserl's writings, let us begin by recalling briefly Husserl's first descriptive characterization of what he later called the "world of the natural attitude" (*Welt der natürlichen Einstellung*).[1] By this Husserl means the world in which we find ourselves at every moment of our life, taken exactly as it presents itself to us in our everyday experience. This world is indefinitely extended in space and time; it comprises both natural material things and cultural objects, like utensils, tools, objects of value; we encounter in it animal creatures as well as fellow human beings, to whom we stand in manifold relations. It is in this world that we have our existence,

---

[1] Edmund Husserl, *Ideas: General Introduction to Pure Phenomenology,* tr. from the German by W. R. Boyce Gibson, London, 1931, §§ 27 ff. (hereafter referred to as *Ideas*).

carry on our activities, pursue all our goals. We always take our bearings on this world of our daily experience, and have a certain familiarity with what we encounter in it.

This familiarity, it must be stressed, is of an entirely different kind and style from scientific knowledge, especially in the modern sense, and in no way depends on, or is derived from, that knowledge. In fact, when Husserl in his last works came to denote the "world of the natural attitude" as "life-world" (*Lebenswelt*), he did so in order to contrast explicitly this world as it is given to our immediate experience, independent of and previous to scientific knowledge, with the universe as constructed and elaborated by science, especially modern physical science – to contrast it, that is, with the mathematized universe or with the universe seen under the aspect of its possible mathematization.[2] Obviously the social scientist, the philosopher of the social sciences and of social life, takes as his point of departure not the idealized and mathematized constructs of the physical sciences, but rather the world of common sense as the scene of all social relationships and actions.

A primary characteristic of our experience of, and our attitude toward, the life-world is the fact, insisted on by both Husserl and Schutz, that this world is taken for granted. Its existence is never doubted or questioned, and this holds for its natural as well as its socio-cultural aspects. To be sure, doubts may and do arise, and as often as not are resolved in the course of experience; it may and does happen that things turn out to be different from what they were believed to be at first. Such questions, doubts, corrections, however, always concern details within the world, particular mundane existents, and never the world as such and as a whole. Whatever activity we engage in, whether practical, theoretical, or other, is pursued within the life-world, whose simple acceptance proves an essential precondition of every activity. It is through its role as general background or horizon with regard to all our mental activities that the life-world appears and discloses itself as accepted and taken for granted. To express it differently, the belief in the existence of the life-world – a

[2] Husserl, *Die Krisis der Europäischen Wissenschaften und die transzendentale Phänomenologie*, The Hague, 1954, §§ 9 ff. and 33 ff. (hereafter referred to as *Krisis*); *Erfahrung und Urteil*, Prague, 1939; Hamburg, 1954, § 10.

belief that as a rule is not even formulated – accompanies, pervades, and permeates all our mental life, since this life takes place within the world of common experience and is always concerned with certain particular mundane existents.[3] This holds also in the case of doubting and questioning. Since doubt concerns only particular things or their properties and particular events in the life-world, it cannot occur except on the basis of the general belief, silently and implicitly accepted as a matter of course, in the existence of that world. The unquestioned and unchallenged certainty concerning the world at large underlies, supports, and enters into every particular mental activity.

We do not, each one of us, experience the life-world as a private world; on the contrary, we take it for a public world, common to all of us, that is, for an intersubjective world.[4] Not only do we encounter our fellow-men within the life-world as this world is given to us, but we also take it for granted that they are confronted with the same world and the same mundane existence as we are. Every one of us perceives the world and the things within the world from the particular point of view at which he happens to be placed at the moment, and hence under aspects and from perspectives that vary in dependence on, and in accordance with, the point of view. But notwithstanding such differences as to manner of appearance and presentation, we regard the life-world, as a matter of course, as identical for us and for our fellow-men and, quite in general, for everybody (*Jedermann*). Finally, we take it for granted that our fellow-men take the world for granted in substantially the same way we do. Because of this thoroughgoing reciprocity we can act and work with our fellow-men in the multiple forms that such cooperation can assume. We orient our actions with regard to what we anticipate theirs to be, and we expect them to do the same.

---

[3] *Ideas*, § 30; *Erfahrung und Urteil*, § 7.
[4] *Ideas*, § 29; *Formale und transzendentale Logik*, Halle, 1929, §§ 95 ff.; *Cartesian Meditations*, tr. from the German by Dorion Cairns, The Hague, 1960, § 43; *Krisis*, pp. 166 ff. In the fifth of his Cartesian Meditations, Husserl develops a theory of intersubjectivity in the setting of transcendental and constitutive phenomenology. Schutz devoted a thorough critical analysis to Husserl's theory in one of his last publications, "Das Problem der transzendentalen Intersubjektivität bei Husserl," in *Philosophische Rundschau*, Vol. V, 1957. An English translation is included in the present volume. Here I can but mention Schutz's analysis, for a discussion of it would lead us too far afield.

To complete this necessarily sketchy survey of Husserl's theories used by Schutz as points of both reference and departure, mention should be made of the "horizonal structure of experience," especially perceptual consciousness. Here I have in view mainly what Husserl calls "inner horizon." [5] Every particular perception yields more than merely what it offers in genuine sense experience. Through every perception the object perceived appears, according to the point of view from which it is observed, under a certain aspect, from a certain side, in a certain orientation. Yet its unilateral appearance includes references to other appearances, to aspects under which the object will present itself when it is seen from a different point of view, to phenomena that will be observed under certain conditions not realized at the present moment, and so on. By virtue of the horizonal structure of experience, every object, even a novel one, appears under the horizon of a certain pre-acquaintanceship, however schematic and inarticulate, a certain familiarity, however dim and vague. That is to say, it presents itself in the light of a certain typicality, and with a sense determined by that typicality.[6] Apart from those beings (rather few in number) that have for us the character and value of uniqueness, the objects we encounter and with which we deal do not present themselves as individual and singular things, but rather as things and creatures of some sort and kind. What we perceive are houses, trees, animals, and the like. We expect of them a more or less well defined type of behavior – for example, a typical mode of locomotion – even though the animal perceived displays no such behavior at the present moment.

Typification as a general feature of perceptual experience denotes a very important and fundamental problem of general phenomenology, for typification is certainly at the origin of conceptual consciousness, if it is not itself conceptualization in an incipient or at least germinal form. Seen from this general perspective, the phenomenon of typification calls for further analysis and elucidation along the lines of constitutive phenomenology in Husserl's sense. Schutz, however, did not orient his work in this direction, though he was of course fully aware of it as a possible line of research. Intentionally he abides by what Husserl calls

---

[5] *Ideas*, § 44; *Cartesian Meditations*, §§ 19 ff.; *Erfahrung und Urteil*, § 8.
[6] *Erfahrung und Urteil*, §§ 80 and 83a.

the "natural attitude," that is, he deliberately abstains from raising questions of transcendental constitution and pursues his phenomenological analyses within the framework of the "natural attitude."

II

For the presentation of Schutz's conception of the common-sense world as social reality,[7] the phenomenon of typification may well serve as point of departure. Rather than dealing in general terms with typification as such, Schutz concerns himself with its specification, and especially with the variation of specified typification. Encountering an animal, I perceive it one time as a quadruped, another time as a dog, still another time as a dog of a special sort. In every case the animal is perceived as typified; it appears with the sense of a certain typicality. According to the type in question, certain aspects, features, and characteristics of the animal acquire emphasis and prominence, while others may pass almost unnoticed. My present interests and the system of relevances corresponding to them determine which form of typification will prevail at a given moment, every shift in my interest being accompanied by, and entailing, a change in typification.

Of still greater importance is that specification of typification which differs from society to society and, within the same society, varies in the course of its history. This is best illustrated by cultural objects like tools, instruments, and utensils of all sorts, which serve, and refer to, specific human activities and needs, the latter also being of a typical nature. To a stranger not familiar with our society and civilization, the things and utensils we use, whose typical use and typical meaning are with us a matter of course, will appear in a light highly different from that in which we perceive them. Conversely, if we come to a strange society or discover the material remainders of a civilization of the past,

---

[7] This account is based mainly on the following articles by Schutz: "Phenomenology and the Social Sciences"; "On Multiple Realities"; "Choosing Among Projects of Action"; "Common-sense and Scientific Interpretation of Human Action"; "Language, Language Disturbances, and the Texture of Consciousness"; "Concept and Theory Formation in the Social Sciences"; "Symbol, Reality and Society"; "Husserl's Importance for the Social Sciences." All these articles are republished in *Collected Papers I: The Problem of Social Reality;* cf. p. XXIV for the journals in which they first appeared. I here refer to these articles once and for all, and shall refrain from giving a special reference every time a conception is discussed.

we are more often than not at a loss to "understand" those utensils, since we do not know, at the outset, their typical purposes or, consequently, their typical uses.

Hereby we are brought before the social nature and origin of the world in which we find ourselves, and which as to both its natural and cultural aspects is an interpreted world throughout. Obviously, this interpretation is not of our own making. On the contrary, it has been handed down to us by our elders and has silently been accepted by us as a matter of course. We have been told and shown by our teachers and parents what the things mean, how they are to be used – that is, how they are interpreted and typified in our society. Not only were we born into our socio-cultural world, but also we have grown into it. Growing into our world and into our society, we have acquired a certain language that embodies the interpretations and typifications in question and is their vehicle as well as their medium of expression. Our lifelong intercourse with both our elders and our contemporaries appears in a certain sense as one continuous process of acquisition of, and practice in, the typifying interpretations that prevail in our society and come to be accepted by us as patterns to be followed unquestioningly.

Along with the language spoken in our society, we acquire a great number of recipes of all sorts: rules for handling things, modes of conduct and behavior in typical situations. We learn that we have to apply typical means in order to obtain typical results. Such knowledge is continuously confirmed in the course of our experience, in circumstances both trivial and consequential. Riding on a train, we are to display a certain typical behavior, which we know is expected from a railway passenger. Whoever desires to enter a career or a vocation knows that he has to comply with certain prerequisites, to fulfill certain conditions, to pursue a typical course of action, if he is to satisfy his desire.

Two features are characteristic of all these acquisitions, recipes, rules, modes of conduct and behavior. In the first place, they are socially approved. This does not necessarily mean that they are sanctioned by laws or in some other formal way, or that they are enforced by special agencies. The overwhelming majority of the rules and recipes are complied with as a matter of course, and are hardly ever explicitly formulated, still less reflected upon.

They define the modes of procedure and conduct regarded as correct, good, and natural by the society in question; they are the ways in which "one" does things.[8] Their social approval in the form of inexplicit and silent acceptance and compliance is but another expression and aspect of their social derivation. Secondly, the recipes under discussion are followed and observed because, and only because, of their usefulness. According to Schutz, the pragmatic motive dominates our daily life in the common-sense world. Hence as long as the recipes permit us to obtain desired typical results, they are unquestioningly applied and complied with; they are not put into question or doubt unless the results fail to materialize.

All the acquisitions under discussion – language, the multiple typifications embodied in language, the recipes of all sorts, the rules for handling and manipulating things, the modes of conduct, behavior, and action in typical situations – constitute together what Schutz calls the "stock of knowledge at hand." This is the sediment of the whole history of my life; it comprises what was passed on to me by those who taught me and whose teachings I accepted on the strength of their authority, as well as what I acquired through intercourse with my associates. Hence my "stock of knowledge" is never completed; on the contrary, it enlarges as long as my life goes on.

Only a very small part of it has originated in my personal experience; the bulk of it is socially derived, handed down to me and accepted by me. In fact, going beyond Schutz's explicit formulations, but keeping in line with the trend and spirit of his theory, we may say that all my personal acquisitions presuppose some socially derived "stock of knowledge at hand," inasmuch as they are inserted into and have to find their place within this socially derived setting. No personal acquisition is ever isolated. Whatever new acquisition I make in the course of my experience must fit into my "stock of knowledge at hand," must be in continuity, even in some conformity, with what at the moment in question I know about the world; and what I know includes both my previous personal acquisitions and what I have been taught and

---

[8] It would be of interest to compare Schutz's analysis of conduct in everyday life – socially determined because socially derived – with Heidegger's interpretation of the anonymity of *"das Man,"* in *Sein und Zeit,* § 27.

told by others in the course of my growing into the socio-cultural world in which I live. The "stock of knowledge at hand" forms the frame of reference, interpretation, and orientation for my life in the world of daily experience, for my dealing with things, coping with situations, coming to terms with fellow human beings.

With his concept of "stock of knowledge at hand" Schutz, I submit, made an important contribution toward further elucidating our specific familiarity with the world of daily experience, a familiarity that Husserl distinguished from scientific knowledge, especially in the modern sense. That the world of common sense is taken for granted – not only its existence but also the way in which it is interpreted – is a consequence and another expression of unquestioned acceptance of the "stock of knowledge at hand." Just as only details within the common-sense world, only particular mundane existents, may become doubtful, and never the world as a whole, so does the "stock of knowledge" in its entirety never become questionable, but only certain elements pertaining to it. This happens when we are confronted with a situation in which the conventional rules fail us in the furtherance and pursuit of our practical goals and interests.

As mentioned before, we take it for granted that fellow-men exist and that they are human beings like ourselves. This implies that we "assume" them to have a "stock of knowledge at hand," as we have one, and furthermore that we "assume" their "stock of knowledge" to be of substantially the same kind as ours. It must be stressed that this "assumption" is not explicitly, still less deliberately, made, as though we were free to choose a different assumption. Nor is it an assumption in the sense of an hypothesis that we expect to be confirmed by future experience but for whose invalidation we must equally be prepared. The term "assumption" must not be understood in the proper sense; it carries no theoretical connotations. Like the acceptance of the life-world itself, it is an unquestioned belief and certainty, on which we act and proceed but which is not made a topic for reflection and is not even rendered explicit, unless we engage in philosophical inquiries. In fact, the task of philosophy may be defined as disclosure and scrutiny of "assumptions" that are taken for granted and even pass unnoticed.

To return to this "assumption" concerning my fellow-men, it has its roots in the fact that I encounter them in the same world in which I find myself. They were born and have grown into the same world. Their "stock of knowledge at hand" derives from the same social source as mine. But the "assumption" that their "stock of knowledge at hand" is substantially the same as mine calls for some qualifications. In the first place, the stock of knowledge admits of degrees of clarity, distinction, and precision, and therefore even when I know the same things as one of my fellow-men, I may and do know them differently. In the second place, I am an expert only in a very small field, in which I have had genuine experience and have acquired first-hand knowledge; in all other fields I am a layman. Thus I know different things from those known by my fellow-men. I know, however, that there are experts in those fields in which I am a layman, and that, if circumstances demand it, I can resort to the advice of the several experts, the doctor, the lawyer, the architect, and so on. Especially in a society like ours, in which division of labor and specialization prevail, the available knowledge is not in its entirety in the possession of every member, but rather is distributed among professional groups. Awareness of this social distribution also belongs to the "stock of knowledge at hand."

Living in the world of daily experience, I am normally not a disinterested observer, still less a theoretician, but an actor who pursues certain aims and goals and tries to accomplish his objectives. The world in which I find myself is not given to me, at least not primarily, as a field of observation that I survey in an attitude of neutrality. On the contrary, in my very pursuing my goals and objectives I am involved in whatever interests I have to further. Because of this involvement I do not simply belong to society at large, but occupy a certain place and position within it: as a member of the profession I have chosen, of the subgroup into which I was born, and so forth. From the vantage point of my position within society I perceive the world in which I live and pursue my goals and purposes. That I occupy my present position within society is the result of the whole history of my life. It is due to the circumstances, partly imposed on me, partly chosen by me, which in the course of my personal history have contributed toward making me become what I am. In the terminology of Schutz, I am in a "biographically determined situation," which is the sediment of my personal past and continues to change as long as I live, developing in continuity with my past. My "biographical situation" is given to me, and to me alone; I do not share it with anybody.

My "because motives," sharply distinguished by Schutz from "in-order-to motives," have their roots in my past, which determines my present "biographical situation." Questions as to why somebody acts as he does, pursues certain goals rather than others, has conceived for himself this life plan and not a different one, refer to "because motives" and cannot be answered except in terms of the life history of the person concerned. As an actor, however, I know hardly anything about my "because motives," since I am involved in my actions and live in them. To become aware of my "because motives" I have to suspend the ongoing action, turn back to my past, and refer to it the goals I am pursuing. I am free to do so, but then I transform myself into an observer of myself and am no longer an actor. In contradistinction to my "because motives," my "in-order-to motives" are always given to me in my very acting. In fact, I act in order to bring about a certain state of affairs, and I endeavor to find and apply the means that will permit me to reach that goal. Hence I am always aware of my "in-order-to motives" as the centralizing factor of my conduct.

All my goals and objectives form an hierarchical order and originate in my "biographically determined situation." The latter is also the source of my systems of relevancy, both my permanent ones and those that are transient, shifting with my "purpose at hand." The system of relevancy that prevails at a given moment depends on the goals I am pursuing and also, as mentioned before, determines my typifications. My actions as well as my projects are oriented toward my goals and purposes, and are organized in terms of my systems of relevancy. Planning is defined by Schutz as acting in imagination, more precisely as rehearsing in imagination a course of action that I endeavor to lay out for myself. In all my acting as well as my planning I am guided by my "stock of knowledge at hand," faulty and deficient as it may be. Circumstances beyond my control may occur, which I had no means of anticipating. It may also happen that I misjudge

circumstances, act without sufficiently complete knowledge of
them, fail to allow for future developments I could have foreseen,
and the like. Whatever criticism I may later come to express with
regard to any of my actions, they are always oriented and directed
by the knowledge at my disposal. That is to say, my actions and
plans have a certain meaning for me. They have that meaning
with respect to the goals, more or less ultimate, that I am pursuing, that is, my goals in their hierarchical order and in the
light of my "stock of knowledge at hand." This notion of the
meaning that an action or plan of action has for the actor himself
is what Max Weber has in mind in speaking of *subjektiver* or
gemeinter Sinn.[9] It will presently be encountered again within
the context of my understanding of my fellow-men, but it must
be pointed out that the notion arises even when I consider my
own action and planning.

It is taken for granted by me that my fellow-men perceive the
world and act within it at their places and positions as I do at
mine, and that, like me, each of them has his unique "biographically determined situation" given to him and to him alone. Yet
we all live in one and the same world. My fellow-men see the
same things I see, though they see them differently, from different
perspectives. While I see a thing from "here," that is, from the
place where I happen to be now, the Other sees it from his standpoint, which is different from mine and for me is "there." Accordingly, certain objects are now "within my reach" – of hearing,
seeing, grasping, for example – or within my manipulatory
sphere, but outside his, and vice versa. Furthermore, our goals
and systems of relevancy cannot be the same, since the "biographically determined situations" in which they originate must by
necessity differ for different persons.

Two idealizations, termed by Schutz the "general thesis of the
reciprocity of perspectives," come into play here. The first is
the "interchangeability of standpoints." I take it for granted that
I can put myself at the place now occupied by a fellow-man,
so as to see things from his point of view and his perspective, and
that he can place himself at my actual point of observation; and
by the same token, that objects beyond my actual reach but

---

[9] Max Weber, *Gesammelte Aufsätze zur Wissenschaftslehre*, Tübingen, 1922, pp.
405 ff., 503 ff., 508 ff.; see also pp. 334 and 336.

within the reach of my fellow-man can be brought within my reach and still, under certain conditions, remain within his as well. The other idealization leads us to the congruency of different systems of relevancy. We take it for granted – and we "assume" our fellow-men to do the same – that differences of perspectives originating in differences of "biographically determined situations" can be eliminated or considered immaterial, and that therefore different systems of relevancy can be made conformable. Thus we arrive at a common world comprising identical objects with identical qualities and properties, identically interpreted by all of us – "identical" to the extent to which such identity is required for practical purposes of cooperation and collaboration.

With his notion of "stock of knowledge at hand ," his theory of the social origin of that knowledge, and his "general thesis of the reciprocity of perspectives," Schutz makes a most important contribution toward the analysis of the phenomenon of intersubjectivity. To see this, one has only to consider these conceptions in conjunction. The world of our common-sense experience and daily life is an interpreted world, having sense and meaning for us; and as thus interpreted it is taken for granted. Its interpretation is socially derived, and this holds not only for the bulk of the content and detail of the interpretation but also, and chiefly, for its style, that is, the general lines along which the world as a whole as well as particular mundane existents are conceived and understood. Knowledge socially derived – which, it may be added, is to be communicated and passed on to others – is by its very nature socialized knowledge throughout. Socialized knowledge obviously stands under the condition of the "reciprocity of perspectives."

Intersubjectivity denotes in the first place the character of the life-world as a public world. Herein is implied the possibility of tuning in my understanding of things and events, my planning and acting, with that of my fellow-men. This, in turn, means that my acts and activities contain references to fellow human beings, both to my contemporaries, who within the limits of the aforementioned qualification may be said to share with me a "stock of knowledge at hand," and to my elders, from whom I derived that "stock of knowledge." Such references, however, are not to determined particular individuals, but rather to "whomever it may concern," that is, to everybody and anybody who lives in our socio-cultural world, is a member of our group, whose systems of relevancy are not only compatible but also congruent and conformable with those that prevail in our society because they are approved in it. The references are to fellow-men of a certain specified kind but, within the limits of this specification, to anonymous ones. By the same token, the world of daily experience appears as social reality, as a world common to all of us and hence as objective, the sense of its objectivity being essentially determined by its anonymity.[10] This anonymity manifests itself most clearly in the case of cultural objects. A utensil, for example, refers both to an anonymous producer and to anonymous users – to anyone who avails himself of it in a typical way in order to accomplish a specific typical purpose.

III

Both intersubjectivity and, closely connected if not identical with it, the social character of the world of common experience can be disclosed and brought out by analysis of the planning and acting of a single individual considered as solitary – without allowing for actual social relationships in the proper sense. This possibility seems to suggest that the life-world's character as a social world is not acquired through additional features being superimposed on it, as though it had not initially exhibited such features. One of Schutz's original contributions consists in his contention that the social character belongs to the life-world essentially and intrinsically. That world is a social and intersubjective world from the outset and throughout; it does not become so subsequently, as was maintained in a certain sense by Husserl.

Turning to social relationships in the proper sense, we have to distinguish, according to Schutz, what he calls the "face-to-face relationship" between "consociates" from all other relationships. The face-to-face relationship is defined as actual co-pre-

---

[10] It goes without saying that anonymity is constitutive of the notion of objectivity on every level, but the connection between these two concepts cannot be pursued here, since we have to confine ourselves to that form of objectivity which prevails on the level of common sense.

sence of consociates, who share a community of space during a certain length of time, be it even for only a short moment. Of such a nature is the meeting of old friends exchanging ideas or planning some common action; but in a fugitive and superficial form the face-to-face relationship also obtains in the casual conversation between strangers who have never seen each other before and do not expect to meet again – for example, passengers who happen to be seated side by side in a railway car. Whatever degree of intimacy or fugacity the relation may have in a given instance, consociates share a "vivid present." By means of the words they exchange and by their immediate observation of gestures and other physiognomical expressions, consociates grasp one another's thought, plans, hopes, fears, though only partially and fragmentarily. As long as the face-to-face relationship lasts, the consociates partake in one another's lives; their biographies intertwine; as Schutz used to formulate it, "consociates grow older together." Here, and here alone, do the partners grasp one another in their unique individuality; the selves of consociates mutually reveal themselves more or less superficially, fragmentarily, and fugitively, according to the lesser or greater degree of intimacy in their relation.

No other social relationship exhibits those distinctive features by virtue of which the face-to-face relationship acquires the quality of a meeting of persons as unique individuals. In all other forms of social relationship we have to resort to typification. We have to typify the personality of our partner, his motives, his attitudes, his general behavior, and the like – even if in the past we had with him a great many face-to-face relationships of an intimate nature. When I write a letter to my absent friend and submit him a proposal, I have to typify what I know about him and form some idea of his likely reaction, in order to formulate my proposal in terms acceptable to him. These typifications admit of varying degrees of anonymity. When anonymity becomes complete, the typified individuals appear as interchangeable, as is illustrated by an example to which Schutz repeatedly refers. Putting a letter in a mail box, I expect that people whom I never met, and in all likelihood will never meet, will behave in a certain typical way (called handling the mail), so that my letter will arrive at its destination and be read by the addressee, whom perhaps I also do not know or expect ever to meet, and the final result will be that within some "reasonable" time I shall receive the commodity I ordered.

In all our activities within the social world we have to rely on our fellow-men conducting themselves in typical ways in typical situations. Except in the face-to-face relationship, we do not deal with consociates, that is, individuals as such, but rather with typified individuals to whom a certain typical role or function (socially approved) is assigned, and according to the degree of anonymity of the typification, these individuals appear more or less exclusively in the light of the functions they are expected to perform in typical ways (also socially approved if not institutionalized or explicitly sanctioned by the legal order). But in typifying my partners, unknown to me, I must also typify myself – assume a typical role, see myself in it, and perform it in the way I assume my typified partners expect me to perform it. While riding in a train, for instance, I have to conduct myself in the way I know the typical railway employee expects the typical passenger to behave.

Such typification and self-typification permit me to tune in, and interlock my typical behavior with what I may reasonably expect to be the behavior of my typified partners. All social interaction is based on the unformulated assumption that I stand a chance to attain my objectives provided I act in a typical, socially approved way, an assumption implying the equally unformulated expectancy that my more or less anonymous partners will also conduct themselves in accordance with the requirements of the roles assigned to them. With increasing typification, and corresponding standardization of the ways in which the functions are performed, the chance is obviously enhanced.

This brings us to the phenomenon of "understanding" our fellow-men. What is here in question is not understanding in a theoretical sense, or the kind that a detached and disinterested observer might have, but rather the form of understanding prevailing in the actual practice of social life, without which no cooperation or social interaction would be possible. To refer to the example mentioned before, writing to an addressee unknown to me, I expect him not only to read my letter, but also to act on it; that is, I expect him to appropriate and to assume my motives in a certain sense. I write him that letter *in order to* obtain the commodity in question, and I expect him to ship it to me *because of* my desire as expressed in my letter. In other words, typifying my partner, in whom I see a seller of the commodity, I rely on an expectancy that my "in-order-to motive" will become his "because motive" (this "reciprocity of motives," as Schutz calls it, depends on the aforementioned "general thesis of the reciprocity of perspectives").

Understanding as here meant has the sense of anticipating my partner's likely actions and reactions. Such an anticipation, which is always based on typification, proves of utmost importance whenever for the attainment of my goal or the realization of some project I depend on the cooperation of others. My prospective partner may pursue interests that not only differ from mine but even conflict with them. To obtain his cooperation, or to bring about some sort of compromise or agreement, I have to form some idea of what my project might possibly mean to him. Unless I had such an idea, it would be impossible for me to come to terms with him, to interlock my course of action with what I may expect his to be; there would be nothing to orient and to guide me in the negotiations on which I am about to enter.

Obviously, my project cannot have the same meaning to my prospective partner that it has to me, since even in the absence of a conflict of interests his "biographical situation" differs from mine. To conceive of the meaning my project might have for my partner, I have to impute to him typical goals, interests, motives, attitudes, and so on. I have to construct the image of a certain type of person who holds a certain type of position and pursues typical interests – those that the position of the type in question requires him to pursue, or at least those that are congruent with his position. To this construct I have to refer my project, in order to see it in the light and from the perspective of my partner's goals, motives, interests, as typified by me. And I have to impute to my partner some knowledge of the meaning the project has to me, a knowledge that I suppose him to attain in substantially the same way I form my knowledge of my project's meaning to him. A reciprocity of this sort prevails in all social interactions.

Again we arrive at the notion of *subjektiver* or *gemeinter Sinn*, already encountered. Previously we were confronted with the meaning that an action or project of action has for the actor himself. Now we are dealing with the meaning of that action or project of action as imputed by the actor to his actual or prospective partner, that is, to another actor (for the sake of simplicity I ignore here the meaning for the onlooking disinterested observer, whom Schutz still distinguishes from the social scientist as a theoretician). At once it is clear that, as Schutz repeatedly emphasizes, the notion of *subjektiver* or *gemeinter Sinn* must not be mistaken for a particularity of Max Weber's sociology, or for a specific methodological device peculiar to the social sciences. On the contrary, "subjective interpretation of meaning" proves to be a common practice of social life in the world of everyday experience. Therefore, as we shall see presently, this notion must be allowed for within the context of social theory. Schutz's analysis provides a definitive clarification and justification of the concept of *subjektiver Sinn*, for this concept is referred to, and shown to arise out of, the total contexture of our experience of social reality and our life within it.

Needless to say, "subjective interpretation of meaning" has nothing to do with introspection: indeed, how could introspection ever lead me to grasp the meaning my action or project of action has for somebody else? Nor should it be misinterpreted as my identifying myself with my prospective partner, who may in fact pursue interests at variance with mine. When for the realization of my project I depend on his cooperation, I must foresee his likely reaction and even endeavor to influence it. But in trying to come to terms with him, I am far from relinquishing my interests and appropriating his. Throughout my negotiations and whatever other dealings I have with him, my project retains the meaning it has for me in the light of my "biographical situation," even though for the sake of its furtherance I must have some knowledge of its meaning for my partner, a knowledge to which I cannot arrive except by referring it to the described typifications.

IV

In the present context I am concerned only with Schutz's conception of the common-sense world as social reality, which I have sketched in only its broadest outlines. On the basis of Schutz's conception and in continuity with it, a theory of the social sciences could be established. Schutz did not develop such a theory in a fully elaborated and coherent form, though he has given a great many most valuable hints toward it, which should be gathered and systematized. Here I must forgo a discussion of the problems related to the theory of the social sciences, but one of them, centrally important in Schutz's thinking, must not be permitted to pass unmentioned. The problem in question, which is closely connected with the notion of *subjektiver Sinn*, concerns the difference between the natural and the social sciences, the latter understood in so broad a sense as to include all sciences dealing with man.

Guided by the scientific knowledge available in his special field (the "corpus" of his science), following and applying the rules of procedure and method generally accepted in his science, the natural as well as the social scientist selects and interprets the phenomena he sets out to explain. Both, in their scientific activity, proceed along the lines of their specific interests, which depend on their scientific situation, that is, the state of the science in question at this particular phase of its historical development. The natural scientist, however, does not have to take into consideration any preinterpretation of the facts and events upon whose study he embarks. Whatever interpretation his objects are subject to derives from him and from him alone. His objects are not expected to interpret themselves or the environment or field in which they are located and move. The theoretical constructs pertaining to the natural sciences are characterized by Schutz as "constructs of the first degree," a term deliberately meant to express the absence of precedent or underlying constructs.

In this respect the position of the social scientist differs from that of the natural scientist. The objects of the social scientist are actors in the social world, human beings involved and engaged in all kinds of social relationships. These actors have "biographical situations" and a "stock of knowledge at hand;" they pursue interests, have goals, motives, and the like; they have a certain conception of the world they live in, and of themselves as living in that world; in some way or other they interpret whatever they encounter in their world; their actions as well as those of their fellow actors have meaning to them. Among the data, facts, and events with which the social scientist has to deal as the subject matter of his studies belong all such preinterpretations and preconceptions. They have to be taken into account in the elaboration of organized knowledge of social reality in its full concreteness, that is, as experienced by the social actors themselves in their daily lives.

Like the natural scientist, the social scientist contrives theoretical constructs, but his are, as Schutz expresses it, "of the second degree," for in conceiving them allowance must be made for the interpretations that the social actors have of themselves, of one another, of their world. These constructs are homunculi, or puppets endowed with consciousness, which the social scientist creates at his discretion, in accordance with the scientific problem he sets to himself. A model of the social world is thus created by means of homunculi, or "ideal types" in Max Weber's phrase. The construction of ideal types is subject to the condition (among others) that understandable relations obtain between what is attributed to the homunculus and the actual conduct of the corresponding actor on the scene of social reality. That is to say, the actor must recognize himself in the homunculus and see in it an idealization of himself. The construction of homunculi is, I submit, an idealization of those typifications and self-typifications that are continually practiced in everyday life.

Since about the turn of the century, the problems related to the philosophical foundations of the social or humane sciences – both their difference from the natural sciences and their proper nature — have been much discussed by thinkers like Windelband, Rickert, Max Weber, Simmel, Dilthey. Especially Dilthey, himself a most eminent historian of philosophy and of ideas (*Geistesgeschichte*), perceived with increasing clearness the urgency of laying down the philosophical foundations of historical knowledge and understanding. According to him the great German historians of the nineteenth century successfully attempted to reconstruct the socio-historical and intellectual life of the past, but they were not able to give an account in conceptual terms of what they were actually doing. Dilthey concerned himself through almost all of his life with the justification of the science of history and philosophical explanation of the very possibility of such a science.[11]

He was well aware that for the advancement of his problems specific concepts were required, concepts related to the interpretation and self-interpretation of life in the intellectual and cultural, not the biological, sense. Such concepts could not be provided by the philosophical trends prevailing in Dilthey's time, since these trends were almost exclusively oriented toward the mathematical science of nature. Nor could they be provided by the new experimental psychology that had begun to develop since the end of the nineteenth century. Hence Dilthey came to conceive the idea of a "descriptive" (*beschreibende*) in contradistinction to "analyzing" (*zergliedernde*) psychology; [12] he seems to have been the first to advocate a psychology of a new style, one that would not simply emulate the procedures of physical science. Hence also Dilthey's interest in the beginnings of Husserl's phenomenology. In Husserl's *Logische Untersuchungen* Dilthey believed he discerned intentions akin to his own. He regarded this newly rising trend of philosophical thinking as a possible source from which those concepts might be derived which he needed for the advancement of his problems.[13]

Schutz is related to the later and even latest phase of Husserl's thought, rather than to the beginnings. Bringing the methods, points of view, and general theoretical orientation of Husserl's phenomenology in its latest form to bear upon the analysis and description of the life-world and of common experience, Schutz laid down a series of notions whose relatedness to, and relevancy for, the problem of interpretation and self-interpretation of life (in Dilthey's sense) are so obvious as to need little elaboration. I therefore venture the opinion that Dilthey's expectations may find fulfillment in the original development that Schutz gave to Husserl's phenomenology, at least to some of its parts. To be sure, it is the problem of history and historical knowledge that occupies the focus of Dilthey's thinking, whereas that problem

---

[11] One of the best presentations of Dilthey's problems and ideas is to be found in L. Landgrebe, "Wilhelm Dilthey's Theorie der Geisteswissenschaften," in *Jahrbuch für Philosophie und phänomenologische Forschung*, Vol. IX, 1928.

[12] W. Dilthey, "Ideen über eine beschreibende und zergliedernde Psychologie," in Wilhelm Dilthey, *Gesammelte Schriften*, Vol. V, Leipzig, 1924.

[13] On the relations between Dilthey and Husserl see G. Misch, *Lebensphilosophie und Phänomenologie*, 2nd ed., Leipzig-Berlin, 1931.

does not play a role of primary importance for Schutz, who concerned himself rather with the relations between contemporaries living in the same world. Yet there is, I believe, a possible continuous transition from the problem of intersubjectivity and the understanding of contemporaries to the problem of reconstruction of the past. Clarification of the foundations of the social sciences (in a more restricted sense of the term) prepares for and contributes to the clarification of the foundations of the historical sciences. For this reason I suggest as a desirable and promising enterprise a study of Schutz's concepts and theories from the point of view of their significance for the work inaugurated by Dilthey and continued by some of his successors.

*Studies in
Phenomenological Philosophy*

WILLIAM JAMES'S CONCEPT OF THE STREAM OF THOUGHT PHENOMENOLOGICALLY INTERPRETED

Future historians of philosophy will certainly agree that it was mainly the thought of three thinkers which helped to remodel the contemporary style of philosophizing: James, Bergson, and Husserl. Although from the beginning of their activity James and Bergson found themselves attracted to each other, entered into correspondence, and met personally several times, there is no reference in James's books or in his correspondence to Husserl's *Logische Untersuchungen* (1900–1901). On the other hand, we know Husserl's admiration for James's *Principles of Psychology*, which he studied carefully with the intention of writing a critical review for a German philosophical journal – a project never realized. Certainly such a document from Husserl's pen would have opened for all friends of James's psychology the best approach to Husserl's own thought.

If, in the following, we venture to seek out the way toward a phenomenological interpretation of some basic tenets of James's *Principles of Psychology*, we are doing so exclusively for the purpose of showing that certain essential starting points as well as principal views are common to both philosophers. It is not at all our intention to transform James into a phenomenologist or Husserl into a pragmatist. We neither pretend that James's concept of psychology as a "natural science" nor his ascription of thought to its cerebral conditions is acceptable from the phenomenological point of view, nor that Husserl's concept of transcendental subjectivity is compatible with James's basic ideas. And we would by no means dare to reduce an original and powerful thinker such as James to a precursor of phenomenology or to simulate an influence of James on Husserl, who approached the same topics from quite another side. But, mindful of all the

differences which separate both men's personalities, their philosophical style, and their philosophical goals, we feel strongly that
it is sometimes more important for the cause of philosophy to
find out where the ideas of great masters coalesce than where
they differ. And I am sure that this attempt would be welcomed
above all by the broadminded James, who once said that his
effort had been to offer in a "natural science" of mind a *modus
vivendi* in which the most varied schools may meet harmoniously
in the common basis of fact.[1]

We are intentionally restricting ourselves to dealing with two
topics of James' *Principles:* the stream of thought and the theory of fringes, though other parts of this important book as well as
parts of his later philosophy, e.g., his theories of "The Meaning
of Truth" and of intersubjectivity, also lead to problems which
stand in the center of phenomenological philosophy.

Discussing the methods of investigation open to psychologists,[2]
James points out that all people unhesitatingly believe that they
feel themselves thinking and they distinguish the mental state
as an inward activity from all the objects with which it may
cognitively deal. *"I regard,"* he says, *"this belief as the most fundamental of all the postulates of Psychology,* and shall discard all
curious inquiries about its certainty as too metaphysical for the
scope of this book." "That we have *cogitations* of some sort is the
inconcussum in a world most of whose other facts have at some
time tottered in the breath of philosophic doubt."

First of all, this basic position is the common platform from
which both James's psychological research and Husserl's phenomenological meditation begin. The first indubitable fact to
start from is the existence of a personal consciousness; the
personal self rather than the thought has to be treated as the
immediate datum in psychology and the universal conscious
fact is not: "feelings and thoughts exist" but ,"I think" and "I
feel." [3] Within each personal consciousness thought is sensibly
continuous and changing, and as such, comparable to a river or a
stream. "Stream of thought," "stream of experiences or cogi-

[1] Preface to the Italian translation of *Principles*, quoted by Ralph Barton Perry,
The Thought and Character of William James, Boston, 1935, Vol. II, p. 54.
[2] *The Principles of Psychology*, New York, 1893, Vol. I, p. 185
[3] *Principles*, Vol. I, p. 226.

tations," "stream of personal conscious life" – both philosophers use these terms for characterizing the essence of inner personal life. For both, the unity of consciousness consists in its through-and-through connectedness. It is, says James, but our abstract conceptual thought that isolates and arbitrarily fixes certain portions of this stream of consciousness.[4]

For both philosophers this concept involves the total rejection of the atomism prevailing in the psychology of Locke, Hume, or John Stuart Mill. These thinkers have reduced mental life to its elementary data (sensations of all sorts) and have concluded from their distinctness for analysis that these elements are in reality originally separate and isolated. They were, then, unable to reconstruct from this heap of atomistic data the unity of consciousness. For James as for Husserl psychical life is not made up of a multiplicity of elements which have to be reunited, it is not a mosaic of juxtaposed sensations, but, from the first, a unity of continuously streaming cogitations. Both, therefore, criticize the associationist theories, and sometimes with the same arguments; both, therefore, reject Locke's simile of a "white paper" soul. James, intentionally limiting its scope to psychology, declares that the idea of a personal soul as well as Kant's concept of the transcendental ego is, at least, superfluous for

---

[4] As Professor John Dewey states in his impressive study, " The Vanishing Subject in the Psychology of James" (*Journal of Philosophy*, Vol. XXXVII, 1940, pp. 589–599), "There is a double strain in the *Principles of Psychology* of William James. One strain is official acceptance of epistemological dualism. According to this view, the science of psychology centers about a *subject* which is 'mental' just as physics centers about an *object* which is material. But James's analysis of special topics tends, on the contrary, to reduction of the subject to a vanishing point, save as 'subject' is identified with the organism, the latter, moreover, having no existence save in interaction with environing conditions. According to the latter strain, subject and object do not stand for separate orders or kinds of existence but at most for certain distinctions made for a definite purpose *within* experience" (*op. cit.*, p. 589). Professor Dewey quotes different passages of James's work, proving that both views can be found therein and that the equivocal account given by James of the nature of the self and our consciousness of it is, above all, the source of the controversy. It may be admitted that Professor Dewey's interpretation leading to reduction of the subject to a vanishing point corresponds in a higher degree to James's later philosophy than the dualistic view. But even Professor Dewey agrees that the important chapter on the "stream of consciousness" is verbally the most subjectivistic part of the whole book and he comments on this statement in a footnote as follows: "I say 'verbally' because it is quite possible to translate 'stream of consciousness' into [the ongoing], 'course of experience' ['of experienced things'] and retain the substance of the chapter." The present paper, limiting its topic to James's concept of the stream of thought, neglects intentionally the second strain emphasized by Professor Dewey and deals exclusively with the first, the subjective one.

scientific purposes. The passing Thought is itself the only
Thinker. But James refutes the concept of a transcendental ego
only within the realm of psychology, leaving open the question
of its possible applicability to other provinces of speculation.[5]
For psychological purposes, he says, it suffices to state that
personality implies the incessant presence of two elements: an
objective person – the Empirical Self or Me – known by a passing
subjective Thought – the I – and recognized as continuing in
time.

For Husserl the personal life of consciousness as an indubitable
fact leads to the apprehension of and theoretical inquiry into the
"realm of pure consciousness in its own self-contained Being."
Let us examine this position more closely. From the beginning
Husserl's problem was a twofold one: first, to establish an *a
priori psychological* discipline, able to provide the only secure
basis on which a strong empirical psychology can be built;
second, to establish a universal *philosophy*, starting from an
absolute "principium" of knowledge in the genuine sense of this
term.[6] We are chiefly interested in the first.

Husserl starts with the explanation of the characteristics of
psychological experience. While just living along, we live *in* our
experiences, and, concentrated as we are upon their objects, we
do not have in view the "acts of subjective experience" themselves. In order to reveal these acts of experience as such we must
modify the naive attitude in which we are oriented towards
objects and we must turn ourselves, in a specific act of "reflection,"
towards our own experiences. As yet Husserl's ideas do not
differ from James's concept. Obviously the latter means the same
things with his famous "four data of psychology": [7] (1) the
psychologist, (2) the thought studied, (3) the thought's object,
(4) the psychologist's reality.

Husserl's next step is to reveal the insight into the "intentionality" of consciousness. Our cogitations have the basic character
of being "consciousness of" something. What appears in reflection
as phenomenon is the intentional object, which I have a thought
of, perception of, fear of, etc. Every experience is, thus, not only

[5] *Principles*, Vol. I, pp. 370, 400 f. Cf. footnote 4.
[6] E. Husserl, "Phenomenology," *Encyclopaedia Britannica*, 14th ed.
[7] Vol. I, p. 184.

characterized by the fact *that* it is a consciousness, but it is simultaneously determined by the intentional object *whereof* it is a consciousness.[8] Types and forms of this intentionality can be described. This description can be performed on two different levels: first, within the natural attitude – and all that has been stated so far refers to this level; secondly, within the sphere of phenomenological reduction. This basic concept of Husserl's theory needs further explanation.

In our everyday life, or, as Husserl says, "from the natural standpoint," we accept as unquestionable the world of facts which surrounds us as existent out there. To be sure, we might throw doubt upon any *datum* of that world out there, we might even distrust as many of our experiences of this world as we wish; the naive belief in the existence of *some* outer world, this "general thesis of the natural standpoint," will imperturbably subsist. But by a radical effort of our mind we can alter this attitude, not by transforming our naive belief in the outer world into a disbelief, not by replacing our conviction in its existence by the contrary, but by suspending belief. We just make up our mind to refrain from any judgment concerning spatiotemporal existence, or in technical language, we set the existence of the world " out of action," we "bracket" our belief in it. But using this particular "epoché" we not only "bracket" all the common-sense judgments of our daily life about the world out there, but also all the propositions of the natural sciences which likewise deal with the realities of this world from the natural standpoint.

What remains of the whole world after this bracketing? Neither more nor less than the concrete fullness and entirety of the stream of our experience containing all our perceptions, our reflections, in short, our cogitations. And as these cogitations continue to be intentional ones, their correlative "intentional objects" persist also within the brackets. But by no means are they to be identified with the posited objects. They are just "appearances," phenomena, and, as such, rather "unities" or "senses" ("meanings"). The method of phenomenological reduction, therefore, makes accessible the stream of consciousness in itself as a realm of its own in its absolutely unique nature. We

[8] E. Husserl, *Ideas: General Introduction to Pure Phenomenology*, translated by Boyce Gibson, § 36.

can experience it and describe its inner structure. This is the task of phenomenological psychology. Incidentally, we have to state that this science, to become aprioristic, cannot deal with "matters of fact" in the sense of Hume. It has to deal with the "Eidos," with the essence of thoughts and must therefore use *eidetic* methods. But to explain this procedure is beyond the scope of our topic.[9]

The transcendental reduction is important for phenomenological descriptive psychology not only because it reveals the stream of consciousness and its features in their purity, but, above all, because some very important structures of consciousness can be made visible only within this reduced sphere. Since to each empirical determination within the phenomenological reduction there necessarily corresponds a parallel feature within the natural sphere and vice versa, we can always turn back to the natural attitude and there make use of all the insights we have won within the reduced sphere.

Let us take as an example Husserl's theory of noesis ("the experiencing") and noema ("the experienced") which leads us to the neighborhood of some tenets of James. As all cogitations are by their intentional character "consciousness of" something, a double manner of describing them will always exist: the first, the noematic, dealing with the "cogitatum," that is, with the intentional object of our specific thought as it appears in it, for instance as a certainly, possibly, or presumably existent object, or as a present, past, or future object; the second, the noetic, dealing with the acts of cogitation, with the experiencing itself (noesis) and with its modifications as: with the perceiving, retaining, recollecting, etc., and their peculiar differences of clarity and explicitness. Each specific noesis has its specific noematic correlate. There are modifications of thought which touch equally upon the whole noetico-noematic content as, e.g., the attentional modifications do; others which transform preponderantly either the noematic or the noetic side. But closer analysis (which can be performed only within the reduced sphere) shows that there is always a noematic nucleus or kernel in each intentional object which persists through all the modifications

[9] Cf. for this problem, Husserl, *Ideas*, § 3 ff. (and see the author's "Some Leading Concepts of Phenomenology," *Collected Papers*, Vol. I.)

and which can be defined "as the meaning of the thought in the mode of its full realization." [10]

As far as I can see, this theory of Husserl's matches James's theory of fringes revolving around a kernel or topic of a thought. And the theory of noema and noesis is but the radicalized expression of James's statement that the object of thought is "all that the thought thinks, exactly as the thought thinks it." Under a universal aspect there is open to our noetic description the total of our life of consciousness, to the noematic description the total of our world as it appears to our consciousness.

As far as my topic is concerned, I might conclude here the account of Husserl's phenomenological reduction. For psychology and even phenomenological psychology (both in its empirical and eidetic disciplines) is a "positive" science promoted in the "natural attitude" with the world before it as the basis for all its themes. For the purposes of such a psychology, therefore, the phenomenological reduction is a pure methodological device for analyzing the life of consciousness. But phenomenological reduction is also of basic importance for the foundation of *transcendental phenomenological philosophy*. Just to round off my summary, I should like to indicate the starting point of the latter.

By performing the phenomenological reduction, the psychological subjectivity on its part loses just that which makes it something real in the world that lies before us, namely its meaning as a "soul," as a human ego in the universal, existentially posited world. To use James's terms, we may say that the Empirical Self, the Me, is to be reduced (together with the whole posited world of which it is an element) to its "appearance." What remains is the "I," the "I myself," which is, as Husserl says, [11] "that subjective conscious life itself, wherein the world and all its content is made for 'me.'" So far, we feel, James would have no objection to Husserl's "transcendental ego." Husserl's statement just quoted is but the translation of James' adage, "The judging Thought is the Thinker" into a language appropriate to the reduced sphere.

But transcendental subjectivity means far more for Husserl:

---

[10] This presentation of Husserl's thought is, of course, throughout but a rough draft of a first approximation.
[11] "Phenomenology," *op. cit.*

the pure transcendental *"Ego cogito"* is no longer *"mens sive animus sive intellectus,"* as Descartes, in misinterpretation of his own discovery, had supposed; it is no longer a mind belonging to a body that exists in an objective spatiotemporal Nature being interested in the world, but exclusively the self-identical subject of all its cogitations, their identical focus. That means: All the "intentional objects" of its cogitations are objects only for the ego and by the ego; they are intentional objects for the stream of its cognitive life or, to use Husserl's technical term, they are constituted by its synthetic activities. To explore this transcendental realm, to explain its existential meaning, and to describe its constitution is the great task of phenomenological philosophy.

Certainly, that is not the way James chose in his later philosophy. As far as the *Principles* are concerned, I can heartily agree with Professor R. B. Perry's statement that the composition of the *Principles* found James with a half-finished theory of knowledge and that his dualism was a half-thought compromise.[12] Nevertheless, his book contains important tendencies in the direction of Husserl's philosophy which might have been developed. An excellent example is James's very ingenious and original theory of *fringes* or psychic overtones, which we are now going to examine.

James's theory of fringes embraces many different problems, only three of which we propose to discuss in this paper: (1) The problem of the unity of consciousness and the horizon. (2) The problem of the object and the topic of the thought. (3) The problem of so-called articulated syntheses.

Ad (1) James starts his analyses with the examination of the transition between the thought of one object and the thought of another. The continuity of the stream of consciousness can be explicated by a necessary relation between the emergent object of the thought and its surrounding objects. "What we hear when the thunder crashes is not thunder *pure*, but thunder-breaking-upon-silence-and-contrasting-with-it." [13] There is no isolated object within our stream of thought, but only "substantive parts,"

---

[12] Ralph Barton Perry, *The Thought and Character of William James*, Vol. II, p. 75.

[13] *Principles*, Vol. I, p. 240. In a specific footnote James refers here to the *Psychology* (Vol. I, pp. 219–220) of Franz Brentano (the teacher of Edmund Husserl) and says: "Altogether this chapter of Brentano's on the unity of consciousness is as good as anything with which I am acquainted."

such as sensations, perceptions, images, whose peculiarity is that they can be held before the mind for an indefinite time, and "transitive parts" which are thoughts of relations, static or dynamic, between the substantive parts. "If there be such things as feelings at all, then so surely as relations between objects exist *in rerum natura*, so surely, and more surely, do feelings exist to which these relations are known." [14] There are, moreover, always "feelings of expectancies," of "tendencies, relating the 'present' feeling with the future and the past." In short, each of our thoughts is, so to speak, surrounded by *fringes* of not explicitly felt relations, it carries with it a "halo" of psychic overtones, or as James likes to call it, its "horizon."

The same topic under the same name is a central theme of phenomenological research.[15] Husserl distinguishes between the inner and the outer horizon. Each experience, for instance, of a corporeal thing [16] has its *inner horizon* which refers to the "stream of different appearance-aspects" in which the thing came to our native perception. Analysis of perceiving reveals a continuous variety in the "appearance" of the object according to differences in the point of view from which it is seen (differences in "perspective"); differences between the actually seen front and the unseen, only supposedly existent, indeterminate back, etc. Each phenomenon, thus, has its own intentional structure, its inner horizon of appearance-aspects, and it is characteristic that, although every phase and interval of this stream of appearance is already in itself a consciousness of "something," the total consciousness of one and the same object keeps its synthetic unity.

But founded on this inner horizon, there is an *outer horizon* too. First, a *spatial* one, formed by the coexistent co-objects, which I do not have actually in view, but which I can possibly bring into view since I can anticipate the typical style of experiencing them. Analysis of the spatial outer horizon starts with

---

[14] *Principles*, Vol. I, p. 245. It must be remembered that James uses the term "feeling" as synonymous with "thought" and consciousness. Cf. Vol. I, p. 186.

[15] In Husserl's *Erfahrung und Urteil* (Part I, Chapter III) it is even treated under the caption "Experience and Relation."

[16] For the sake of avoiding too great complications we restrict our presentation to the experience of a corporeal thing. The problem of the horizon, however, is a universal one and subsists, *mutatis mutandis*, for all kinds of experience.

the relations of the perceived object with the background from
which it detaches itself, and ends with the totality of the surrounding world as the last horizon for each of its objects. Secondly, a
temporal horizon, first and foremost temporally extended in
objective time: the actually perceived object is the same as the
one perceived yesterday or to be perceived tomorrow.

All the horizons discussed so far refer to the categories of
acquaintance and strangeness. Experience in the strict sense can
be realized only by explicating the implications hidden in the
various relations to other experiences just called horizon. It is
our interest, the cognitive or the practical, which determines the
limits up to which we have to unravel all these preformed syntheses in order to get a sufficient knowledge of the object in question.
Here we meet again, as the result of Husserl's analysis, two
conclusions James derives from his own theory of fringes:

(*a*) He distinguishes [17] between "knowledge-about" an object
and mere "acquaintance with" it, and states that the former
includes knowledge of the object's relations, i.e., of the "fringes"
of unarticulated affinities about it. In Husserl's terminology:
knowledge of an object requires at least partial explication of its
spatiotemporal horizon.

(*b*) James's "Principle of constancy in the mind's meaning."
"The same matters can be thought of in successive portions of
the mental stream, and some of these portions can know that
they mean the same matters which the other portions meant. The
mind can always intend, and know when it intends, to think of
the Same." [18] This principle called by James the "very keel and
backbone of our thinking," [19] is named by Husserl the synthesis
of identification; and he recognizes "the possibility of synthetic
unity as the central viewpoint in phenomenology." [20] In discussing the syntheses hidden in the inner horizon of the object
we have already met this principle of sameness.

So far we have characterized the temporal horizon only in objective time. In order to understand fully the interconnectedness
of the stream of thought we have to glance at the unifying synthe-

---

[17] *Principles*, Vol. I, p. 221.
[18] *Principles*, Vol. I, p. 459.
[19] Cf. also *Principles*, Vol. I, p. 272: "*Sameness* in a multiplicity of objective
appearances is thus the basis of our belief in realities outside of thought."
[20] *Ideas*, § 86.

sis of *subjective time* – or in James's terminology – the sense of time. The continuity of the stream of thought, Husserl points out, is based on the character of temporality as the relational form which necessarily connects experiences with experiences. In necessary continuity each "now" transforms itself into a "just now"; another "now" matches the former "now" and becomes a "just now" matching the former "just now" and so on. The actual present, therefore, is not an instantaneity, but the persisting form for continuously changing contents. Actual impression is nothing else than the limiting phase of a continuous series of retentions, or, in the other direction, of a continuous series of anticipations, both chains to be interpreted as continuous successions of intentional relationships. Therefore, says Husserl, each actual experienced present carries along its horizon of the experienced past, which is necessarily always filled with content, and its horizon of the future, which is empty or filled merely with the content of the anticipated future present. This means that every present moment has about it a "fringe" [21] of experiences which constitute the one primordial fringe of the pure ego, its total primordial now-consciousness. What student of James would not recognize the latter's famous theory of the "specious present" [22] in this basic concept of Husserl's?

Ad (2) In all our voluntary thinking, says James,[23] there is some kernel or topic of the thought about which all members of the thought revolve. Half the time it is a problem, a gap we cannot fill with a definite picture, word, or phrase, but which it is our thoughts' destiny to fill up. Or instead of a definite gap we may merely carry a mood of interest about with us. At any rate there is a feeling of relation, a *fringe* of relations to the topic in which the object cognized, substantive qualities, and things, appear to the mind. Through its relation to the kernel every element of the thought is bathed in that original halo of obscure relations, which, like a horizon, then spread about the meaning. Hence we need to distinguish between the topic and the object of the thought: the topic is what the thought is "about," the

---

[21] Cf. *Ideas*, § 82. Professor Boyce Gibson, the English translator, has chosen the term "fringe" here for Husserl's term *"Horizont"* (horizon) and has by this translation alone anticipated our whole topic.

[22] *Principles*, Vol. I, pp. 608 ff.

[23] *Principles*, Vol. I, pp. 259 ff.

object what is thought about it.[24] The object of the thought is its entire content or deliverance, neither more nor less. Let us not be mistaken by the fact that in conceptual terms, the thought seems to have object-parts. It has only time-parts, but, however complicated its object may be, the thought of it is one undivided state of consciousness, one single pulse of subjectivity.

As the foregoing very incomplete quotations [25] show, James feels strongly the eminent importance of his great discovery of the theory of fringes for the distinction between the "topic" and the "object" of thought. Unfortunately, his rather aphoristic comments on this matter deal with most heterogeneous questions on very different levels and he abstains from breaking down systematically the different problems involved.

It is certainly impossible to analyze all the implications and connotations of the concept of fringes within the frame of this paper. Such an examination would lead immediately into the theory of prepredicative experience and, thus, of constitution.* I restrict myself, therefore, to point out that one of the possible interpretations of James's theory of the elements of thoughts related by fringes to the kernel refers to the phenomenological problem of the "noematic nucleus" as against its noetic modifications. For James, the "topic" is the "meaning" of the thought, as, according to Husserl, the noematic kernel is the "meaning" of the intentional object.

Ad (3) But there is certainly another connotation involved in the "topic of the thought" related by fringes to its elements. Sometimes James speaks of a *train of thought,* and the topic or meaning of such a train is its "conclusion." "That is what abides when all its other members have faded from memory.... It stands out from the other segments of the stream by reason of the peculiar interest attaching to it. The interest *arrests* it ... induces attention upon it and makes us treat it in a substantive way. The parts of the stream that precede these substantive conclusions are but the means of the latter's attainment ...

---

[24] Cf. R. B. Perry, *op. cit.,* Vol. II, pp. 75 ff.; *Principles,* Vol. I, pp. 275 ff.

[25] We have neglected entirely, e. g., the function of the "topic" as "grammatical subject" and the problem of a general grammar based on the concept of fringes. According to James, a feeling of "and," of "if," of "by," also pertains to the fringe relation (*Principles,* Vol. I, pp. 245 f.).

* See *Collected Papers,* Vol. I, pp. 112–113, 274 ff.

when the conclusion is there, we have always forgotten most of the steps preceding its attainment.... The practical upshot of a book we read remains with us, though we may not recall one of its sentences." [26] He emphasizes "the sensible continuity and unity of our thought as contrasted with the apparent discreteness of the words, images, and other means by which it seems to be carried on." "Between all their substantive elements there is 'transitive' consciousness, and the words and images are 'fringed,' and not as discrete as to a careless view they seem." [27]

This idea corresponds to the phenomenological concept of so-called "articulated" or "polythetic" syntheses, namely those in which discrete, discontinuous acts of experiencing are bound together in an articulated unity, in the unity of a synthetic act of a higher order.[28] It is the peculiarity of such polythetic synthe-ses that consciousness can grasp their step-by-step formation only in a "fan of several rays of thought," whereas the integrated object, once synthesized, can be experienced in one single ray of thought, in a "monothetic" act. This is above all important for Husserl's theory of "syntactic forms" of all kinds and for his theory of the constitution of "ideal objects." And again James comes to the same conclusion when he declares [29] that his doctrine of fringes decides the controversy between nominalists and conceptualists in favor of the latter. For "the power to think things, qualities, relations, and other elements isolated and abstracted from the experience in which they appear, is the most indisputable function of our thought."

Here we have to call a halt and forego a discussion of the amazing parallel between great parts of both philosophers' theo-ries of attention, perception of space and time, and reality. Our aim was to show that phenomenology is not quite a stranger in this country. Not without pride she considers herself as working on the same genuine philosophical proplems which the great William James established as the American philosophical tra-dition. And although between Husserl and James there are incontestably great differences in methods and goal, we dare say that whoever has seized the full dept of James's admirable

[26] *Principles*, Vol. I, p. 260.
[27] *Ibid.*, p. 271.
[28] *Ideas*, pp. 118 f.
[29] *Principles*, Vol. I, p. 472.

concept of the stream of thought and its fringes has not only found an excellent approach to several essential provinces of phenomenological psychology: nay, far more! he has already wandered through some of their most remarkable parts.

EDMUND HUSSERL'S IDEAS, VOLUME II*

I. PRELIMINARY REMARKS

The first volume of Edmund Husserl's *Ideas pertaining to a Pure Phenomenology and to a Phenomenological Philosophy*, subtitled "General Introduction to Pure Phenomenology" was published in 1913.[1] It became a standard text of Husserl's philosophy. A second volume should have been dedicated to analyses of certain concrete problems leading to the clarification of the relationship between phenomenology on the one hand and the physical sciences of nature, psychology, and the sciences of the mind on the other. A third concluding volume should have dealt with the idea of Philosophy. Husserl drafted the second volume in 1912 – no draft of the third volume has been found in the manuscripts – but, being dissatisfied, left it unpublished. He worked on the pertinent manuscripts with some interruptions until 1928. The *Archives Husserl* at Louvain under the splendid direction of Professor H. L. Van Breda have again rendered a highly appreciated service to all friends of phenomenological philosophy by publishing for the first time these important studies of Husserl's in two volumes: *Ideas* II: "Phenomenological Analyses Relating to the Problems of Constitution," and *Ideas* III: "Phenomenology and the Foundation of the Sciences." Both volumes are excellently edited by Mrs. Marly Biemel, who had the exceedingly difficult task of establishing, as far as *Ideas*

---

[1] English translation by W. R. Boyce Gibson, London-New York 1931, reprinted 1952.

* Edmund Husserl, *Ideen zu einer reinen Phänomenologie und phänomenologischen Philosophie, Zweites Buch: Phänomenologische Untersuchungen zur Konstitution*, Herausgegeben von Marly Biemel, Husserliana Band IV. Auf Grund des Nachlasses veröffentlicht vom Husserl-Archiv (Louvain) unter Leitung von H. L. Van Breda, Den Haag, 1952.

II is concerned, a readable text from three versions prepared by Husserl's assistants, Edith Stein and Professor Ludwig Landgrebe, and from many additional manuscripts, all of them re-worked, corrected, and supplemented by Husserl but never brought into shape for final publication.

In the concluding sections (149–153) of the published volume I, the main problems to be treated in the continuation are clearly indicated: 1. The problem of "objective regions" and their transcendental constitution; 2. the problem of intersubjectivity; 3. the relations of phenomenology to the various sciences, especially to psychology and ontology. Already in the beginning of volume I (section 9) we learned that every concrete empirical objectivity together with its material essence finds its place within a highest material genus, a "region" of empirical objects. To the pure regional essence belongs then a regional eidetic science or, as we can also say, a regional ontology. Moreover, as shown at the end of volume I, there are specific phenomenological problems connected with the idea of a "region." Every objective region is "constituted" in the transcendental consciousness. For example, an object determined through the regional genus "real thing" has prescribed *a priori* its modes of being perceptible, conceivable, etc., originating in its noematic-noetic structure, in its positing-intuitional meaning: it is extended, it has its "form" in time, it is a unity of causal connections, etc. More generally speaking, each region prescribes rules for the course of possible intuitions and serves, thus, as a guiding clue (*Leitfaden*) for the systematic description of the correlation between the determinate appearing object as a unity and the determinately infinite multiplicity of its appearances. The problem of constitution, so we read at the end of section 150 of volume I, betokens nothing further than the analysis of this correlation and its underlying rules by means of eidetic description.

The problem of constitution has to be solved for all material regions, that of the material thing, of animal nature and of the spirit. But these intentional analyses of the objectivities of the various regions are interlaced: the inanimate thing is not anything isolated over against the experiencing subject, it is an intersubjectively identical thing, a constitutive unity of higher order, related to an indefinite plurality of subjects that stand in a

relation of "mutual understanding." The intersubjective world
as the correlate of intersubjective experiences, mediated through
empathy, plays a constitutive part in "objective" experience.
Empathy gives unity to the separate manifolds belonging to the
different personal subjects and streams of consciousness.

Thus far we have presented the program, as developed at the
end of volume I, which has been closely followed by Husserl's
first draft for volume II. Why did he withhold its publication? In her introductory remarks the editor, Mrs. Biemel,
rightly points out that the problem of the constitution of the
object in consciousness became during the fifteen years in which
Husserl worked on the manuscript a main problem of his philosophy and the very task of phenomenology. In 1934 Husserl told the
present writer that he left the second volume of the *Ideas*
unpublished because he had not at that time found a satisfactory
solution for the problem of intersubjectivity, which he believed
to have achieved in the fifth *Cartesian Meditation*.[2] As a matter
of fact, nearly all basic concepts of transcendental phenomenology underwent a radical change during the period in question.
A comparison of Husserl's philosophy as stated in the *Ideas* with
that of the *Cartesian Meditations*, with Husserl's article in the
Encyclopaedia Britannica,[3] or Eugen Fink's essay in the *Kant-
Studien* of 1934 [4] shows this clearly. The concepts of phenomenological reductions, of transcendental subjectivity, of constitution,
of the relationship between phenomenological psychology and
transcendental phenomenology, the substitution of methodological idealism by transcendental idealism, the various attempts
to overcome the issue of solipsism are just examples. Husserl's
manuscripts published in *Ideas* II partially reflect this struggle.
Sometimes three or four different and irreconcilable attempts are
made toward the solution of a particular problem, and, as shown

[2] *Méditations Cartésiennes, Introduction à la phénoménologie* traduit par G. Pfeif-
fer et E. Levinas, Paris 1931; the German original published as Volume I of Husserliana (*Cartesianische Meditationen und Pariser Vorträge*), edited by S. Strasser,
Den Haag 1950.
[3] "Phenomenology," translated by C. V. Salmon, *Encyclopaedia Britannica*, 14th
ed., (1929), Vol. XVII, pp. 159–172.
[4] Die phänomenologische Philosophie Edmund Husserls in der gegenwärtigen
Kritik, *Kant-Studien*, Vol. XVIII, 1933, pp. 319–383, which Husserl endorsed as expressing his own views. For a careful presentation and illuminating discussion of this
important article see Marvin Farber, *The Foundation of Phenomenology*, Cambridge,
1943, pp. 543–560.

by Husserl's various marginal notes, carefully reproduced by the
editor in the annex, large parts of the now published text were
rejected by the author in the latest state of the manuscript.

In what follows we try to give a condensed summary of the
main problems treated in *Ideas* II, conscious of the shortcomings
involved in such an enterprise. No attempt will be made to
reconcile the various phases of phenomenological thought or to
connect the views developed in the present text with other
writings of Husserl; nor is it our aim to bring the internal
contradictions within the text into focus. We have here to deal
with a significant phase of a work in progress, the more significant
as the topics treated therein are of decisive importance for the
foundation of the social sciences. It is a transitional phase in the
development of phenomenology, a camp erected for the still
unachieved conquest of the Himalaya in the thin air of an awe-
inspiring altitude.

II. THE MAIN ARGUMENT OF HUSSERL'S IDEAS II

1) The Region of Inanimate Objects

The constitution of the material inanimate object in the outer
world, of the thing proper, is the first region of reality analyzed
by Husserl. That the thing is extended in space and has its duration in time, that it has qualities, being heavy or elastic or
colored, that it stands in relations to other objects, that it is
moved or unmovable – all this is experienced in our perception.
But can we perceive also its materiality, its being a real object?
The phantom, too, has spatiality, duration, qualities, colors, is
moved or is at rest. We perceive also the rainbow and the blue
sky. What the thing and also the phantom reveal to our perception is merely its *sensorial schema*, as Husserl calls it, which
changes continuously with the aspects under which we experience it. Its specific materiality however, which distinguishes the
real material thing from the phantom, cannot be ascertained as
long as we take the particular thing as being experienced in
isolation, that is, as being detached from its relations to "circumstances." The reality of the thing, its materiality, cannot be
referred to the *sensorial schema* alone. This schema changes if

the circumstances change, but the changing schemata are apprehended as manifestations of a determined unity and their changes as being dependent upon the pertinent real circumstances. The various real states of the qualities of the thing, say its various colors under different lighting, are apprehended as mere modifications of the same objective color, the color which the thing has in darkness as well as in sunlight, and especially as modifications which depend upon the changing circumstances, such as the light. It is this "realizing apprehension" by which not only any "objective" "real" quality of the phenomenal thing is constituted but also the reality of the thing itself as substratum of its changing qualities. By this apprehension the changing qualities are not perceived as mere *sensorial schemata* but as manifestations of a real quality of the state of a "substance" at the time of such apprehension. In other words, the quality itself is originarily * given just in the ongoing course of functional dependencies upon the pertinent circumstances. These dependencies are causal dependencies, not merely supposed but "seen" or "perceived" causalities. What the thing is in its materiality can only be revealed by the progress of our experiencing, it being understood that the resulting experiences may corroborate, rectify, invalidate, or annihilate one another during this process. To know a thing means to know how it will behave under pressure, heat, etc., in brief, all its causal dependencies upon other things which are also experienced as real and material objects in the outer world. Substantiality, reality, and causality are, thus, inseparably interconnected and real qualities are *eo ipso* causal qualities.

It has to be emphasized that the material thing and its causalities thus described are not the thing and its causalities in terms of the natural sciences but the thing as it is constituted in the sensorial perception of an experiencing subject and even a subject assumed to be isolated, that is, detached from any connection with its fellow-subjects. As such, the material thing refers from the outset to the body of the experiencing subject and its normal sensorial apparatus. The body participates in all

---

* "Originarily" (and related forms such as "originary" and "originariness") is an adaptation from Husserl's German (*originär*) and should not be understood as meaning "originally," since the term is used in a structural and not a temporal sense.

acts of perceiving. It is the carrier of our sensations, more precisely of two sets of sensations which both contribute to the constitution of a spatial object: the first set contributes directly to the constitution of the qualities of the thing (its color, smoothness, etc.); the other set, the system of kinaesthetic sensations, bodily movements, in brief of the spontaneity of perceiving functions freely performed in accordance with an inherent order, *motivates* the first series. For example, any actual perception refers to a possibility of other perceptions of the form: if my eyes move in this way, then the image perceived will change in this way; if in that way, it will change accordingly. Thus, the same unchanged thing presents itself in various aspects dependent upon the situation of my body. Among these various aspects one will prove to be the optimal one (e.g., the object seen in sunlight under a clear sky) and will be considered the "normal" one. The world apperceived in "normal" experience is taken as the "real," the "true" world. All deviations from this normalcy are interpreted as originating in psycho-physical conditions to which also all somatological anomalies of the sensating body belong. Thus, even on the level to which the present investigations are by pedagogical reasons artificially restricted, namely under the solipsistic assumption, certain motives are at work which lead to a distinction between the merely appearing thing and the thing as it "really" is. Therefore, there is an "objective nature," so to speak, even within the solipsistic sphere. Of course, the term "real" may also have another meaning, namely the identical stock of qualities which can be ascertained by disregarding everything related to the psycho-physical subject and which can be couched in logical-mathematical terms. The "real" thing in this second sense is, however, not the object of my subjective experience; it is the physical thing of the natural sciences.

2) The Region of "Animalia"

Over against the material nature of inanimate things there stands out a nature in a second and enlarged sense, another region of reality, namely animal nature. A soul or psyche is predicated to the *animalia* which also include human beings. Psyche is from the outset always incarnated, and that means that it appears as an element of nature in connection with a material thing, the animal or human body. In order to investigate the constitution of the realm of nature as psyche, we have to analyze our originary intuition of the psyche which precedes all theoretical thinking and which no theory can invalidate. Such an analysis has, therefore, to forego any reference to the achievements of the science of psychology; it has to be performed in several steps: (a) our experience of the sphere of the psyche by "inner perception"; (b) the problem of the "reality" of the psyche; (c) our experience of its incarnation in our body; (d) our experience of other bodies as animated ones and, therefore, as manifestations of other psyches.

(a) *Our experience of the psyche by inner perception.* Given to our inner perception is the stream of our experiences (*Erlebnissen*) without a beginning or an end, with its perceptions, recollections, phantasies, emotions, etc. We do not experience this stream as a mere annex to our material body. Its unity is rather a form of inner time. Yet, within this unified stream of experiences we may, by adopting an appropriate reflective attitude, grasp intuitively units of a particular structure contained therein. Of special importance for the problem at hand are the egological units, the various forms of the I. Husserl distinguishes here three egological forms: (i) the unity of the pure or transcendental ego; (ii) the real psychological I, the empirical experience of the psyche as being interconnected with the reality of the body; (iii) I, the human being, the I-man (*Ich-Mensch*), the concept of the I as used in everyday thought.

To begin with this last concept, we find that man using the pronoun I in everyday life refers to the whole man with body and soul, to his states of mind, his bodily feelings, his acts, personal qualities and characteristics, his dispositions and faculties, permanent and passing attitudes, etc. He does not say: I am a body, I am a soul, but: I have a body, I have a soul. But even here the psychological aspect has a paramount position among all the others. I call my body *mine* because its states and qualities are mine, and this means that they have some psychological significance. To be sure, I speak also of certain objects outside of the body as mine: my possessions, my performances, my objects of use and enjoyment, my clothes, etc. But the qualities of these objects, in contradistinction to those of the body, are not considered as being my qualities, unless as signs, symptoms or reflexes of my psychological qualities.

The first of the other two egological concepts, the pure or transcendental ego, is known to the student of Husserl's philosophy, especially of the first volume of the *Ideas*, as one of the basic concepts of phenomenology. It can only be grasped in transcendental reduction by performing an act of reflection upon the intentional experiences already performed. Turning back in recollections to its previous cogitations the pure ego can become conscious of itself as the subject of these recollected cogitations. It is then revealed as the "sum cogitans," as the numerically identical, undivided, and in itself unchangeable subject, constituted as a unity of inner time, which functions in all the active (and also passive) experiences pertaining to the same stream of consciousness. As such, the pure ego is the center, the *terminus a quo*, the pole of all conscious life, of all cogitations in the broadest sense, including actions, affections, theoretical, evaluating, and practical attitudes; the other pole of these manifold forms of intentional relatedness, their *terminus ad quem*, are the *cogitata* of these cogitations. The objects of these cogitations, the noemata, are, however, always objects within an environmental field, themes within a thematic field surrounded by a margin of potentially intentional units which form, so to speak, the spiritual field of vision. It is a field of determinable indeterminateness. To it belongs the whole real world, included therein the real (empirical) I's, mine as well as that of others.

Whereas any cogitation arises and passes away, the pure ego can never do so. It functions continuously as the performing ego in its actual cogitations although it may withdraw from them in certain modifications of their actuality. Thus it makes, so to speak, its entrances and exits ("*es tritt auf und ab*"), it goes into or out of action, it may be wide awake or sleeping or at any intermediary grade. But it is always there. It is in this sense that Husserl interprets Kant's famous statement that the pure ego must be able to accompany all my cogitations. In other words, all data of consciousness, states of mind, and noetic forms, which can be accompanied by the identical ego of an actual or possible cogito, belong to a single monad. Yet within this absolute stream of consciousness certain unifying formations enter into existence which are, however, entirely different from the unity of the real I and its qualities. To these formations belong, for instance, the "lasting opinions" of one and the same subject, which could be called habitual ones if this term did not lead to a dangerous confusion with the current use of "habits" emanating from "dispositions" which belong to the I-man, the empirical human being. These lasting opinions or convictions become the possessions of the pure ego, always subject of course to modification, correction, corroboration, or annihilation by supervening experiences.

In contradistinction to the pure ego, the psychological subject or psyche forms a substantial-real unity with the body of man and animal. The psychological I is the substratum of the individual qualities in a broad sense, including the intellectual, practical, emotional character, mental capacities, gifts, etc. These qualities are unities of manifestations on different levels in manifold forms of transition and interconnectedness. All this stands under a certain order which becomes patent by an analysis of the pertinent subjective experiences.

(b) *The "reality" of the psyche.* To understand why Husserl speaks of the reality of the psyche and psychological life we have to keep in mind that according to him there are two kinds of real experiences or, better, experiences of reality: (1) the outer (physical) experience of material things; (2) inner experience. Either kind is fundamental for particular types of empirical sciences, the former for the sciences of material nature, the latter for the sciences of the psyche.[5]

Why does Husserl predicate reality to both matter and psyche? The analogy is based upon a common ontological form. As the material thing is the unity of its qualities, so is the psyche the unity of the individual qualities such as character or gifts which are founded upon but not identical with the underlying sensorial faculties. These qualities are organized in a particular hierarchy; and this unity and nothing else is the psyche. Moreover, the material thing, as well as the psychological I, is causally referred to circumstances, and this in a manner regulated by them. But

---

[5] The problem of the foundation of these sciences is one of the main problems of *Ideas* III.

this analogy refers merely to the *formal* generalization, to the ontological *form* of reality, to which both realms belong. In any other respect they show important differences: (a) The material thing is constituted as the unity of *sensorial schemata*, which unity is nothing else than the unity of causal dependencies upon other material things. The psyche is a unity of the stream of consciousness as the life of an identical I, of a unity extended in time. It does not schematize itself; (b) Material things may, at least as a possibility, remain unchanged whereas psychological life is in a permanent flux; (c) A *res extensa* may be cut into pieces, the unity be divided into parts. The psyche is absolutely indivisible; (d) The interconnectedness of the material states of things belongs to the sphere of the transcendent outer world of which I have consciousness, that of psychological states to my consciousness itself, that is, to the immanent flux which alone constitutes the psychological I. To be sure, understood in a psycho-physical sense, any thing may function as an origin of "stimuli" but the fact that it influences the experiencing subject in some way is not a constitutive property of the material thing. Conversely, nature remains what it is, whether or not the psyche interferes. That the schema of the thing appears to me as dependent upon my kinesthetic movements in these and those adumbrations is sometimes referred to the so-called psychophysical causality. But this causality proves to be just a dependency of the psyche upon the functioning of the body in which it is incarnated. (e) Dependency of the psyche upon circumstances has a threefold meaning: (i) the psycho-physical (better: physio-psychical) aspect of such dependencies (e.g., all sensations, including emotional ones and those of needs, depend upon the body, therewith upon the physical nature and the system of interconnectedness prevailing therein); (ii) ideo-psychical dependencies: consciousness is, so to speak, dependent upon itself, e.g., the present stock of experiences upon the previous one, any emergent psychological datum upon the preceding psychological life. All dispositions are sedimentations of this previous history and thus "auto-conditioned." There is no analogy to this kind of dependency in the realm of inanimate nature, the realities of which are without history; (iii) the intersubjective dependencies of the psychological life, to be discussed later on.

(c) *The Constitution of Psychological Reality through the Body*. The psyche is always incarnated in a body and the problem of the constitution of this body as an animated one (not as a mere spatial object among other spatial objects) in the experience of the subject has now to be investigated. Touching my left hand with my right one, I have a double series of sensations: the right hand has tactile sensations by which my left one is experienced as a physical thing, as matter, which has extension, a certain shape, warmth, smoothness, etc. But I find also in my left hand a series of sensations localized therein which are not qualities of my body *as the* physical thing, but which appear if, where, and when my body is touched. This localization of sensation is principally different from all material determinations of the extended thing. All sensation belongs to the psyche, all extension to the material thing. The body is, thus, a physio-aesthesiological unity, the carrier of the sense organs and localizable sensations of motion and pain. It is also the organ of my will, namely the only object *immediately* and spontaneously movable by it, and by this very fact, a means of producing a *mediate* and spontaneous motion of other things. By this reason the subject, the counterpart of material nature, has the particular power of "I can," namely: "I can move this body freely" and "I can perceive the outer world by these movements."

(d) *The Constitution of Psychological Reality through Empathy*. A fellow-man (as all the other *animalia*) is from the outset given to me as both a material object with its position in space and as a subject with its psychological life. The former, like all other material objects, is given to my original perception (although in always changing orientations) or, as Husserl calls it, in originary presence. Certain material objects of my environment which are of the same type as the material thing previously experienced by me in the solipsistic attitude as my own body are apprehended by me as human bodies, that is, I bestow upon them by way of empathy ("*ich fühle mich ihnen ein*") an "I-subject" with everything pertaining thereto. The localization of my sensations is transferred ("*überträgt sich*") upon the other bodies, but this their psychological life is not given to me in originary presence, merely in co-presence, it is not *presented* but *appresented*. By the mere continuous visual perception of the

Other's body and its movements a system of appresentations, of
well-ordered indications of his psychological life and his experiences, is constituted; and here is the origin of the various forms of
the systems of signs, of expressions, and finally of language.*

To the sphere of the appresentations of the Other's psychological life belongs also the system of appearances in which an outer
world is given to him. Perceiving his body as a body, that is, in unity
with his psychological I-subject at a certain place in space and time,
I also posit by way of empathy that this second I has in a way
analogous to my own sensorial data, changing appearances and
things appearing therein. The things posited by others are also
my things, by empathy I co-perform their positing: Included here
is the notion that to him his own body is a "Here" over against
which all the other objects in the outer world are "There." I
identify the thing before me in the modus of appearance A with
the thing posited by him in the modus of appearance B. Included
therein is the possibility of exchanging places and the assumption
that every human being has at the same place in space the same
appearances of the same thing, provided that all of them have
the same sensibility. But never can the Other, being there, have
at the same time the same appearances of the same object as I
being here. Only by way of appresentations can I grasp his
appearances and his Here to which they are related by his co-
given body. And vice versa as well. Looking from his appresented
Here at my own body as an object of Nature being There I
conceive my own body exactly in the same manner in which it
is given to my fellow-man. Placing myself at the standpoint of
the Other, and *any* Other, I become aware that everyone finds
any fellow-man as the natural being Man with whom, from the
point of view of outer perception, I have to identify myself. Thus,
empathy leads to the constitution of an intersubjective objectivity
of things and of human beings as physio-psychological unities. Only
by intersubjectivity is the objective world fully constituted. This
refers even to my own body which can, strictly speaking, be
apprehended as a body merely because I may look at it from the
point of view of the other, in the modus of There.** By the same

* See the author's "Symbol, Reality and Society," *Collected Papers*, Vol. I.
** See the listings for "Here and There" in the Index to *Collected Papers*, Vols. I
and II.

token, our assumed *solus ipse* would not be an *"ipse."* Any objectivity presupposes intersubjectivity, and normalcy and anomaly also have to be re-interpreted in terms of intersubjectivity.

3) The Region of Spirit

(a) *The Personalistic Attitude and the Communicative Common Environment.* So far Husserl's analysis of the constitution of the world has dealt with the constitution of Nature, first as the reality of material things, secondly as the reality of the psyche. Now we have to investigate subjectivity which is no longer nature but spirit (*Geist*). *In the naturalistic attitude* the psyche is but a layer of aesthesiological experiences of events occurring on the body.* The animated body is an object of nature within the objective spatio-temporal world. Animals, human beings (our fellow-men as well as ourselves) are – always in terms of the naturalistic attitude – animated bodies, each with its localized sensibility; all consciousness is founded upon the body, localized upon it, and co-ordinated with it in time. Thus they belong to the context of substantial-causal Nature. All this refers also to the empirical (psychological) I which lives in these states. From this point of view the emergence of a "cogito" is a fact of nature.

From this naturalistic attitude we have to distinguish the *personalistic attitude* in which we find ourselves in everyday life among our fellow-men with whom we are connected in manifold relationships. A person is what he is as a subject of an environment. The personal environment is the world which is apperceived, remembered, believed, etc., by the person in his acts, which exists for him and towards which he adopts a theoretical or practical or evaluating attitude. Thus, the physical objective reality as such is not the actual environment of any

---

* Events occurring "on" the body should not be confused with events occurring "in" the body. In *Collected Papers*, Vol. I, the author writes: "The physical object 'the Other's body,' events occurring on this body, and his bodily movements are apprehended as expressing the Other's 'spiritual I' toward whose motivational meaning-context I am directed." In connection with this passage, Dr. Schutz wrote on July 25, 1954 to Prof. Maurice Natanson: "What I had in mind are events taking place on the 'surface' of the Other's body such as blushing or smiling, but it would be erroneous (because transforming the body into a mere thing) to speak in such a case of a *surface*."

person whatsoever. The personal environment is not a world "in itself" but a world *for* the person, who has to *know* of it either by actual apperceiving or positing it or by having it at least in the horizon in a more or less clear and determined way, ready to be apperceived. It is a world experienced by the person in his intentional experiences as having a particular meaning-structure, which, to be sure, is always changing and subject to modification by cancellation and regrouping of meaning contents. This being the case, the personal environment is always in a state of becoming. Its foundation is the world actually perceived as given to our senses, but the I finds itself referred to it in new acts of theoretical or practical evaluations. For this reason, the objects within the personal environment are not mere things of nature but objects for use and enjoyment, foodstuffs, clothes, arms, tools, works of art and literature, means for legal or religious ends. Husserl calls these environmental objects upon which a new intentional meaning has been bestowed *"founded objects."* From the naturalistic point of view a "mere thing" in the psychophysical reality may act as a stimulus upon the animal; this is a causal relationship. In terms of the relationship between personal subject and environmental object this causal relationship of stimulus and response is superseded by a system of motivations. Phenomenologically speaking, the noematic unities called "things as apprehended by the personal I" are starting points of more or less strong tendencies attracting the subject to turn to them in practical, cognitive, evaluating, etc. acts. Whether the I follows or resists these tendencies, it experiences itself as being motivated by them either in its actions or in its passively enduring them.

The subject does not merely find things in its environment but also other subjects and it apprehends them as persons with their environments, but, nevertheless, as being referred to the same objects to which it itself is referred. To be related to a common environment and to be united with the Other in a community of persons – these two propositions are inseparable. We could not be persons for Others, not even for ourselves, if we could not find with Others a common environment as the counterpart of the intentional interconnectedness of our conscious lives. This common environment is established by comprehension, which in

turn is founded upon the fact that the subjects reciprocally
motivate one another in their spiritual activities. Thus, relationships of mutual understanding (*Wechselverständnis*) and consent
(*Einverständnis*) and, therewith, a *communicative common
environment* originate. It is characterized by the fact that it is
relative to the persons who find one another within this environment and the environment itself as their counterpart (*als ihr
Gegenüber*). The person participating in the communicative
environment are given one to the other not as objects but as
counter-subjects, as consociates in a societal community of
persons. Sociality is constituted by communicative acts in which
the I turns to the Others, apprehending them as persons who turn
to him, and both know of this fact. Nevertheless, the comprehension of the other person occurs merely by appresentation,
everyone having only his own experiences given in originary
presence. This leads to the fact that within the common environment any subject has his particular subjective environment, his
private world, originarily given to him and to him alone. He
perceives the same object as his partner but with adumbrations
dependent upon his particular Here and his phenomenal Now.
Any subject participates in several time dimensions: there is
first his particular inner time, the flux of immanent time, in
which the constituting experiences have their place; second
the time dimension of the constituted experiences, the (still
subjective) space-time. By reason of the relationships of
simultaneity, of "before" and "after," prevailing between both
dimensions, the primarily constituted unity of the appearing
thing is, as to its duration, simultaneous with the continuity of
perception and its noetical duration. There is, third, the objective intersubjective time which forms *a priori* a single order
of time with all the subjective times: the objective time and the
objective space "appear" as "valid" phenomena in the subjective
orders of space-time. This is the true reason for the exchangea-
bility of places mentioned herein before. The communicative
common environment presupposes that the same thing given to
me *now* (namely in an intersubjective Now) in a particular
adumbration can be given to the Other in the same modus
thereafter in the flux of intersubjective time, and vice versa. The
concept of normalcy and anomaly of experience, which we en-

countered in the solipsistic analysis, now receives a new, inter-subjective, meaning.

According to Husserl, communicating subjects constitute personal unities of a higher order, social subjectivities (collectivities) which have as their environment the world in existence *for* these social subjectivities, the world of social or cultural objects, sciences, arts, etc. Proceeding on these lines we may even arrive at the concept of the sum-total of all social subjectivities which stand in actual or potential communication, and their counter-part: the spiritual world.

(b) *Motivation as the Basic Law of Personalistic Life.* It has been mentioned before that the causal relationship prevailing between objects in nature is superseded by the relationship of motivation prevailing between the subject and the environmental objects in the personalistic attitude. The *personal*, or as Husserl calls it, the *spiritual subject* is the subject of intentional-ities, and the environmental object is object for it, thematic object for this I within its defining cogito as this object is therein perceived, remembered, etc. The point is that this relationship is not a *real* relationship but a relationship of *intentionality*. A real relationship prevails between the reality "I-man" and the real object which stands in real causal-relationship of nature with his body. The real relationship drops out if the thing does not exist; the relationship of intentionality, however, persists, even if not realities but phantoms are posited by the spiritual I as the noematic object of its environment. This object incites, motivates the subject to attend to it, to take, actively or passive-ly, an attitude to it, to contemplate it theoretically, to handle it practically, to evaluate it, etc. Motivation is, thus, the basic law of spiritual life, and the all-pervading stream of conscious-ness is a unity of motivations. In personalistic interpretation even all experiences of things of nature with their intercon-nectedness by space, time, and causality are dissolved into a texture of immanent motivations according to which the noetic experiences progress from positing to positing, from doxic thesis to doxic thesis in the way of *"in-consequence-of."* The motivations may be of different types: (1) motivations of reason (*Vernunftmoti-vationen*), that is, motivations *of* acts *by* acts which stand under the jurisdiction of reason, as in the case of logical reasoning where I bestow my doxic thesis upon the conclusion "in consequence of" having bestowed it upon the premises; or (2) motivations by association and habit, that is, relations between earlier and later experiences within the same stream of consciousness, in which case the motivating experiences may be sedimentations of previously performed reasonable acts or even perfectly unreasonable ones, imposed upon us; they may be distinct or hidden, eventually even "unconscious" within the meaning of psycho-analysis.

The comprehension of other human beings by empathy is based upon the fact that they are apprehended as subjects of an environment of things and persons to which they react and upon which they act as persons, as spiritual I's, that is, subject to the laws of motivation. Of course, the Other's person is given to my comprehension as referred to his body and in unity with his body. But if we talk with the Other and he with us, if we give him orders or follow his, then the relationship between the Other's spiritual I and his body is to us merely the unity of an expression of his spiritual life and that which is expressed therein. No search of causal factors can help us understand the Other and his behavior. We have to understand his motives, the "reasons," for his actions, and to obtain knowledge of their context. Nor is my being motivated by his actions (and vice versa) a real causal relationship. As physical objects and events his body and bodily movements are articulated in accordance with a particular meaning-structure; it is an animated body expressing the Other's spiritual I to whose motivational meaning context I am directed. Empathy in other persons is nothing else but that form of apprehension which grasps this meaning. This situation prevails also with respect to what Husserl calls animated objects, generally called objects of culture. If we read a book we perceive it as an outer object, a material thing. I see it as it appears to me, here on my desk to my right, but I am not directed towards it as an outer object, but toward that which "animates" this material object, namely towards the meaning of what is written therein: I "live in its meaning" by comprehending it. The same holds good for "animated things" in everyday life, a tool, a house, a theater, a temple, a machine, etc. The spiritual meaning of all these objects is apperceived as being founded upon the really

appearing object which is not apprehended as such but as expressing its meaning.

(c) *The Spiritual I.* The apperception of the Other's spiritual
I is also transferred to my own I. The I which apperceives other
minds is not necessarily given to itself in this manner, namely as
a comprehensive unity. Only by comprehending my fellow-man
as apprehending me as a social human being, do I become myself
an I in my relationship to Others, creating, thus, the constitutive
possibility for the "We," the community of all human beings
which includes me.

The particularity of the spiritual subject consists in the fact
that within it the apperception "I" emerges, in which apperception this "subject" is the "object" (although not always the
thematic object). We have therefore to distinguish "I who I am"
on the subjective side, and "I who I am" as object for me, the
Me, which is in a specific sense represented, constituted, eventually intended within the being "I am." Under the Me we understand the person, constituted for me, the I which is conscious as
a Self.

The I as a unity is a system of faculties of the form "I can."
Here we have to distinguish the physical "I can," the bodily one,
and the spiritual one. I can – practical normalcy being presupposed – move my body and its organs of perception in a natu-
rally free way. I can freely perform my mental activities, e.g.,
penetrate into my recollections, compare, distinguish, etc., all
this in a typically normal way depending upon circumstances,
such as my age, health, etc. Again the "I can" as a practical
possibility and the "I can" as a logical possibility have to be
distinguished. I may make a decision merely between practical
possibilities, they alone may become a theme of my will. This
practical "I can" may or may not meet resistance. If it does,
there subsists a graduality of the active power to overcome the
inertia of resistance. The resistance may prove to be unsur-
mountable: I cannot, I do not have the force.

Another category of the "I can" reveals itself in an analysis
of what can be imagined as possible. A centaur is a possible
object, intuited as the identical object of these or those quasi-
perceptions. This possibility is a doxic-logical possibility. I
cannot, however, intuitively imagine that two times two equals

five. I can merely imagine that I perform such a judgment in a
figurative, confused way. I can imagine that I commit a murder
and yet I cannot imagine that I could do it. Is this not an antinomy? Husserl's answer is that the first "I could do it" refers
merely to the imagined practical possibility as such; the second
"I could not do it, nevertheless" means that the action contradicts the "nature" of my person, the style in which I become
motivated. This leads to the insight that the "I can" is motivated
in the knowledge of my own person. I know myself by experience,
I have an empirical self-consciousness. My cogitations are acts of
an I-subject, and the I has been constituted by its activities and
its habits and faculties to an apperceptive unity, the kernel of
which is the pure ego. Hence the evidence "I am." By analogy
to previous experiences, to previous forms of behavior and their
motives I expect to behave in a certain way in the future. I may
also in my imagination place myself in possible contexts of
motives, in possible situations, and decide how I would behave
under the then prevailing circumstances. The personal life
shows a certain typicality. Everyone is first typical as a human
being, (e.g., the general typicality of the human body is a prerequisite of all empathy), second as this particular individual
character. Association and apperception are principles of the
typification of all psychological acts. This typicality is the origin
of my expectations of future behavior, of my own as well as of
my fellow-men, but as any expectation, it carries along apperceptive horizons of indeterminate determinability within a
general intentional frame of reference. In terms of these typi-
calities I comprehend the behavior of my fellow-man and its
motives. When I co-perform his acts in phantasy his motives
become my quasi-motives, and thus comprehensible. The Other's
comprehensibly motivated spiritual life and its individual typical
course is, thus, apprehended as a variation (*Abwandlung*) of my
own spiritual life. In both I can distinguish two levels: the higher
one is the specifically spiritual level, the level of the *intellectus
agens*, of the I in its free acts, including therein all acts of reason
proper; this level, in turn, depends upon the dark background of
character dispositions which in turn depend upon nature. Here
is the origin of the classic distinction between reason and sensibility. Mind is not the abstract I of the positing acts but the full

personality, the I-man, who takes an attitude, who thinks, evaluates, etc. But this I is founded upon its past experiences. They can be questioned as to their history and genesis.

4) The Ontological Precedence of the Spiritual World

Thus the personalistic and the naturalistic attitude are interconnected in a certain way. The stream of experiences is dependent upon the psyche in a specific sense: the psyche through the animated body is dependent upon nature. The mind in its freedom moves the body and gears through the body into the external world. Working upon nature, mind does not, nevertheless, exercise a causal influence upon it, provided that we understand under causality the relationship of a reality with its correlative circumstantial realities. We may say that the body has a dual reality: as aesthesiological body it depends upon the material body in naturalistic terms; as organ of the will (*Willensleib*), as freely movable body, it constitutes a specific reality in personalistic terms. In the same manner the psyche has a double aspect: as bodily determined it depends upon the physical body, therewith upon nature. As spiritually determined it stands in a context of reality with the mind. Hence we have two poles: physical nature and spirit, and in between, body and psyche. And it follows that body and psyche are, strictly speaking, Nature in a second sense only with respect to their facing physical nature. On the other hand, the appearing body with its sensations and the psyche belong to the spiritual environment and receive as such the character of a spiritual reality. As Paul Ricœur [6] puts it, in naturalistic terms everything can be interpreted by reification, even spirit, which manifests itself merely in its performances. In personalistic terms everything can be spiritualized, even the material things which are just the theater and the impact of action and endurance. The body is, so to speak, the converter of spiritual motivation into physical causality.

Nevertheless, the spiritual world has ontological precedence over the naturalistic one, and Husserl proves this by a careful refutation of the theory of a psycho-physical parallelism. We have

---

[6] In his remarkable review of *Ideas II* in *Revue de Métaphysique et de Morale*, Vol. LVI, 1951, pp. 357–394 and Vol. LVII, 1952, pp. 1–16.

to forgo a presentation of his subtle but involved argument. Its
outcome is that spirit cannot be determined by its dependencies
upon nature by reducing it to physical nature in terms of the
natural sciences. Subjects cannot be dissolved into Nature because
then that which gives meaning to Nature would have been
eliminated. Nature is principally relative, Mind principally ir-
relative (absolute). If we eliminate all minds from the world,
then there would be no Nature at all. If, however, we eliminate
Nature, the "true" intersubjective-objective reality, then Mind
would still remain as individual mind; it would merely lose the
possibility of sociality, the possibility of comprehension which
presupposes the intersubjective constitution of the body. This
individual mind would no longer be a person referred to a material and, therewith, personal world. But in spite of this tre-
mendous impoverishment of "personal" life, an ego with its
stream of consciousness would remain and would safekeep its
individuality, its specific way of judging, of evaluating, of being
motivated in its positing and attitudes. In the realm of nature no
thing has in itself individuality. What distinguishes two equal
things is the real-causal context which presupposes a Here and
Now, and these two terms refer to an individual subjectivity with
respect to which the determination of place and time has been
constituted. Mind, however, in contradistinction to the thing, has
in itself its motivation. It is not individualized because it exists
at a certain place within the world, but because it is the sedimentation of its habitualities and has, thus, its individual history.
The same mind cannot exist twice and cannot return to its
previous states. This is so because minds are not unities of
appearances but unities of absolute contexts of consciousness,
more precisely, egological unities. And appearances are correlates
of contexts of consciousness, which contexts have absolute
existence. If the appearances are constituted intersubjectively,
then they are referred to a plurality of persons who can inter-
communicate. The absolute existence of persons and their experiences precedes the relative existence of the appearances. All
individuation of the latter depends upon the individuation of the
former, all existence of Nature upon the existence of absolute
minds. Nature is the X, and principally nothing but the X.
which is determined in accordance with general determinations,

Mind, however, is not an X, but that which is given as such in the spiritual experience.

III. SOME CRITICAL OBSERVATIONS

It is hoped that, in spite of its obvious imperfections, the preceding account of the mainstream of Husserl's argument has brought out the central importance of the problems dealt with. The American reader might be surprised to recognize the similarity of certain themes with those of William James, Santayana, Dewey, George H. Mead, Cooley, and others. On the other hand, it can be clearly seen how deeply certain European philosophers such as Scheler, Heidegger, Sartre, Merleau-Ponty are indebted to Husserl.

Space does not permit a full critical evaluation of Husserl's argument, and some of his problems such as his treatment of intersubjectivity and sociality would deserve a separate study of considerable length. The following remarks should be read as an abridged and incomplete catalogue of some open questions which require further critical analyses. They are based exclusively upon the volume under scrutiny, without taking into consideration writings of Husserl so far unpublished.

(1) Husserl points out that the same unchanged thing presents itself in various aspects dependent upon the situation of my body. One of them will prove to be the optimal one and will be considered as the "normal," the "real," the "true" one, which leads to the constitution of an objective nature within the solipsistic sphere. The identification of the "optimal" with the "normal" aspect is highly questionable. Rather should not the habitually recurrent aspect be considered as the criterion of normalcy? And in either case, how can this "solipsistic normalcy" lead to the constitution of "intersubjective normalcy"?

(2) The distinction between the three I's (the I-man, the psychological I, the transcendental ego) is full of difficulties and at least the terminology oscillates considerably: (a) Where is the place of the fourth I-concept, the spiritual I, the person, especially in its relationship to the pure ego? In just the manuscripts published in the volume under scrutiny Husserl makes four or five attempts to answer this question (Annexes X–XIV,

Section 57); in later phases of his theory the concept of the pure or transcendental ego will undergo a complete reformulation; (b) With respect to this distinction of three or four I's within the same stream of consciousness, what is the relationship between the I-subjects and the I-objects, that is, in the language of William James and G. H. Mead, between I and Me? Are there also three (or four) Selves as there are three (or four) I's? (c) Is this trichotomy equally applicable with respect to the Other? Which one is, then, the *terminus a quo* and the *terminus ad quem* of the rather unexplained function of empathy? The problem of empathy itself remains entirely unclarified; the reference to the underlying relationship between presentation and appresentation involves the crucial phenomenological problem of how the appresented objectivity is constituted by the presented one, or, in the language of the fifth Cartesian Meditation, how the relationship of "pairing" (*accouplement*) originates.

(3) Closely connected with the previous group of problems is the questionable allocation of habitualities (lasting opinions) to the pure ego, of individual qualities, such as character or gifts to the psyche, and of the unities of "I can" to the spiritual I, the person. The difficulties are increased by the introduction of the concept of ideo-psychical dependencies as characteristic of the psyche, and of motivation as the basic law of personal life. Is motivation different from ideo-psychical dependencies? If the latter have to be conceived as causal dependencies upon "circumstances," are these circumstances not necessarily environmental ones and therefore motivating? And does the concept of motivation not cover very heterogeneous elements if equally applied to the I as being attracted by an object, the I as the system of faculties of the form "I can," and the social interrelationship?

(4) According to Husserl, the "localization" of sensations in my body is "transferred" (whatever this means) by way of empathy to that material thing appearing within my solipsistic environment which is "of the same type" as my own body, and this in such a way that this material thing is apprehended as the body of another human being with its psychological life. (a) Is there not the fallacy of hysteron-proteron involved? Are there objects within my solipsistic environment thinkable which are

"of the type of my body," my body in its aesthesiological structure and its movements being experienced from "within," the appearing object "of the same type" from "without"? (b) Have we not to distinguish with Sartre *"le corps pour moi"* and *"le corps pour autrui"*? Or to introduce with Merleau-Ponty the concept of *"le corps propre"*? (c) Have we not to say with Max Scheler that the "localization of sensations" belongs to the sphere of vitality (*Vitalsphäre*) and is, therefore, essentially incapable of being "transferred by empathy"? (d) And if such a transfer were possible, would it refer merely to the belief in the Other's general capacity of "localizing his sensations on his body" or also to the specific system of such localizations? In the latter case, how can I, being a male, grasp by empathy the localizations of certain sensations in a female body?

(5) The least satisfactory part of the analysis is that dealing with sociality and social groups. From the outset actual or possible communication between persons is taken for granted and sociality defined as being constituted by communicative acts. The communicative environment, basic for all constitution of the intersubjective world, originates, according to Husserl, in relationships of mutual understanding and mutual consent, which in turn are founded upon communication. But communication presupposes already a social interrelationship upon which it is founded, such as the relationship of being "tuned in" one upon the other, of being motivated to address the other or to listen to him.* And the vehicles of such communication – significant gestures, signs, symbols, language – have necessarily to belong to the common environment in order to make communication possible and, therefore, cannot constitute it. Even if we assume, for the sake of argument, that the Other as a person is apprehended with his environment and also that this environment is from the outset, at least partially, a common one, such apprehension of the Other alone would not involve the possibility of my comprehending him and even less of communicating with him and of reaching with him mutual consent.

(6) The assumption that communicating subjects constitute personal unities of a higher order, social subjectivities (collectivities) which have as their environment the world of social and

* See *Collected Papers*, Vol. II, p. 161 f.

cultural objects is entirely unclarified. Does this theory have its root in Hegel or Durkheim or the "organic" school of the social sciences (Wundt, for instance) ruling in Germany at the beginning of the century? Or in Rudolf Gierke's legal theory of the "*Sozialer Verband*" (a term persistently used by Husserl)? The attempts of Simmel, Max Weber, Scheler to reduce social collectivities to the social interaction of individuals is, so it seems, much closer to the spirit of phenomenology than the pertinent statements of its founder. Doubtless the present work of Husserl is full of the most profound insights relating to the foundation of the social sciences. But they have to be looked for in other parts than in those dedicated to the analysis of communication and social groups.

These few remarks are submitted for further consideration. There is not space enough to summarize the positive contributions of this outstanding philosophical achievement. It is hoped that the lengthy presentation of its content speaks for itself.

PHENOMENOLOGY AND THE FOUNDATIONS
OF THE SOCIAL SCIENCES

(IDEAS, VOLUME III BY EDMUND HUSSERL)[1]

Husserl's "Ideas II," published at the same time as the present volume, were discussed at length in the previous chapter. There the reasons why Husserl in 1913 published only the first volume of his work were explained and a brief survey of the history of his manuscripts forming the content of "Ideas II" was given. The present volume, briefly entitled "Ideas III," is based upon a manuscript of 1912, drafted at the same time as "Ideas I," and, unlike the manuscripts forming volume II, was never rewritten by the author or his assistants. It is, therefore, more unified than its twin volume on which Husserl worked with interruptions until 1928, but it represents an earlier phase of the development of the thought of the founder of modern phenomenology which cannot always be reconciled with the statements of volume II, let alone the later phases of phenomenological philosophy. Some readers who are familiar with volume I might find it helpful to study Ideas III first before turning to the more complicated and highly elaborated problems presented in Ideas II.

Husserl starts in the first chapter with an investigation of the various realms of reality – the material thing, the animated body, the psyche – in order to ascertain the fundamental kinds of apperception corresponding to each of these realms and the character of the various sciences originating therein. Material things are originally given in acts of material perception, that is, of things in the outer world. Material perceptions in this sense are just a special case of perceptions of extended objects;

[1] Edited by Marly Biemel and published as Volume V. of *Husserliana* by the Husserl Archiv, Louvain, under the direction of Professor H. L. Van Breda, Den Haag, 1952.

the latter would also include the perception of phantoms. That which distinguishes real material things from phantoms is not, however, their being a "substance" in the sense of Descartes or Spinoza. Their reality, according to Husserl, is principally relative, namely relative to the circumstances by which they are causally determined. In perception the real thing is only given unilaterally, its causal relations remain undetermined. The objectivity of Nature is constituted only in the unified spatial-temporal causal context of the experiences of a plurality of Egos which enter into intercommunication, through the intermediary of their bodies. When one passes to the theoretical attitude, a science of material Nature becomes possible. It follows that all sciences of reality (in the sense just explained) must be causally explanatory if they aim at determining what reality is.

A second basic form of apprehension is that referring to the animated body, not as a material thing but as the carrier of sensorial fields localized therein, as a universe of sensations of sensorial impressions, briefly, as an object characterized by the fact that all perceived bodily experiences are experienced with their localization. The science of somatology (which, of course, presupposes the material experiences of material existence) has to study the somatic perceptions which any scientist makes not only by the experience of his own body, but also by the experiencing apperceptions of the Other's body given to him by way of appresentation in the form of empathy. This concept of somatology as a theory of sensations, (treated customarily by physiology and psychology) presupposes the elimination of the sensations from the texture of apprehensions in which they are interwoven. Just the same sensations which in the realizing apprehension of material perceptions function as "presenting contents" (*darstellende Inhalte*) for material characteristics, receive localization in the new realizing apprehension which we call "our bodily experiences," namely as states of sensation; yet they are under the heading "perceptual states of the I" components of the psychical state, thus belonging to the third realm of reality, that of the psyche or of the egological sphere. That is the true reason why psychology, understood as the science of the psyche, has also to deal with sensations. But whereas from the point of view of somatology the sensations are manifestations of the *"aistheta"* of the body, of its sensibility, and have to be investigated by the theoretical somatologist as to the causal relations to which they belong, sensations, from the point of view of psychology, are the hyletic foundation of perceptual apprehensions; their function is, then, a double one: as kinesthetic sensation they are motivating, as presentational sensations motivated. And all these apprehensions are occurrences within the egological consciousness and undergo as such a particular apprehension, namely as states of the psyche. A human being or animal is not a mere body with sensorial states of consciousness; it has a particular psychological structure by reason of which it becomes conscious of the sensations mediated by its bodily existence, taking towards them a theoretical, evaluating, acting attitude, etc. The psyche, as the unity of these experiences which fall under the heading of consciousness, is a reality of its own, although always founded upon the reality of the body which, in turn, is founded upon the reality of the material thing.

Psychology, as the science dealing with the reality of the psyche, has to deal with the genesis and the transformations of the I and its dispositions, with the ideo-psychical regularities pertaining to the I and its acts, etc. But these characteristics are insufficient for a description of the particular realm of a science of psychology and its methods. In order to determine the foundation of psychology, we have to investigate its relationship to phenomenology. This is the purpose of the second chapter of Husserl's study.

This relationship can only be understood as a special case of the relationship prevailing between phenomenology and all the empirical sciences. All discoveries of the latter take place within the frame of an *a priori*, which cannot be grasped by the dogmatic empirical sciences but is accessible to the eidetic methods of phenomenology. The method of all empirical sciences is determined or at least co-determined by the general essential structure of the realm of reality to which these sciences refer. The examination of this structure as to its constitution in pure intuition would lead to an ontology of this particular realm. Thus, ontology refers to the various regions of objectivities and to the methods which any empirical science dealing with facts belonging to these regions has to observe. There must *a priori* exist as many ontologies as there are regional concepts and, consequently, all radical classification of the sciences depends upon the concept of the "region" (such as thing, animal, psyche, etc.) and its essence which can be disclosed by noematic intuition. Starting, for instance, from the concrete perception of a material thing, I may perform the transition to the eidetic attitude, abstracting from the existential positing of actual experience and moving in free arbitrariness in the realm of "empty possibilities." In whatever way I transform the "Gestalt" of the thing in free phantasy, vary its qualitative determinations, change its real properties – all these products of my phantasy still show particular regularities: they refer to things created, destroyed, transformed, etc., but still to *things*. The thing perceived appears to me only under a certain aspect, its meaning transcends that which appears, but it does so in a still undetermined way, which refers to future perceptions. We may ask how this object looks in other perspectives, what might be the appearance of its unseen side; we may imagine, by a procedure of our phantasy, a course of experience which would reveal the perceived objects from all sides, completely and consistently. We may even construct entirely different worlds for the same thing from which we started with different laws of different natural sciences. Phantasy may act as freely as it pleases, but it can not annihilate the world; it can only build up an infinity of new and ever new worlds. If within this realm something is experienced at all, then it is experienced as a *res extensa*, and this term designates not merely a content but a form for all possible objects of possible experiences of this kind in general. Thing, therefore, is not merely a general concept (universal) such as mineral. All material contents of a thing are contingent; they all may change, but not its general form as a thing. In eidetic attitude I can, thus, determine the essential structure of a thing, the eidos "thing." In this manner in the world of essences a differentiation is established between *a priori* and *a posteriori* concepts. And what has been stated with respect to the region of things is just an example for the determination of regions in general. The *a priori* within the sense of region is the fountainhead of all ontologies which prescribe to all empirical sciences their field and methods.

As far as nature is concerned, its ontology encompasses geometry, phoronomy, and the a prioristic discipline dealing with the structure of pure time. An ontology of the psychical or animated realities has to deal with the animated in general, including the psyche. Take, for instance, perception as a "state" of real existing individuals. How experiences of this kind occur with respect to human beings and animals, under what real conditions and with what consequences, according to what general and special natural laws, all this can and must be determined by the methods of the empirical sciences, by observation and experiment. Yet we may perform the "eidetic reduction," discarding all questions as to the actual existence of these "states" called perceptions within actual unities of consciousness, and turn to the eidos of perception, the eternally identical meaning of possible perceptions in general. We can do the same with respect to recollections, phantasies, expectations, cognitive, emotional, volitive experiences of any kind. Directed toward the essences in eidetic-intuitive apperception, the full contents of these experiences and their intentional correlates, such as they are given to psychological experience are fully preserved in the eidos. What is lost is merely their relation to the facts of an experienced reality within nature. To the empirical psychologist, however, the "psychologically real," namely the actual experiences as actual states with their relations to space and time, is given. The same situation prevails even where a region of reality can be originarily determined in such a way that it functions as the foundation of two kinds of sciences: empirical sciences which refer to existence, and eidetic sciences, which refer to essence and determine therewith the "content" of all possible existing in general, and, therefore, also of the actually existing. Everywhere the eidetic science precedes (in terms of foundation, not genetically) the empirical one.

The eidetic science of the realm of the psyche is a part of phenomenology. Husserl calls it rational psychology. It has, however, to be well understood that phenomenological method no more enters into competition with experimental psychology, than mathematical method in physics competes with experimental physics. Husserl emphasizes that he has never written a word which would run counter to the profound respect due to experimental psychology. His aim is merely to render experimental psychology more fertile by referring it to its phenomenological foundations and to make it, in the true sense, a rational explicating science.

But is phenomenology then not mere description and do we not have a highly developed "descriptive psychology?" In any realm of reality there are descriptive sciences, but all description refers to real existence and states what has been really experienced and what supposedly can be experienced again and again in the future. Phenomenological description does not refer to existence and real experience of existence. Its aim is the investigation of the apodictically posited frame of possibilities within which the empirical realities occur. In addition, it has to be considered that description means something different in the so-called descriptive sciences of nature and in descriptive psychology. The descriptive concepts of the former originate on a level on which realities are already fully constituted for the intuition but are, from the point of view of the final idea of objectivity of nature, mere "appearances" of the things themselves, the things of physics. Appearances refer to intercommunicating subjects of normal sensibility, and physics rejects such normalcy and also the relationship to normal circumstances as yardsticks for objectivity. Physics, as an objective natural science, does not have any interest in the systematic description of these subjective and intersubjective appearances. They interest the physicist merely in so far as they are manifestations of objective qualities. The description of the really experienced colors in their manifold adumbrations does not as such interest him; to him, the experienced color is merely a manifestation of those cognitively determinable objective optical events for which mathematical optics establishes the theory.

Of quite a different character is psychological description. The psyche is not a substratum of "appearances." The psychological unity constitutes itself directly in its states, which are given to consciousness adequately within immanent time and without the intermediary of appearances. The "relativity" to the intuiting subject drops out, and these experiences which pertain to the true existence of the psyche itself are the very *theme* of psychology, not merely media from which this theme could be distilled. In psychology there are no "appearances" of the psyche; there is merely our experience of the psyche itself. If we understand under "description" the conceptual expression of that which has been perceived, then psychological description determines the psychological events as such, whereas the description of the natural sciences determines merely appearances but not that which has to be determined. Thus the field of psychological experiences (*Erlebnisse*) becomes for psychology an infinite field of determining description in terms of rigorous conceptual schemes. For the performance of this task, however, phenomenological analysis is required in order to ascertain the eidetic context which underlies the conceptual scheme. This task cannot be performed by empirical psychology, but only by rational psychology which is (in Husserl's view of 1912) a part of phenomenology. It has to be kept in mind, however, that any kind of psychology deals with psychical events as the states of a psyche, that is, of a human or animal I, which is a reality founded upon Nature. Phenomenology aims at dealing with the eidetic of the transcendentally purified consciousness, with the pure Ego. As such, phenomenology is neither rational psychology nor a rational discipline of Nature. To call the eidetic discipline of psychological *states* of consciousness phenomenology, as this has been done above, and also in earlier writings by Husserl, is only justified by the fact that the pure experience enters with its full essence into the psychological state and undergoes there a particular apperception which, however, does not change its essential character. The task of transcendental phenomenology proper can best be ascertained by an investigation of the relationship between phenomenology and ontology, and this study forms chapter III of the present book of Husserl.

This chapter is very important for the methods of phenomenology but of a highly technical nature. It would deserve a presentation surpassing by far the space at our disposal. It deals with a certain paradox encountered by transcendental phenomenology. After the performance of the phenomenological reduction, so we learned in volume I, we have bracketed all "transcendent being" and also all empirical sciences referring thereto. What has been left is the pure consciousness with its acts and the correlates of these acts, the noemata. Thus the epoché of the transcendental reduction refers also to all ontologies. On the other hand, as it

has been stated above, all ontologies are rooted in their fundamental concepts and axioms, and these can be interpreted as
essential contents of pure experiences which as such belong to the
realm of transcendental phenomenology. But if this is true, then
the consequence has to be accepted that all the disciplines
founded upon these fundamental concepts and axioms are also
preserved in the transcendental reduction. This is indeed a very
serious dilemma which goes to the roots of the basic principle of
phenomenology, the transcendental reduction.[2]

Husserl overcomes this difficulty by distinguishing between a
science of the transcendental consciousness on the one hand, and
an intuitive discipline dealing with the essential structures of
this consciousness on the other hand. The former would include
the sum total of essential knowledge referring to experience in
general, therewith also the transcendental interpretation of all
ontologies. The "same" concepts and propositions may, therefore,
appear in ontologies and in pure phenomenology proper. But
there is an important difference. If we deal as ontologists with
the eidos of space, of material nature, of spirit, we are still
concerned with dogmatic science, we judge of spatial configu-
rations as such, men as such, etc. We state what belongs to these
objectivities (*Gegenständlichkeiten*) in truth, that is, in unre-
stricted necessity and generality. These propositions of eidetic
generality find their application within the sphere of empirical
knowledge, since we know *a priori* on the one hand that nothing
can occur within the existential sphere that is essentially excluded by the structure of the essences particularized therein,
and, on the other hand, that everything happening within the
empirical sphere must happen as postulated by the structure of
these essences as its necessary consequence. Phenomenology
proper, however, is not concerned with things, psyches, etc.,
"as such" in eidetic generality, but with the transcendental
consciousness, its acts and their correlates, briefly with Noeses
and their Noemata (correlates). Noema and essence should not

---

[2] Such an eminent student of phenomenology as Professor Eugen Fink, although
starting from a different point of departure, has recently pointed out that the ontological problem has been dodged by Husserl's phenomenology in all phases of its
development. See his paper "L'analyse intentionelle et le problème de la pensée
spéculative" in H. L. Van Breda (Ed.), *Problèmes actuels de la phénoménologie*, Brussels,
1952, pp. 53–87, especially p. 66 ff.

be confounded, although it is essentially possible by a change of attitude to transform the apprehension of a noema into that of the corresponding ontic essence. Nevertheless, to posit a noema does not involve the positing of the objectivity which "corresponds" to the noema, although this objectivity is "objectivity meant by" the noema. "Phenomenological judgment of the noemata" is one thing, "ontological judgment of essences and essential singularities" is another. To be sure, as phenomenologists we also perform positing acts in a theoretical attitude, but these acts are exclusively directed towards experiences (*Erlebnisse*) and their correlates. As ontologists, however, we perform acts of actual positing which are not directed towards correlates and "objects" in quotation marks, but towards objects as such. We have to distinguish between the positing of meanings and the positing of objects. The noema is nothing else than the generalization of the idea of meaning applied to the total realm of the act.

The analyses of the preceding section are just an example of one of the most important devices of phenomenology, the method of clarification, which Husserl describes in the fourth and final chapter of the present volume. As a rigorous science, phenomenology postulates the reduction of all its concepts and propositions to the highest degree of clarity. But also all dogmatic sciences are in need of clarification. They all are far from a satisfactory understanding of their foundations, which originate in the imperfect and naive empirical knowledge of everyday life. They frequently simply re-symbolize that which was relatively intelligible on a lower level, but which now, by this very process of re-symbolization turns out to be entirely obscure on the scientific level. In this way the sciences became what they are, namely factories of very valuable and practically useful knowledge for the domination of the world; but the progress of science has not enriched us with treasures of insight. The most urgent task is to refer the sciences to their origin and to transform them by the intuitive method of clarification into systems of understandable knowledge.

The process of clarification has to start with the conceptual material with which the sciences operate. These are of a threefold kind: a) logical formal concepts such as object, quality, relation, number, but also concepts which express forms of meaning such as "proposition," etc. They are common property of all sciences; b) regional concepts, which express the "region" as such, e.g. "thing," "quality of a thing," "relations of things," etc. They are common to all sciences, referring to the same region; c) material concretizations of these regional concepts such as color, sounds, the various kinds of sensorial feelings, etc. Systematic clarification would have to deal with these various concepts in the sequence just enumerated, that is, the clarification of the ontologies has to precede that of the pertinent empirical sciences. It is the ideal of phenomenology to establish a complete realm of fully clarified ideas, that is, a complete system of all intuitively knowable essences. By the technique of eidetic reduction phenomenology, so Husserl thinks, can perform this task.

We have, however, to distinguish between the explication (*Verdeutlichung*) and clarification (*Klärung*) of a concept. The explication of a concept, of that which is meant by a word as such, takes place only within the cognitive sphere. The meaning of the term "decaeder," for example, can be successfully elaborated in cognitive terms to "a geometric body limited by ten congruent planes." There are many "equivalent" expressions for the same state of affairs and we have to distinguish the unexplicated, unanalyzed concepts from the analytically explicated ones and both from "analytic propositions" in the sense of Kant, namely propositions designating the noematic object of the first and the second as the same. More precisely, we have to distinguish the unanalyzed concept and another concept which in relation to the first one will later on function as its explication. In the process of clarification, however, we transcend the sphere of the mere meaning of a term and of the thinking of meanings: we bring the noematic object of the meaning to congruency with the noematic object of our intuition. But the analysis of verbal meaning, the establishment of a congruency as nearly perfect as possible between the cognitive noema and the intuitive noema, has merely a propaedeutic function for the process of clarification proper to be performed on the side of intuition. Such clarification has by eidetic methods to follow exactly the levels of constitution of the particular intuited object which is actually taken as an example or exemplar of the eidetic noema: the object as it is meant has to be brought by the process of clarification to perfect self-givenness, to perfect lucidity and vividness. Again we recognize here the general task and the of course infinitely remote ideal of Husserl's phenomenology: to grasp in intuition and perfect clarity as well as in systematic completeness the universe of ideas, of all possible essential kinds of possible objectivities in general; to determine on the ground of the noemata included in such intuitions all possible conceptual essences; to allocate to these essences words and meanings of words which express them in purity and unequivocally; to arrive, thus, at a complete stock of fully clarified concepts, respectively, terms. Phenomenology can perform this job because all eidetic axioms find their place within its context; thus phenomenology is the matrix from which all ontological insights originate.

THE PROBLEM OF TRANSCENDENTAL
INTERSUBJECTIVITY IN HUSSERL *

I

The central significance of intersubjectivity was already made
clear by Husserl in the first volume of *Ideen* [1] on the occasion of
an analysis of the natural attitude. The objective, spatio-temporal
reality of a surrounding world (*Umwelt*), accepted not only by
me but also by other ego-subjects (*Ich-Subjekte*), is taken for
granted without question as an element of the general thesis
(*Generalthese*) of the natural attitude. It is part of this general
thesis that other ego-subjects are apprehended as fellow-men
(*Nebenmenschen*) who have consciousness of the objective world
as I do in spite of differences in perspectives and in degrees
of clarity. It is also taken for granted that we can communicate
with one another (Par. 29). How, in the frame of the natural
attitude, is mutual understanding (*Einverständnis*) in principle
possible? The answer given by Husserl in *Ideen I* (Par. 53), on
the occasion of the preparatory analyses of pure consciousness,
refers to the experience of a linking of consciousness and body
(*Leib*) to form a natural, empirical unity by means of which
consciousness is located in the space and time of nature, and
which, in acts of "empathy," makes possible reciprocal under-

* The present paper was read and discussed at the Husserl-Colloquium in Royaumont on April 28, 1957. The German text from which this translation was made
appeared in *Philosophische Rundschau: Eine Vierteljahrsschrift für philosophische
Kritik*, edited by Hans-Georg Gadamer and Helmut Kuhn, Vol. V, 1957, pp. 81ff.
The translation is by Frederick Kersten in collaboration with Professor Aron Gurwitsch and Professor Thomas Luckmann.

[1] Edmund Husserl, *Ideen zu einer reinen Phänomenologie und Phänomenologischen
Philosophie*, I. Buch: *Allgemeine Einführung in die reine Phänomenologie*. II. Buch:
Phänomenologische Untersuchungen zur Konstitution. III. Buch: *Die Phänomenologie
und die Fundamente der Wissenschaften*, Husserliana, Vols. III to V, Den Haag,
1950–1952.

standing between animate subjects belonging to one world. "The experiences of others manifest themselves to us," we apprehend them by virtue of the fact that they find bodily expression. This "apprehending" ("*Ansehen*") by way of empathy is an intuiting, presentative act, although not an *originarily* (*originär*) presentative one. There is consciousness of the Other and his mental life as "present" in his body. However, his mental life is not given originarily, as his body is (Par. 1). For this reason the possibility that any other consciousness posited by me in empathic experience, does *not* in fact exist cannot be compellingly refuted by any experience of mine. My own empathic experience, however, is absolutely and originarily given in the stream of my immanent perception (Par. 46). Empathic evidence thus excludes, in principle, originary verification (Par. 140).

Even though mutual understanding in the way of empathy does not in fact occur among *all* ego-subjects, it is always possible in principle. Hence it is possible that factually separated worlds of experience are joined together through interconnections of actual experience to form a single intersubjective world. This world would be the correlate of the unitary world of minds (*Geisterwelt*), "the universal extension of the human community reduced to pure consciousness and the pure I" (Par. 46).

The sense of the world as determined by intersubjectivity is still preserved in the subjective manners of appearance of noematic constitution after performance of the phenomenological reduction (Par. 135).

Thus, for instance, in the transcendental constitution of things, various levels can be distinguished within the originary conscious experience: the first level is that of the substantial-causal thing related to a single stream of consciousness, viz., to the possible perceptions of a single ego-subject; a second level is that in which the intersubjectively identical thing, as a constituted unity of a higher order, is related to an open plurality of subjects who are in agreement (Par. 151). What is shown here in the example of the constitution of material things is likewise valid for all regions of objects as, for instance, all concrete cultural formations (state, law, custom, church) and all communities; these objects of a higher order are essentially founded on psychic realities, which in turn are founded on physical realities, animal or human communities (Par. 152).

The theme of intersubjectivity is only indicated but not developed further in the volume of *Ideen* published during Husserl's lifetime. It had been Husserl's intention to reserve these investigations for the second volume of *Ideen*, whose early appearance had been planned. In fact, the posthumously published second volume contains significant analyses of the constitution of mental reality and the cultural world in empathy – to which we shall return later. In his *Nachwort zu meinen Ideen*, Husserl felt justified in noting that the presentation of the first volume of *Ideen* suffered from incompleteness with respect to the problem of transcendental solipsism or transcendental intersubjectivity, that is, the problem of the essential relatedness of the objective world (taken for granted by me) to Others whom I also take for granted. The main thesis of transcendental-phenomenological idealism, he writes there, is that only transcendental subjectivity has the ontological status of absolute being, while the real world is essentially relative to it. This thesis acquires its full sense only when, by phenomenological disclosure of the transcendental ego, "the fellow-subjects who present themselves as transcendental in my transcendental life can be reached as transcendental fellow-subjects belonging to a transcendental We-community which also presents itself to me" (Par. 14). "Transcendental intersubjectivity is thus the one in which the real world is constituted as objective, as existing for 'everyone' " (Par. 15). *

The problem of intersubjectivity is a central motif also in *Formale und Transzendentale Logik*.[2] On the one hand, the transcendental subjectivity of consciousness, by whose operations the world as accepted by me is constituted with all its contents – things, my own self, Others – is first of all, I, that is, my own self. On the other hand, the world is the objective world common to all of us and as such it has the categorial form of a world

---

* . . . "die in meinem transzendentalen Leben sich als transzendental ausweisenden Mitsubjekte in der sich mit-ausweisenden transzendentalen Wirgemeinschaft auf-zuzeigen vermag" (Par. 14). "Die transzendentale Intersubjektivität ist also diejenige, in der sich reale Welt, als objektive, als für "jederman seiende konstituiert" (Par. 15).

[2] *Formale und Transzendentale Logik, Versuch einer Kritik der logischen Vernunft*, Halle, 1929.

truly existing once and foreever not only for me but for everyone. World-experience is not my private, but shared experience. But the world as the "world for all of us" is primarily "my" world.

This primal fact, Husserl says, must be faced by the philosopher, and he must not shut his eyes to it for one moment. "For philosophical children this may be the dark corner haunted by the ghosts of solipsism, psychologism, or relativism. The true philosopher, rather than avoiding it, will throw light on it" (Par. 95). The task is, to answer "the painfully puzzling question" of how another psychophysical ego comes to be constituted in my ego, since it is essentially impossible to experience mental contents pertaining to other persons in actual originarity. The constitution of the Other must therefore be distinguished in principle from the way in which my own psycho-physical I is constituted. Because it is in the consciousness of the transcendental ego – which precedes all that is mundane – that the world is constituted as an intentional unity, the Other has sense only with reference to me; yet evidently the reference is not to me as a transcendental ego, but to me as a human self: his body referring to my body as "another's body," his psychic life referring to my psychic life as the "psychic life of another." Furthermore, an Other's psyche refers, in turn, to *an Other's transcendental ego*, which the Other must apprehend from himself on the basis of the world as given to him in his experience.

It must therefore be made intelligible how my transcendental ego can constitute in itself another transcendental ego and, thereafter, how it can also constitute an open plurality of such egos. Since they are egos of others, they are absolutely inaccessible to me in their original being, and yet they have existence for me and are apprehended by me as having certain determinations.

In the *Formale und Transzendentale Logik* Husserl does not only present the central significance of the problem of intersubjectivity for overcoming the "transcendental illusion" of solipsism and for the constitution of the objective world in the everyday sense as a world opposed to me, but he also suggests a solution to the problem which he then developed in the *Cartesianische Meditationen*.[3] We turn now to this text, as it

---

[3] *Cartesianische Meditationen und Pariser Vorträge*, Husserliana, Band I. Den Haag, 1950. Martinus Nijhoff.

contains the most thorough presentation of the constitution of transcendental intersubjectivity and the problems related to it. In doing so we bear in mind Fink's warning [4] that in *Cartesianische Meditationen* Husserl has done no more than outline an approach to the interpretation of the universe of transcendental monads. According to Fink, the goal of the analysis of the experience of the Other, offered in the *Fifth Meditation*, was not a thematic interpretation of "empathy," but an exposition of the transcendental reduction. Making full allowance for this limitation, we shall, in what follows, attempt step by step to examine the solution of the problem that is offered in *Cartesianische Meditationen*. We shall try to show that extraordinary difficulties are connected with each of these steps. These difficulties make it doubtful that Husserl's attempt to develop a transcendental theory of experiencing Others (empathy) as the foundation for a transcendental theory of the objective world was successful, and, what is more, they make it doubtful that such an attempt can succeed at all within the transcendental sphere. This analysis is not only important for deciding whether or not the problems of intersubjectivity, which are fundamental for the whole system of constitutive transcendental phenomenology, can be solved successfully. It is also relevant for the question whether the results of phenomenological constitutional analysis are applicable to all social sciences.

II

After the first three Meditations have shown that existents have sense for me only by virtue of the operating intentionality of my conscious life and its constitutive syntheses, the Fourth Meditation deals with the constitution of the ego itself (inseparable from its experiences), which, as an existent for itself, is an "object," and which "maintains its identity" in experiencing its flowing *"Cogitationes."*

Husserl distinguishes (Par. 31–33) (1) the "identical I" that as continuously constituting I lives in all of its experiences; (2) my personal I, which – in being a substratum of habits, i. e., of

[4] Eugen Fink: *Die Phänomenologische Philosophie Edmund Husserls in der gegenwärtigen Kritik*, Kantstudien, Band 18, 1933, p. 368.

"acquisitions" from previous experiences rather than an empty pole of identity – constitutes itself actively out of the centering I; and (3) the ego in its full concreteness, the ego taken in the manifold stream of its intentional life, including all the objects constituted for it in this stream. This is the ego which embraces all the real and potential "contents" of its conscious life. This ego in its full concreteness is called a "monad" by Husserl who deliberately borrows this term from Leibniz. Hence the problem of the self-constitution of this monadic ego must embrace all problems of constitution. But in order to approach this ego, I must, in free variation, extend my factual transcendental ego into the universal Eidos "transcendental ego at large," that is to say, into the universe of all forms of experience that can possibly be conceived by my factual transcendental ego. (Par. 34). It then appears that to the Eidos "transcendental ego at large," which has been attained in this manner, there belongs a universal apriori that embraces an infinite multiplicity of types of conceivable actualities and potentialities of life, ordered as to coexistence and succession, subject to specific laws of motivation within the universal unitary form of time-consciousness, in short, ordered according to the formal laws of egological genesis (Par. 36 and 37). *

Now we must turn to the question which forms the subject matter of the Fifth Meditation. How can the objectivity of the

---

* Husserl unterscheidet (Par. 31–33) (1) das identische Ich, das als kontinuierlich konstituierendes Ich in allen seinen Bewusstseinserlebnissen lebt; (2) mein personales Ich, das sich in eigener, aktiver Genesis aus dem zentrierenden Ich dadurch konstituiert, dass dieses keineswegs ein leerer Identitätspol ist, sondern ein Substrat von Habitualitäten, d.h. von "Erwerben" vorgängiger Bewusstseinserlebnisse; und (3) das in voller Konkretion genommene Ego in der strömenden Vielseitigkeit seines intentionalen Lebens und der in diesem als für es seiend konstituierten Gegenstände, das Ego also, welches das gesamte wirkliche und potentielle Bewusstseinsleben mitumfasst. Dieses Ego in seiner vollen Konkretisation nennt Husserl in bewusster Anlehnung an Leibniz "Monade". Das Problem der Selbstkonstitution dieses monadischen Ego muss also alle konstitutiven Probleme mitumfassen; um ihm nahezukommen, muss ich aber mein faktisches transzendentales Ego in freier Möglichkeitsabwandlung zum universalen Eidos "transzendentales Ego überhaupt", also zum Universum aller möglichen, für mein faktisches transzendentales Ego irgend erdenklichen Erlebnisformen erweitern (Par. 34). Es zeigt sich dann, dass zu dem so gewonnenen Eidos "transzendentales Ego überhaupt" ein universales Apriori gehört, das eine unendliche Mannigfaltigkeit von Typen erdenklicher Aktualitäten und Potentialitäten des Lebens umfasst, geregelt in Koexistenz und Sukzession, in den eigentümlichen Gesetzen der Motivation, in der universalen Einheitsform des Zeitbewusstseins, kurz in der formalen Gesetzmässigkeit der "egologischen Genesis" (Par. 36–37).

world as a world for everyone, and the existence of Others be established within this egological cosmos? How is it possible to derive the intersubjectivity of the world from the intentionalities of my own conscious life? We shall restate the several phases of Husserl's attempt to solve this problem.

III

As the first step, a further reduction – Husserl calls it a second epoché – must be performed within the egological sphere which is already the result of a prior phenomenological reduction. By the further reduction the results of intentional activities referring directly or indirectly to other subjectivities are excluded, or, as Husserl also says, are screened off (*abgeblendet*).

Thus, to begin with, one abstracts from all "that is other than myself" ("*Fremden*"). This means that one abstracts not only from Others as living beings but also from everything that refers to other minds such as the cultural objects which determine or co-determine my phenomenal world and, finally, from the character of my now "remaining" world as a world for everyone. After the performance of this "second epoché," there remain in the thematic field only those actual and potential intentionalities in which the ego is constituted in its "proper sphere" ("Eigenheit"); thus there always remains a uniformly interconnected stratum of the phenomenon "world" which is, of course, no longer a world for everyone, but is "nature reduced to the ego's proper sphere" ("*eigenheitlich reduzierte Natur*"). Within this universe of what is peculiarly my own (*des Selbst-eigenen*), a "transcendent world" appears as, so to speak, an immanent transcendence which is still a determining part of my own concrete being. For this reason, Husserl calls it, primordial world or primordial transcendence. In contrast to this primordial transcendence, the transcendence of the objective world proves to be a transcendence of a higher level insofar as the constitution of the Other is already presupposed in the latter (Par. 44).

Let us examine more closely the way in which this "second epoché" is performed. Within the phenomenologically reduced egological sphere this epoché aims to separate all that is "properly" of the ego from all that is not of it. Before the second reduction, one must recall, the world is straightforwardly given as a transcendental phenomenon and it is so given in congruent experiences. This implies, however, that that which is not "properly" of the ego still co-determines the sense which the world has for the ego – even though its existence is no longer merely accepted in consequence of the phenomenological epoché. Even within the transcendentally reduced conscious life, the phenomenon "world," including the Other, is not experienced as my private synthetic product, but as an intersubjective world whose objects are accessible to everyone.

Exclusion of what is not "properly" of the ego is brought about (Par. 44) by abstraction "first of all from what gives to men and animals their specific sense as, so to speak, ego-like living beings" * and further by abstracting from all determinations such as cultural predicates which refer to Others in their sense as ego-subjects; and finally, the surrounding world in its being and sense as world for everyone is affected by the epoché, whereby, so far as cultural objects are concerned, their being for everyone means for "everyone of the corresponding cultural community, e.g., the European or the French cultural community" (Par. 43).

The ego's entire transcendental field of experience is divided into two strata by the second epoché: first into the sphere of what is "properly" of the ego, including the cohesive stratum of its world-experience in which whatever is not of the ego is screened off: second, into the sphere of what is *not* of the ego. But it should be noted here that, according to Husserl's reiterated assertion (Par. 44 and Par. 55), my actual and possible experiences *of* the second sphere, every consciousness *of* it, every manner of appearance *of* it, belongs in the first sphere – the sphere "properly" of the ego. Only in as much as the very subjectivity of an Other is in question are the "products" of that subjectivity "screened off" in the sphere that is "properly" of the ego (Par. 45).

The negative determination of the sphere that is "properly" of the ego in terms of what is *not* "properly" of the ego involves at least five major difficulties. (1) Within the

---

* "zunächst von dem was Menschen und Tieren ihren spezifischen Sinn als sozusagen ich-artigen lebenden Wesen gibt."

transcendentally reduced sphere as an intentional constitu-
ent of the phenomenal world of experience one must be able
to identify what is not "properly" of the ego and to identify
it *as such* in order to be able to abstract from it. As far as I can
see, this corresponds also to the exact wording of the text of
Cartesianische Meditationen. Several texts, including passages in
Formale und Transzendentale Logik, point to a "preconstituted
substratum" (*Unterstufe*) of what is not "properly" of the ego.
Of what kind is the preconstitution of that substratum, and
how does it come about? What is that substratum, and must
not a radical clarification of the constitution of what is not
"properly" of the ego begin with an analysis of that substratum?
And furthermore, how does that which is not "properly" of the
ego – the not-I from which I must abstract in order to disclose
primordial transcendence – manifest itself as such?

(2) The concept of "that which is not 'properly' of the ego",
from which abstraction is to be made, fluctuates considerably.
Even the equation of animals and men as "ego-like" living
beings is highly doubtful. Moreover, who are the "Others" in the
sense of "ego-subjects" and what is their noematic-ontic manner
of givenness which would serve as a transcendental clue for a
constitutional theory of the experience of Others? Are they the
other personal egos? Or are they the "centering" other egos as
substrata of habits? Or are they the other egos in their full
concreteness? The same ambiguity appears in the correlated
concept of "everyone." Apparently, everyone is any living
being that is ego-like (*ich-artig*); then another time it may be
"any human being," and a third time – at least as far as cultural
predicates are concerned – it may be "everyone of the corresponding
cultural communities".

(3) Husserl explicitly states (Par. 44) that every reference of
sense to a possible Us and We is excluded by the second epoché.
But how is this compatible with the retention of all actual and
possible experiences *of* Others (the *Other*'s ways of appearing
to me) within the sphere of what is "properly" of the ego? Do
not these experiences *of* Others already institute (*stiften*) a We or
Us?

(4) A particular difficulty, it seems to me, lies precisely in the
distinction between our consciousness *of* what is not "properly"

of the ego and our consciousness of the subjectivity of others insofar as it determines or co-determines sense. Let us recall that as a consequence of the second epoché the former, i.e., the actual and potential experiences *of* what is not "properly" of the ego, were defined as belonging to the sphere "properly of the ego," while the latter, i.e., the "products" of sense-determining other subjectivities, were assigned to the second sphere. Are not many and perhaps all of our experiences of what is not "properly" of the ego instituted in the natural world – which is retained as intentional correlate in the egological sphere – as "products" of other subjectivities, or are they not at least interpreted by us as being instituted in this way? And is it not precisely because of this that they have the sense "experiences" *of* something that is not "properly" of the ego? I do not see how this differentiation can be maintained.

(5) In the *Kantstudien* essay, fully endorsed by Husserl, Fink pointed out (l.c., p. 355f.) the importance of distinguishing between the three egos involved in phenomenological reduction: (1) the mundane ego (I, the human being, undubitably accepted along with all my mundane life); (2) the transcendental ego to whom the world is pregiven in universal apperception and by whom the world is taken for granted; and (3) the detached observer performing the epoché. Fink notes that the transcendental ego that takes the world for granted does not by any means interrupt its believing in the world and thus continues to accept the self-apperception "man", whereas the transcendental theoretical observer makes use of no mundane positing, whether it be theoretical or not. His thematic field is the transcendental meaning of the "world" in positive living functionality. Who is now to perform the second epoché by which the primordial sphere of what is "properly" of the ego would be attained? According to the text of *Cartesianische Meditationen*, it is "I as the one who meditatingly explicates" (Par. 62). This, in the sense of Fink's tripartition, is the observer who performs the epoché. But, on the other hand, it is stated there that "I experience, the Other *in* "me" and know that he is constituted in "me" – although "mirrored appresentatively," and not experienced originarilly. Who is now this "me"? Obviously it is the transcendental ego, to whom the world is pregiven in universal apperception. But is

that which is not "properly" of the ego and which should be excluded or screened off, not the apperception of "another human being," i.e., another mundane ego in his mundane life, even if we grant that it is modified to "another ego for me"? We shall see that this question assumes even greater significance later on.

Previously, the sphere "properly" of the ego was only negatively determined as that which is "not other than 'properly' of the ego." Husserl now adds (Par. 46) a positive determination. The sphere "properly" of the ego (*Eigenheitlichkeit*) is the sphere of actualities and potentialities of the stream of experiences to the extent to which, as the horizon of essentially my own being, the stream in its immanent temporality, including whatever pertains to it, is accessible and pregiven to my explication. "All possibilities of the kind subsumed under the 'I can' or 'could have' set this or that series of subjective processes going . . . obviously belong to me as moments of my own essence." To this sphere belong not only the constitutive systems contained within the stream of experiences but also the unities constituted therein, the latter, however, only insofar as they are inseparable from the originary constitution itself. In other words: the intentional object belongs to the full monadic concretion of that which is "properly" of the ego. Therefore we also find within the original sphere of original self-explication a trancendental world to which belong all phantasies meant as transcendent, all pure possibilities and all eidetic objects, insofar as they are subjected to the reduction to what is "properly" of the ego.

IV

We now turn to the second step, which is to lead to the constitution of the Other's I within the primordial sphere. Among all natural bodies (*Körpern*), after nature has been reduced so that it belongs to the sphere that is "properly" of the ego, one that I call "my living body" ("*mein Leib*") is distinguished by the fact that I ascribe "fields of sensation" to it and control it actively (*über ihn handelnd verfüge*). In the sphere reduced to what is "properly" of the ego, "another human being" appears, first of all as a body. Upon this body I now bestow – and this

is of fundamental importance for Husserl's theory of the experience of the Other – the sense "living body" and more
particularly "living body other than mine"; I do this through
an "apperceptive transfer" from my own living body, through a
process that involves an analogy (*analogisierende Auffassung*)
although it is not an inference by analogy (*Analogieschluss*).

This analogical apperception, or "appresentation," is a special
form of mediate intentionality, the essence of which is that – in
connection (*Verflechtung*) with a presentation (*Gegenwärtigung*)
one that is a genuine self-presentation (*Selbstgebung*) of an
A – there is effected a co-presentation of a B (the "appresented")
that itself never comes to actual presentation but is continually
interwoven with something perceived in self-presentation, the A.
The phenomenon of appresentation is only a special case of the
universal problem of "pairing" which itself is nothing else than
a primal form of passive synthesis. Such a synthesis may be
designated as association in a specific sense. It is characteristic
of pairing association – that two salient data are intuitively
given in the unity of one consciousness. Whether they are noticed
or not, phenomenologically, they provide the basis for a unity of
similarity insofar as they appear as different. An intentional
overlapping takes place between both elements of the pair, a
reciprocal stimulating and coinciding. As a result of this coincidence (which, if total, yields the limiting case of "perfect
likeness)", a transfer of sense is carried out among the paired
elements, i.e., the one is apperceived in conformity with the sense
of the Other unless sense-moments realized in that which is experienced cancel out this transfer in the consciousness of the
difference (*des Anders*) (Pars. 50–51).

In appresentation of the Other, my own primordially reduced
"living body" (*Leib*) is the primal instituting originary phenomenon, always given in immediate presentation. If a body
that is similar to my living body (*Leibkörper*), i.e., a body which
is so constituted that it must enter into phenomenal pairing
with my body, enters my perceptual field, then, by a transfer of
sense, the sense "living body," and, more particularly, "Another's
living body," will be transferred to it from my own body (Par. 51).

Let us pause for a moment to examine this argument. Husserl
refers the apperception of another body that stands out in relief

within my primordial sphere as "an Other's living body" to the fundamental phenomenon of appresentation and consequently to an overlapping of sense which arises in passive synthesis on the basis of similarity. The basic importance of the theory of appresentation, especially its importance for establishing the nexus between sign and signatum, symbol and what is symbolized * cannot be doubted. However, Husserl here uses the theory of appresentation to supply the foundation for the analogical apperception of a body appearing in my primordially reduced sphere as an "other living body." Primordially, the body at first appears only as a determining element of myself in immanent transcendence, since, in nature and the world reduced to what pertains to what is "properly" of the ego, my living body alone is constituted originally as living, as a functioning organ. If I extend this sense analogically to another body appearing to me in that sphere, apprehending it as an Other's living body, the extension depends on the similarity of that body to my living body – the latter being always present and given to me as a primal instituting organ. It is precisely the similarity between the body appearing to me and my living body which makes possible the apperceptive transfer of sense from the latter to the former. To what extent, however, does such similarity obtain?

The other body is visually perceived, but my body is not, as a rule, visually perceived by me, and even if it is, then only partially. My living body is, to be sure, always present and given as the primal instituting organ. But it is present as inner perception of its boundaries and through the kinaesthetic experience of its functioning. It is thus present precisely in a way which is as dissimilar as possible from the external perception of an animate body other than mine and therefore can never lead to an analogical apperception. This was already clearly established by Scheler and later by Sartre in his distinction between the ontological dimensions of the body ("*mon corps pour moi – mon corps pour autrui*") and by Merleau-Ponty in his analysis of the problem of "*corps propre*." Husserl's assumption that an analogical apprehension of an Other's living body takes place on the basis of a similarity to my own living body contradicts the

* See: *Collected Papers*, I. *The Problem of Social Reality*, "Symbol, Reality and Society".

phenomenological finding that my living body "stands out" in my primordial perceptual field in a manner which is fundamentally different from the manner in which the allegedly similar body of the Other stands out in this field.

It seems that Husserl, in this connection, limits the concept of the "Other" to that of the "other man." As already noted above, however, the concept of the Other also embraces, in at least one of its significations, other "ego-like living beings," as, e.g. animals. If we apply to these Husserl's theory of appresentative sense-transference from my organism it proves impossible to explain how it happens that this and that body appearing in my primordial sphere comes to be construed as the body of a fish or as the body of a bird, i.e., as belonging to an "ego-like being" living "in" it.

But let us return to Husserl's line of thought. Mere appresentation is not sufficient for a body appearing to me to be experienced as the living body of another. For if that appresentation is to endure and not prove illusory at once, it must be verified (*bewähren*) in further appresentations that agree synthetically. Thus, through its permanently congruent behavior ("*Gebaren*") the living body of another must continuously manifest itself as what it is, namely, as animated body, in short as the "Other." Appresentation here provides new appresentative contents in a continuous progress (Par. 52).

"Understanding the corporeality (*Leiblichkeit*) of the Other and of his somatic conduct is evidently the first content of appresentation: the understanding that his limbs are hands that touch and feet that walk, that his eyes are eyes that see." Subsequently there is empathic apprehension of certain contents of the higher psychic sphere; these are also indicated somatically as the external conduct of one who is angry, of one who is happy, comprehensible with reference to my own conduct under similar circumstances. It is important that the Other so constituted arises in my primordial world as an intentional modification of my own self, although from the outset with the sense "other self" (Par. 54). That I consider an Other's body as *not* my own rather than as a reduplication of my own body is apparent, among other indications, from the fact that somatically I myself am the center of a primordial world which is oriented around me.

In my primordial world, my body has the index of "here," while the body of the Other appearing in this world has the index of "there," although his body has for him, the Other, the index of absolute "here." By virtue of the fact that the body of the Other "there" enters into an association of sense with my body "here," the Other is appresented, in an apperception of a higher level, as a co-existing ego in the mode of "there" (Par. 53).

A new series of difficulties arises here.

(1) How do I know, when reduced to the primordial sphere of what is "properly" of my ego, whether – and to what extent – the behavior of the body experienced as the living body of the Other is, indeed, congruent? To ascertain this would offer no difficulties in principle, although it would present a whole series of factual difficulties if we were concerned with a theory of understanding the Other in a world the intersubjectivity of which could be already taken for granted, as, for example, in the world of everyday life as it is experienced in the natural attitude. There would still remain the question as to how the concept of "behavior" is to be understood, viz., whether it is to be understood as mere "behavior," as pure somatic functioning, or as an indication of consistently congruent psychic events pertaining to the Other. Husserl's exposition clearly shows that the latter is his view. But, considering that the sphere which has been reduced to what is "properly" of the ego is one which has been attained by abstracting from all of the products of other subjectivity that determine or co-determine sense, what sense can it make within this sphere to refer to congruent psychic events pertaining to the Other? What is congruent here and what is not? Or are we to see the solution in preserving my pre-experiences *of* what is *not* "properly" of my ego even within the primordial sphere that has been reduced to what is "properly" of my ego. If such is the case, what are those experiences *of* what is not "properly" of my ego (which are supposed to yield a criterion of whether or not the behavior of the body of the Other is congruent) if not the pre-experiences of congruous psychic events pertaining to Others in that "pre-constituted" domain of the substratum in which there already is a sense "everyone," viz., "every human being" or, more restrictively, "every human being of my cultural sphere"? If I

must fall back upon pre-constituted substrata for the clarification of congruent behavior, then there are only two possibilities: *either* the "second epoché" has not been carried out radically enough – perhaps it cannot be radically carried out at all – and our attempt to reach the pure sphere of what is "properly" of the ego has miscarried; *or* I can indeed – within this pure sphere – apprehend the other emerging body analogically as living body of a living being or perhaps even as the living body of a fellow-man but am unable within the primordial sphere to grasp the verification of this appresentation as such, viz., the congruent behavior of another human being.

(2) Furthermore, the idea of congruence (*Einstimmigkeit*) already presupposes that the behavior of Others can be typified according to standards of normality – a normality which, however, must be based upon the "products" and the functional contexts of other subjectivities – and, therefore, should have been bracketed by the second epoché.

The relation of normality and anomaly to the idea of congruence did not escape Husserl's attention (Par. 55). He speaks, on the one hand, of the abnormalities of blindness, deafness, etc., which can be explained only with reference to a normality already presupposed; on the other hand, he develops the curious theory that animality and the hierarchical sequence of higher and lower animals can, in principle, be constituted for me only as anomalous variations of my humanity.

(3) Normality is, in a still deeper sense, a presupposition for congruence in the behavior of Others. There are normalities of the most varied kinds for the behavior of man and woman, of youth and old age, of the healthy and the sick, and all of this in all kinds of variations, depending on the culture to which the "Other" and I belong. All of these normalities must belong to the preconstituted substrata in order to make possible the ascertainment of congruent behavior of the Other in the primordial sphere of what is "properly" of my ego. What is congruent according to one order of "normality" is not congruent according to another.

(4) It is not sufficient to consider the "Other" as a modification of myself in the mode of "there," without clarifying the nature of this modification, which again leads to the problem of nor-

mality, and hence to the problem of preconstituted substrata. If, however, I tacitly presuppose the preconstituted substrata within the reduction to what is "properly" of the ego, why then the "second epoché" at all? This second epoché could never yield the constitution of the Other as a full monad within my monad, but at most it yields appresentation of another psychophysical ego beginning from the substratum of my psychophysical ego.

V

The third step which Husserl takes in developing his theory about experiencing Others clearly shows that this was certainly not his opinion. According to Husserl, with the appresentation of another animate body as "that of the Other," everything belonging to the concretization of this other I, first as his primordial world and then as the fully concrete ego, is appresented in analogical modification. In apperception on higher levels, I appresent the Other as an ego co-existing with me "there." "In this way, another monad becomes constituted appresentatively in mine." Both are functionally joined in a single perception that is at once presenting and appresenting. Therefore, Husserl says, the natural entity appearing in the Other's primordial sphere that appears to me as the Other's (living) body "there" is throughout *the same* as the central body that appears as "here" to him; only the *actual* perceptions are not the same since, my varying perspectives refer to my own body "here" as center of reference (thus "from there," as if I were "there"). Thereby objective nature is also constituted as a phenomenon of experience: from experiencing the Other, there accrues to my primordially constituted nature a second appresented stratum, one that can be experienced and is experienced as standing in synthetic unity of identity with my primordially constituted nature. This second stratum is that same nature as it could appear to the Other. This synthesis, identifying the same nature both as primordially given and as appresentatively given and verified, also serves to institute the co-existence of my I and of the Other's I, and thereby a common time-form is instituted (Par. 55).

Here a series of questions arises:

(1) First of all, it is hard to see how, along with the appresen-

tation of another's animated body as "of the Other," his primordial world, the sphere of what is "properly" of his ego, can
be appresented as well. Supposing that the transference of sense
from my body to the co-existing body of the Other succeeds, the
Other would be given to me as another psychophysical I;
however, this would still not suffice to constitute a sphere of
what is "properly" of his ego. That sphere is the sphere of
actualities and potentialities of another's stream of subjective
processes and embraces all the possibilities of "you can" and
"you could." But how do I arrive at an experience of "you can"
and "you could"? By a transference of the sense "I can" or
"I could"? This, indeed, is inconceivable since my being-here
and your being-there involves necessarily "I can from here, but
you cannot from there." This difficulty can by no means be
overcome by an extension of the appresentation to include
"were I there, then I would be able to do what you can from
your here," since this extension by no means admits the converse:
"If you were here, then you could do what I can from here." – Or
should the disclosure of "you can" or "you could" be traced
back to a transference of sense from a preconceived or presupposed
"everyone can" or "everyone could"? That would be still more
impossible since the normality of "everyone can" supposedly
originates in the institution of intersubjectivity between me and
the Other.

(2) It is still less clear how the appresentation of another
psychophysical I should lead to the concretization of a full other
monad. Temporality, immanent to you, belongs to your full
monad, since it is precisely my immanent temporality and yours
which makes you and me monads. And out of this arises the first
form of community, viz., the community of nature with the living
body of the Other, and therefore, common reality and common
time-form. Even if Husserl were right that, by the simultaneous
existence (*Mit-sein*) of the other I "there would be primally
instituted a co-existence of my I and of the other I, of my whole
concrete ego and his, my intentional life and his, my *realities*
and his – in short a common time-form" (Par. 55 in fine);* even

* eine Koexistenz meines Ich – und meines konkreten Egos überhaupt – und des
fremden Ich, meines und seines intentionalen Lebens, meiner und seiner Realitäten
urgestiftet wäre, kurzum eine gemeinsame Zeitform."

if "of itself," as Husserl says, each primordial temporality were thereby to acquire the significance of the manner in which objective temporality would appear merely to a single subject, still that would tell us nothing about how the temporality of the Other, essential to the constitution of the other complete monad, might be disclosed.

(3) Furthermore, it remains open to question whether the accretion of an appresented stratum to natural bodies (*Natur-körper*) belonging to my primordial sphere – "the same natural object in the manner in which it is given to the Other" – is sufficient for the constitution of objective nature, and, subsequently, for the constitution of the objective world. Husserl speaks of the synthetic unity of identity of the natural object as given to *me* in primordial originarity and the appresentative stratum accruing to it from experiencing Others. But does not the constitution of an objective nature presuppose as warranted the systematic unity of identity of the natural object given *to the Other* in primordial originarity with the same natural object as appresented by him as it might be given to me? Does not, therefore, the instituting of a common and objective nature presuppose a we-relationship, and is it not founded upon the possibility of communication?

The problem of founding the intersubjective world on the possibility of communication occupied Husserl in the second volume of *Ideen*; we shall briefly sketch the line of thought developed there.

VI

Husserl distinguishes (*Ideen* II) between the "naturalistic" and the "personalistic" attitude. In the naturalistic attitude – which must not be confused with the "natural" attitude (Par. 49e) – nature is given first as the reality of material things, then as the reality of mental life. In this attitude other animate beings (*Animalia*) appear to me as primally present living bodies (*Leibkörper*) with appresented internality. If, in the sphere "properly" of my ego, (Husserl says here, "in my solipsistic experience"), I encounter material things which resemble my body, I construe them as "living bodies," i.e., I ascribe to them an ego-subject "with all that that implies and with the specific content required from case to case" (Par. 45).* First of all, localizations – familiar to me on my own body – of the several sense-fields (tactual field, smell, pain, etc.) are "transferred" to the other bodies. My indirect localization of mental activities is "transferred" as well. How this "transfer" of localization can occur, and how, subsequently, a continuous coordination of the physical and the psychical is to take place – "legitimately" – is neither explained nor intelligible.

According to Husserl, a mental life "belongs" to the seen body by virtue of transferred compresence (*Kompräsenz*), just as a mental life belongs to my body. It is a mental life which can be understood by me through empathy and to which belongs the system of appearances through which the external world, including my body, is given to the Other from the standpoint of There. This process of empathy, therefore, leads to the constitution of the intersubjective objectivity of the world, of inanimate things as well as of men as physio-psychological unities. For even my body can, properly speaking, be construed only as a natural object by my looking at it from the standpoint of the Other in the mode of There. The natural object "man" is thus a transcendent external object, given in a double layer of experience: external primally presentative perceptions are interwoven into a phenomenal unity with appresenting empathy (i.e. empathy introjecting into the external) (Pars. 46–47).

All this is, however, only, a description of the naturalistic attitude. As a *person* "I" am and every Other is, the subject of a surrounding world, the concepts "I" and "surrounding world" being strictly interrelated (Par. 49). The surrounding world is the world perceived, remembered, conceptually grasped by the person in his acts; it is the world of which the personal I is conscious and to which it is oriented in its conduct. Thus, not physical reality as a whole, but only that sector of it which the person "knows", is his surrounding world (Par. 50). The surrounding world is therefore permanently recreated in continuous transformations of its sense which result from the ego's acts of sense-bestowal and sense-cancellation. Hence it is, in a certain

---

* d.h. ich fühle ihnen je ein Ich-Subjekt ein mit all dem was dazu gehört und mit dem besonderen Inhalt, der von Fall zu Fall gefordert ist."

way, continuously in process (*im Werden*). In this surrounding world, the subject not only encounters things, but also other subjects related to the same objects. Husserl explicitly denies that, in the personalistic attitude, mind (*Geist*) can be "inserted" into the body as though it belonged to the body's reality. He asserts – without giving reasons – that in the "comprehensive experience" of the existence of the Other, we "simply" ("*ohne weiteres*") understand the Other as a personal subject related to the same objects as ourselves (Par. 51).

To live in a common surrounding world and to be in a personal association (*Verband*) "goes hand in hand": the one is constituted essentially along with the other in that relations of mutual agreement arise which lead to a reciprocal relationship between persons on the level of consciousness, and, at the same time, to a unitary relation of the persons to their common surrounding world".* This surrounding world Husserl calls the communicative surrounding world. By its nature it is relative to the persons who live in it and encounter it. Persons who share in the communicative surrounding world are to each other not objects, but counter-subjects (*Gegensubjekte*) or fellow-men (*Genossen*). As such they stand to one another in reciprocal social relations. Sociality is constituted by specific communicative acts in which the I addresses himself to Others, conscious that these Others will understand this and will, on their part, turn to the I. The subjects communicating with one another constitute, as Husserl says, personal unities of a higher order, associations of subjects who also have their surrounding world and stand in communication with one another. Finally, there arises the idea of the totality (*Inbegriff*) of all these social subjects standing in actual or potential communication with one another; the correlate of that idea is the world of the mind (*Geisteswelt*).

Husserl's presentation is not only fragmentary; it also suffers from serious and basic deficiencies.

(1) It is not clear how the mental life of the Other can be constituted in compresence of empathic transfer of localizations on my own body to the seen body of the Other – if such a "trans-

---

* "gehört ohne weiteres zusammen: eins konstituiert sich wesensmässig mit dem anderen und zwar dadurch, dass sich Beziehungen des Einverständnisses bilden, die eine bewusstseinsmässige Wechselbeziehung der Personen und zugleich eine einheitliche Beziehung derselben zur gemeinsamen Umwelt herstellen," . . .

fer" is possible at all. It is impossible that, in comprehensive experience, the Other is grasped "directly" as a personal subject dealing with objects of a common surrounding world. This latter is impossible because, as Husserl correctly establishes, the physical world is part of the surrounding world of a subject only insofar as the subject has some awareness of it. To be sure, Husserl knows quite well that each person, idealiter, has his "ego-istic" surrounding world within the communicative one, provided it is conceived in abstract isolation. But Husserl makes no attempt to explain how the several sectors of the physical world can coincide – a coincidence which, of course, must be known by every one of the persons subsequently communicating with one another. Only such a clarification could show how a common surrounding world can arise at all and how this community (*Gemeinsamkeit*) of "knowledge" could be established prior to the establishment of reciprocal understanding which would be founded on such a community of knowledge.

(2) It is not difficult to show that reciprocal understanding and communication already presuppose a community of knowledge, even a common surrounding world (and social relationships), and not the reverse. The common surrouding world and the social relation, therefore, cannot be derived from the idea of communication. All communication, whether by so-called expressive movements, deictic gestures, or the use of visual or acoustic signs, already presupposes an external event in that common surrounding world which, according to Husserl, is not constituted except by communication. These events take place in the "personalistic" sphere and by no means in the "naturalistic" one; they do not belong to the common nature preconstituted on a lower level but rather to the surrounding world. It is presupposed that I, as personal subject, in producing signs, orient myself to the Other, who has to interpret the signs as my communication; and it is presupposed that I assume that he who interprets the signs is equally, as a personal subject, oriented to me and my communicative acts. This reciprocal orientation, which alone makes communication possible, is the fundamental presupposition of every social relationship, so that social relationship cannot be constituted by communication.

(3) Another entirely unclarified step is that of going from

subjects communicating with one another to the constitution of personal unities of a higher order, associations of subjects which have their own surrounding world and from those associations of subjects to an all-encompassing community whose surrounding world no longer contains subjects – a community of minds (*Geistergemeinschaft*) encountering a world of objects significant to mind as a world *for* the mind (*Geist*). It can be already seen that the meanings of the concepts of person, communication, surrounding world and subjectivity shift so radically in the transition to higher levels that it can be taken only as an excessive metaphorical usage of inadequate terms. To be sure, in the social world of everyday life there arises the problem, serious for all social sciences: the problem of the so-called "social person." But this is not a problem for phenomenological constitutional analysis, and only a regrettable ignorance of the concrete sciences of society led Husserl, whose conscientiousness was otherwise exemplary, to introduce unexamined constructs of everyday thinking and of the social sciences into phenomenological analyses of constitution. How dangerous this procedure is, will be seen as soon as we return to the argument in *Cartesianische Meditationen* which was preceded by the manuscripts incorporated into the second volume of *Ideen*.

VII

In the Fifth Cartesian Meditation, too, it is pointed out (Pars. 56 and 58) that the co-existence of my I and another I and hence the institution of a common temporal form and of a common nature, establishes only the first level of community between ego and alter ego.

Husserl emphasizes that all other intersubjective communities can be "easily" derived from the first one. Thus: the human community – you and I and the Other and everyone as man among other men – who experience each other and whom I experience as such; the transcendental correlate of this, the community of monads of transcendental intersubjectivity, which is likewise constituted in me, the meditating ego, exclusively from the sources of my own intentionality; further, the social communities arising from "I-thou" acts to which there correspond in the objective world social communities considered as objectivities of the mind (*"geistige Objektivitäten"*), among them the "personalities of the higher order"; finally, the "cultural world," which by its constitution presupposes what is already constituted, on different levels, both primordially and secondarily, and whose constitution is itself oriented with regard to a "zero-member" (*"Nullglied"*), i.e., with respect to a personality ("I and my culture").

Let us examine these possibilities for deriving higher communities starting with the human community. According to Husserl, the sense "man," even as individual, carries with it the sense of membership in a community: I (and everyone) as man among men; I, who experience Others and am experienced by them as an Other; and, further, I, who experience Others as oriented to Others who are oriented to me in iterative mediation.

In *Krisis der europäischen Wissenschaften und die transzendentale Phänomenologie* [5] Husserl points out (Par. 54a) that this involves a change of meaning from * "I" – just as I now say I – into "other I," into "all of us," "We, the several egos among whom I am an I." But there it is asked: Are not these egos, is not this We, a mere phenomenon after we perform the transcendental reduction? Is it not the case that the philosopher in the epoché deals neither with himself nor with others as men, but only as poles of transcendental regressive inquiry? Husserl points out further (Par. 54 b) that it must be maintained that the epoché is performed by me, as the one who philosophizes, "and ⟨that⟩ even when many are present and perform the epoché in actual community with me, yet for me in my epoché all other men with their entire act-life belong to the world-phenomenon which is exclusively mine in my epoché. The epoché creates a unique philosophical solitude..." ** The primal I, the ego of my epoché,

---

[5] Edmund Husserl, *Die Krisis der europäischen Wissenschaften und die transzendentale Phänomenologie: Eine Einleitung in die phänomenologische Philosophie*, Husserliana, Vol. VI, Den Haag, 1954.
    * dass dies einen Bedeutungswandel des "Ich" – so wie ich soeben Ich sage – in "andere Ich," in "Wir alle," "Wir mit den vielen Ichen, worin ich ein Ich bin" involviert.
    ** ...dass daran festzuhalten ist, dass ich, der Philosophierende, die Epoché vollziehe "und selbst wenn da mehrere sind und sogar in aktueller Gemeinschaft mit mir die Epoché üben, so sind für mich in meine Epoché alle anderen Menschen mit ihrem ganzen Aktleben in das Weltphänomen einbezogen, dass in meiner Epoché ausschliesslich das meine ist. Die Epoché schafft eine einzigartige philosophische Einsamkeit . . . ."

can never lose its singularity and personal indeclinability. This is only apparently contradicted by the fact that the I transcendentally makes itself declinable for itself by a special constitutive operation peculiar to it, and that the I thus in and of itself constitutes transcendental intersubjectivity, of which the I then considers itself merely as a privileged member, that is, as the ego of the transcendental Others. That "each transcendental ego of intersubjectivity must necessarily be constituted as man in the world and that each man thus contains in himself a transcendental ego can ultimately be understood, as Husserl further shows, only through a methodical explication of the functions and operations of transcendental intersubjectivity. However, the transcendental ego is not a real part or stratum of man's psyche (which would be an absurdity); ⟨but it is contained in man⟩ insofar as man is the self-objectivation of his transcendental ego, which he can ascertain by means of phenomenological self-examination (*Selbstbesinnung*). It is true, however, that any man who performed the epoché could know his ultimate ego operative in all of its human doing."

Here, it appears, we have reached the core of the problem of transcendental intersubjectivity. Yet Husserl only increased the almost insurmountable difficulties when he asserted in his last writing (*Krisis*, Par. 54b) that, although – "for the deepest philosophical reasons which cannot be discussed any further" – allowance must be made for the absolute singularity of the ego and for its central place in all constitution, it was nevertheless methodologically naive to allow humanity, which includes the ego that philosophizes and functions as I-pole of transcendental acts, the same conversion into transcendental subjectivity.

Let us draw up a partial catalogue of the main difficulties connected with transcendental intersubjectivity.

(1) As the Fifth Cartesian Meditation (Par. 56) describes it, an open monadic community, which we designate as transcendental intersubjectivity, corresponds, in transcendental concretion, to an open multiplicity of men; more generally: of animate beings, as subjects of possible mutual community. In view of what we have said thus far, what is this possible correspondence? The open human community stands, at least potentially, in communication. Here, in fact, there is an I and another I as

Thou, a We and an Us; we see the bird in flight – I and Thou; we all experience the change of seasons – I and Thou and everyone; we build a house, write letters to one another, take a walk – I and Thou. But how can one come to the transcendental We, the primal ground of all communities? I, the one who performs the epoché, the transcendental ego, have constituted the Other in the previously described manner; and, similarly, you, another transcendental ego, have constituted me. But how can my full monad in its concretization enter into a transcendental We-relationship with yours? Even if one accepts Husserl's theory of the constitution of the Other, according to which, by virtue of appresentative transfer, your body, appearing in my primordial sphere, leads to the constitution of your full psychic life and further to the constitution of your transcendental ego for me; even if, unlike Husserl, one admits the assumption, that my body appearing in your primordial sphere leads in an analogous manner to the constitution of my full psychic life and of my transcendental ego for you; if one assumes all of this, still no transcendental community, no transcendental We, is ever established. On the contrary, each transcendental ego has now constituted for himself, as to its being and sense, his world, and in it all other subjects, including myself; *but* he has constituted them *just for himself and not for all other transcendental egos as well.*

That in this constitution – and we assume here that it occurs as Husserl describes it – the appresentative Other constitutes the world from the stand-point of his Here, which for me is There, that I know this, and that I cannot consider my own body as a thing belonging to objective nature unless I look at it from the standpoint of the Other – his Here, my There: all of this still does not yield a transcendental community unless we were to define community in such a way that, contrary to meaningful usage, there would be a community for me, and one for you, without the two necessarily coinciding. Nor is (unless one relapses into the natural attitude) communication between a plurality of transcendental subjects and hence the institution of a communicative intersubjectivity possible in the transcendental sphere, since all communication requires events in the natural world and, as shown above, already presupposes intersubjectivity viz., the We-relationship.

Or does Husserl's theory deal with two completely different concepts of intersubjectivity, the first defining intersubjectivity simply as constitution of an objective world inclusive of Others encountered therein; and the second defining intersubjectivity as communication, both actual and potential? In that case, a community in the sense of the first definition would be nothing else than the constitution of a plurality of transcendental egos in the primal ego, that is, in the ego of the meditating philosopher performing the epoché. Community in the sense of the second definition would presuppose, on the other hand, that the egos belonging to a community know about the existence of such a community.

Let us put aside the misleading talk of a plurality of transcendental egos. The main question remains whether my transcendental ego knows about a transcendental Thou or, what is more, constitutes it. How a transcendental We can be instituted by this transcendental ego and this transcendental Thou is an additional problem. Only upon such a transcendental We can a community be founded. In the language of the passage from *Krisis* quoted above, Husserl asks: How can the primal ego, which cannot lose its singularity and personal indeclinability, make itself declinable for itself by a special operation? We raise the same question, but above and beyond this we insist upon the need for an explanation of how the I can be made transcendentally declinable not only for itself, but also for Others.

(2) But is it conceivable and meaningful to speak of a plurality of transcendental egos? Is not the concept of the transcendental ego conceivable only in the singular? Can it also be "declined" in the plural, or is it, as the Latin grammarians call it, a *singulare tantum*?

Fink, in the previously mentioned essay in *Kantstudien* (367f) writes, without pursuing the thought further, as follows: "Interrogation of the intentionality in which the Other is accepted as another man, that is, as part of the world-phenomenon, leads to the transcendental account of an existential connection in a uniquely structured multiplicity of transcendental egos. The "metaphysical" designation monads can serve only to indicate the transcendental egos without adequately characterizing them. By no means are we thereby transposing a massive plurality into the transcendental sphere. Nor can the transcendental ego be conceived under the idea of a worldly oneness. The implication of "monads" is a heading for the great problem of the non-extensive monadic multiplicity, the non-individuated interpenetration, possible only in the transcendental realm." *

Toward the end of the unpublished continuation of *Krisis* (Par. 71), Husserl hints at the same problem.

The chief result of the preceding analyses, according to him, is the proof that the epoché would be abortive if it were limited to a single reduction within a single psyche or to progressive single reductions from psyche to psyche. "All psyches form a single unity of intentionality in which the streams of the single subjects are reciprocally implicated. It is a task for phenomenology to give a systematic account of this unity. What is an outside-of-one-another in naive positivity or objectivity, is, when seen from within, an intentional in-one-another." **

Both hints – and they are mere hints – are extremely paradoxical. It is completely unclear how an intentional in-one-another could account for the reciprocal implication of streams of life belonging to single subjects, and even to all psyches. Perhaps the unpublished manuscripts on intersubjective constitution can provide an explanation. The present study does not go beyond published material.

Another question presents great difficulties. The Fourth Cartesian Meditation considers "the transcendental ego at large" (attained by free variation of my factual transcendental ego) as the universe of possible forms of subjective processes of the Eidos "Ego." Among other things, it says there (Par. 36) that within the framework of the required eidetic phenomenology

---

* "Die Befragung der Intentionalität, in welcher der zunächst im Weltphänomen stehende Andere als ein anderer Mensch gilt, führt zur transzendentalen Ausweisung eines Seinszusammenhanges einer eigenartig strukturierten Vielfalt transzendentaler Iche, die mit dem "metaphysischen" Titel Monaden nur angezeigt, nicht gekennzeichnet werden sollen. Keineswegs ist damit eine massive Pluralität in die transzendentale Sphäre verlegt, ebensowenig wie das transzendentale Ego unter der Idee der welthaften Einsheit gedacht werden kann. Die *Implikation* "der Monaden" ist der grosse Problemtitel, der das nicht extensive Sein der Monadenvielfalt, die nur im Transzendentalen mögliche Weise eines nicht individuierten Ineinander, bezeichnet."

** "Alle Seelen bilden eine einzige durch die Phänomenologie systematisch zu entfaltende Einheit der Intentionalität in wechselseitiger Implikation der Lebensströme der einzelnen Subjekte; was in der naiven Positivität oder Objektivität ein Aussereinander ist, ist von Innen gesehen intentionales Ineinander."

"the fact of the transcendental ego and the particular data given in transcendental experience of the ego have the significance merely of examples of pure possibilities." To be sure, not all single possible types are compossible within the unity of a possible ego. The question arises, however, as to how the multiplicity of reciprocally implied transcendental egos is compatible with the Eidos "transcendental ego at large." The texts state repeatedly that the Other is a modification of myself in the mode of "there." Is not the transcendental alter ego only one of the possibilities of the Eidos "transcendental ego at large?"

Is it not the case that the epoché, which, on principle, every man can perform, discloses his "factual transcendental" ego, which, however, as soon as the eidetic reduction is performed, turns out to be a mere example of one "transcendental ego at large" that is the same no matter who extracts it? Is the constitution of the Other only a matter of specific compossibilities? And what sense would it make to speak of intersubjectivity with reference to the one and unitary Eidos "transcendental ego at large," that is, to speak of transcendental, not mundane, intersubjectivity? Here there seems to be a multiple paradox: How is the principle of the compossibilities that are determining the factual transcendental egos compatible with the compossibilities of the mutual intentional implication of all monads? If there is no paradox here, there surely is an open problem.

(3) Let us once more ask who it is that performs the different epochés and reductions which ultimately lead to the constitution of transcendental intersubjectivity. The *Meditationen* speak repeatedly of "I, the meditating philosopher." Fink speaks of the observer as performing the epoché and this is substantiated by certain passages in *Krisis* (esp. Par. 54b and Par. 69). Here reference is made to the ego as the primal ego of the philosopher performing the epoché. Furthermore, it is described how the epoché creates a unique philosophical solitude which is the basic methodological requirement for a genuinely radical philosophy.

In later passages (*Krisis*, Par. 71, p. 260) too, in the exposition of the phenomenological-psychological epoché, it is established that radical and complete reduction leads to the absolutely unique ego of the ("pure") psychologist who thereby becomes absolutely isolated. According to another passage (*Krisis*, Par.

54b, p. 187), however, several people can "perform the epoché" with me "and even in actual community with me"; undoubtedly, however, "for me and my epoché all other men with their entire act-life belong to the world-phenomenon which is exclusively mine in my epoché." * And, at the end of the Fourth Meditation, after establishing that the common world for all of us is constituted for me by means of constitutions on the part of others which are constituted in myself, we read the following sentence (p. 120): "There belongs also, of course, the constitution of a philosophy common to 'all of us' who meditate together – ideally a single *philosophia perennis* " **

The unsettling question which arises is: How can the isolated philosopher, the nonparticipating transcendental observer who performs the epoché, meditate with someone else? How can he perform the epoché in actual community with others? In short, how is "*symphilosphein*" possible? – It seems that Husserl, as well as Fink, have seen these difficulties. Husserl introduces in the last part of *Krisis* the theory of changes of attitude which he discusses under the peculiar heading "professional periods and professional pauses" (*Berufszeiten und Berufspausen*) (e.g., *Krisis*, Pars. 69, 72; Appendix III, p. 373). And Fink concludes his essay by presenting the three-fold paradox which continually obscures the problem of phenomenology: the paradox of the situation of utterance (*Äusserung*), the paradox of the phenomenological proposition (*Satz*), and the paradox of transcendental determination.

Surveying the single phases, we find intersubjectivity in the life-world, solitude in the primordial sphere, transcendental intersubjectivity, solitude of the transcendental observer.

(4) It is scarcely necessary to refute in detail the completely untenable theory that social communities correspond to personalities of a higher order. It is clear that no single feature arrived at by analysis of individual persons can be encountered in so-called personalities of a higher order.

---

* "und sogar in aktueller Gemeinschaft mit mir die Epoché üben" können, wobei freilich "für mich und meine Epoché alle anderen Menschen mit ihrem ganzen Aktleben in das Weltphänomen einbezogen sind, das in meiner Epoché ausschliesslich das meine ist."

** "dazu gehört natürlich auch die Konstitution einer Philosophie als einer uns *allen* als miteinander Meditierenden gemeinsamen – der Idee nach einer einzigen "philosophia perennis." –

There is, however, another problem related to the structure of the social world, which deserves to be considered seriously. Husserl takes as the model of the social situation the case of the bodily presence of the participants in a community of time and space, so that the one finds himself in the perceptual field and the range of the Other. In the analysis of the experience of the Other Husserl has a preference for using this model, which is similar to his preference for using the visual perception of near objects in the analysis of perception. But the social world has near and far zones: the surrounding world (this term being understood here in a sociological sense) in which you and I experience one another in spatial and temporal immediacy, may pass over into the world of my contemporaries, who are not given to me in spatial immediacy; and in multiple transitions, there are the worlds of both predecessors and successors. – Husserl repeatedly indicates that each ego-subject not only has a perceptual field with open horizons, undetermined but determinable, but also has the "horizon of empathy of his fellow subjectivity" which can be opened up by direct intercourse with the chain of Others who are Others for Others as well as for me. Everyone's oriented world has an originarily given core within a horizon of co-valid and anticipated intentionality. All other egos would already be intentionally implied in the living stream of intentionality that is the life of any ego-subject by way of empathy and the horizon of empathy (*Krisis*, Par. 71, p. 258f.). This may serve as a highly useful first description of the life-world. But how is this analysis to be understood with respect to the reciprocal constitution of of fellow-subjectivity in the transcendental sphere? It must also be asked whether in fact the bodily appearance of the Other in my primordial sphere has the decisive significance which Husserl ascribes to it. I empathize much more with a philosopher spatially and temporally distant than with my neighbor in the subway who is given to me in person (*leibhaftig*) but as a stranger (*Fremder*). And what about social far-horizons involving both temporally and spatially – decreasing acquaintance? Was is not said that only that part of physical reality about which the subject has some "knowledge" belongs to the surrounding world (now in Husserl's sense of the term)? Are the Sumerians and the pygmies of the African bush, who are unknown to me, actually constituted in my meditating ego? Do I constitute Socrates or does he constitute me? Is not "to have in a horizon" something other than constitution?

VIII

As a result of these considerations we must conclude that Husserl's attempt to account for the constitution of transcendental intersubjectivity in terms of operations of the consciousness of the transcendental ego has not succeeded. It is to be surmised that intersubjectivity is not a problem of constitution which can be solved within the transcendental sphere, but is rather a datum (*Gegebenheit*) of the life-world. It is the fundamental ontological category of human existence in the world and therefore of all philosophical anthropology. As long as man is born of woman, intersubjectivity and the we-relationship will be the foundation for all other categories of human existence. The possibility of reflection on the self, discovery of the ego, capacity for performing any epoché, and the possibility of all communication and of establishing a communicative surrounding world as well, are founded on the primal experience of the we-relationship. To be sure, all this must remain preserved within the transcendental sphere and must be submitted to explication. This is the task Husserl set himself in his work; transcendental phenomenology must explicate the sense which this world has for us prior to all philosophy – a sense which philosophy can reveal, but cannot change (*Cartesianische Meditationen*, Par. 62, *in fine*). Here we shall not pursue the question whether the problem of intersubjectivity must not first of all be made the theme of an "ontology of the life-world purely as the world of experience (i.e., as the unitary and consistently congruent world open to actual and possible intuition)" (*Krisis*, Par. 51). It can, however, be said with certainty that only such an ontology of the life-world, not a transcendental constitutional analysis, can clarify that essential relationship of intersubjectivity which is the basis of all social science – even though, as a rule, it is there taken for granted and accepted without question as a simple datum.

On the other hand, our introductory comments have shown

that Husserl made the problem of *transcendental* intersubjectivity the central point of his thinking after *Ideen* I. It is only if the we-community manifests itself in the life of the transcendental ego as transcendental, that transcendental phenomenological idealism can be saved from appearing solipsistic. Only by phenomenologically uncovering transcendental intersubjectivity is it possible to account for the constitution of the real world as existing for everyone. – But how can the appearance of solipsism come about? Obviously only by artificially suspending the hidden intentionality of the founding mundane intersubjectivity and eliminating, by means of the reduction, the essential content of the world accepted by me as a world for everyone. Neither the fact that the world – even in its reduced status as a transcendental phenomeon – is a world for all of us, nor the fact that my experience of the world refers apriori to Others, requires explanation. What does require clarification is the desperate attempt to escape from the appearance of solipsism by introducing the second epoché leading to the primordial sphere – since it is precisely this attempt which gives rise to that appearance.

But there are more essential difficulties. They arise from a transformation of sense which the concept of constitution has undergone in the course of the development of phenomenology. At the beginning of phenomenology, constitution meant clarification of the sense-structure of conscious life, inquiry into sediments in respect of their history, tracing back all *cogitata* to intentional operations of the on-going conscious life. These discoveries of phenomenology are of lasting value; their validity has, up to now, been unaffected by any critique, and they are of the greatest importance for the foundation of the positive sciences, especially those of the social world. For it remains true that whatever is exhibited under the reduction retains its validity after return to the natural attitude of the life-world. But unobtrusively, and almost unaware, it seems to me, the idea of constitution has changed from a clarification of sense-structure, from an explication of the sense of being, into the foundation of the structure of being; it has changed from explication into creation (*Kreation*). The disclosure of conscious life becomes a substitute for something of which phenomenology in principle is incapable, viz., for establishing an ontology on the basis of the processes of subjective life. Here I agree in every respect with the comments made in the beautiful essay which Fink published in *Problèmes actuels de la phénoménologie*.[6] The creation of a universe of monads and of the objective world for everyone proves to be impossible within the transcendental subjectivity of the meditating philosopher, a subjectivity which is supposed to subsist for him, and for him alone. But the *clarification of the sense-structure* of intersubjectivity and of the world accepted-by-me-as-objective is, and remains, a legitimate task for phenomenological constitutional analysis. And Husserl did not only point to this task as an area for research, but to a large extent he fulfilled it.

DISCUSSION

Comments by Eugen Fink on Alfred Schutz's Essay, "The Problem of Transcendental Intersubjectivity in Husserl" (Royaumont, April 28, 1957).

My dear friend, I am not handicapped now in this discussion by friendship, and you have said yourself that friendship does not exclude intellectual controversy. However, I am handicapped in that I am very much in agreement with you and your views on the aporias in Husserl's theory of empathy – although I am not always in agreement with your proposed solutions of these aporias.

First of all, I should like to agree with you that Husserl limited himself in his analysis of the experience of the Other to such Others as are present to me in person (*gegenwärtig anwesenden Anderen*), that is, to Others who stand in my near-field, in my perceptual field. I agree with you, furthermore, that his analysis limits itself to explicating this Other as being present in a body, as having a body (*Leibhaber*) and, to this extent, not differing much from cats and dogs. And if having a body (i.e., "a living body": *Leib*) should serve as a sufficient indication of a transcendental fellow-subject, then one must, consequently, conclude that cats and dogs are also transcendental subjects. But how is one to arrive, from an explication of the Other as having a body at the Other, say, for example, as a lover (from "*Leibhaber*" to "*Liebhaber*")? For the character of the Other encountered in the mode of the opposite, complementary sex cannot be understood by virtue of an appresentation which extends, analogically, the ways and the functioning (*das Walten*) of my body to the body of the Other. In a certain way, Husserl's analysis remains caught in the reduplication of the ego. Even though he sees this danger, he does not succeed in overcoming it methodically.

Schutz: Are we then in agreement or not?

Fink: Yes, completely in agreement. My remarks were by way of amplification rather than criticism. But you said that you would still

6 Edited by H. L. Van Breda, Bruxelles, 1951.

consider appresentation, in another way, as a valuable instrument for
conceptual phenomenological analysis. I would like to say now something
about this concept of appresentation. Appresentation was taken up by
Husserl in the analysis of perceptual objects. The front of a perceptual
thing is itself given: the back is, however, appresented. This appresentation is an anticipation of a possible way of bringing the back itself to
originary givenness by walking around the object. That is, appresentation
has the character of redeemableness (*Einlösbarkeit*). I now ask: Is the
appresentation, in which the Other is given, also determined by this
fundamental sense of redeemableness or is it an appresentation
which essentially cannot be redeemed? I can never and in no way o-
riginarily apprehend what is "within," what it is that acts in the living
body of the Other (*das-Im-Leibe-Walten des Anderen*); that is, I can
never "redeem" this appresentation. The experience of the Other being
of this kind, the use of the concept of appresentation is metaphoric – and
unsuccessful at that – and I believe that Husserl has not commented in
sufficient detail on the difference between appresentations which can and
those which cannot be "redeemed."

A further point is that, as you said before, the experience of the Other
involves a reciprocal relationship: in experiencing the Other I experience
concurrently his experiencing of me. But this reciprocal relationship is,
taken strictly, not only a simple running back and forth from myself to
the Other and from the Other to me. This reciprocal relationship allows,
potentially, infinite reiteration. I can therefore say that I so experience
the Other as he is experiencing me, and that he so experiences me as I
am experiencing him, and this can go on infinitely. This potentiality
need not be actualized; however, we have here an infinite reciprocal
reflectibility somewhat like two mirrors placed one opposite the other
reflecting into each other in infinite reiteration. This infinity of reciprocal
relationships in the encounter of two subjects is not seen by Husserl
insofar as this implication of infinity is concerned. And it is further to be
asked if, on the whole, the reciprocal relationship involved in the encounter of two subjects – this reciprocity of facing and objectivating the
Other – suffices even to clarify the immediacy of understanding by which
the existence of the Other is apprehended in shared situations. (*Unmittel-
barkeit des Verstehens des Mitdaseins mit dem Anderen*).

In this connection, you still referred to Husserl's analysis and showed
with approval that in this analysis the Other is experienced as "là-bas,"
as *there*. That is, spatial differentiation of Here and There is of help in
understanding the difference between my life and the Other's. But now
I ask, what about the Now? You can explicate the differentiation between
Here and There, in the sense that, "There" for me is "Here" for him and
my Here is for him There. But can you say the same about the Now? Is
not the Now the very dimension in which Here and There are given in
contemporaneity, in simultaneity? Can you distinguish the Now of the
Other, as his Now, and my Now? Or is not such a distinction simply
bereft of sense? The difference between Here and There is possible only
within the dimension of a common encompassing Now.

Then you say – forgive me if I proceed so unsystematically, but this
is the way I noted these things in the course of your exposition – that it
was an error of method on the part of Husserl to try to derive the objectivity of the world from intersubjectivity and, in fact, that it might be

just the reverse: the objective world is presupposed for intersubjectivity. And you show in this context that all processes of communication (*Verständigung*) – by language, signs, or however – already presuppose objective things as supports or as a medium, as vehicles of signification in mutual understanding (*Sich-Verstehen*). But this is meant by Husserl in still a different sense, and I would like, in this connection, to refer to the Kantian notion. Kant formulates objectivity of experience – that is, relatedness of experience to objects – in the context in which he formulates the difference between a judgment of perception and a judgment of experience; he formulates objectivity of objects by the character – if one will – of intersubjectivity. Hence it seems to me that one cannot establish between objectivity and intersubjectivity a relationship such that the one or the other is prior; rather, objectivity and intersubjectivity are perhaps co-original.

Then another point which occupied me was the following: you said that the transcendental Ego, in the flux of its life, must constitute the Others with their sense as intramundane Others and also itself as intramundane. The finitude of my life as related to death also belongs, in a fundamental way, to this intramundaneity of myself and my fellow-men. Can the transcendental Ego die? Or is death only an objective fact which belongs to its objectivation in the world and which has no truth for its final transcendental inwardness? Consequently, in a way, is not the intramundane human situation under-determined when one does not keep in view such determinations of human existence as finitude, that is, the fate of death? Does this not concern transcendental subjectivity, too? Here, then, is a question.

In his late manuscripts which were written after *Cartesianische Meditationen*, Husserl comes, to be sure, to questions which are related to the aporias which you have pointed out. He sees the difficulty involved in simply transposing structures of the intramundane multiplicity of subjects into the transcendental realm. He does, indeed, see a certain danger in the transposition of mundane structuring subjectivity into the realm of the transcendental, and in some manuscripts he arrives at the curious idea of a primal ego, of a primal subjectivity which is prior to the distinction between the primordial subjectivity and the transcendental subjectivity of other monads. He seems to try to some extent, to withdraw the plurality from the dimension of the transcendental – thus heading toward a problem which reminds us of the late Fichte. In the same context Husserl also tries to circumvent the difference between essence and fact by going back to the primal facticity of transcendental life which first constitutes possibility and thereby variations, and – as an objectivation (*Vergegenständlichung*) of variational multiplicities – also constitutes essence. According to Husserl's ideas in these very late manuscripts, there is a primal life which is neither one nor many, neither factual nor essential; rather, it is the ultimate ground of all these distinctions: a transcendental primal life which turns itself into a plurality and which produces in itself the differentiation into fact and essence. Consequently, if one takes these texts into account, many difficulties, many aporias, to which you have pointed would appear in a quite different light. The substantive difficulties, however, would be then only increased.*

* The German text of these comments was transcribed from a tape recording by Dr. R. Böhm.

Alfred Schutz's Answer to Comments Made in the Discussion of "The Problem of Transcendental Intersubjectivity in Husserl" (Royaumont, April 28, 1957).

First of all, I wish to thank all participants in the discussion for their highly interesting and instructive remarks. However, to reply to all of them within the time at my disposal in due thoroughness is an impossible task, since most of the questions raised by the speakers touch on fundamental problems of phenomenology. For this reason, I ask to be forgiven if I take up only summarily some of the points brought up in this discussion and perhaps even fail to deal with a few of them.

Allow me to begin with a short personal observation. My attempt at a critical presentation of Husserl's transcendental grounding of intersubjectivity was motivated exclusively by one desire: to present, for discussion before this forum of highly competent phenomenologists, the difficulties involved in this theory – difficulties which I could not overcome in the twenty-five years of studying this theory of my highly respected teacher. My aim was not to offer a solution of my own to the problems of the constitution of transcendental intersubjectivity in terms of the operations of the consciousness of the transcendental ego; nor is the implication of my thesis that – because Husserl's argumentation obviously fails here – the methods of transcendental phenomenology, not to say phenomenology in general, must be rejected. Rather, I strove to show that Husserl's failure to find a solution to this problem is due to his attempt to interpret the *ontological* status of social reality within the life-world as the constituted product of the transcendental subject, rather than explicating its transcendental *sense* in terms of operations of consciousness of the transcendental subject. Undoubtedly, we are confronted with a problem with serious implications and it was my purpose to present this problem for discussion. It affords me great satisfaction that all speakers, especially such prominent and expert phenomenologists as Messrs. Fink and Ingarden, concurred therein.

Dr. Fink's observations especially have such depth that I would like to discuss them in detail. To begin with his observations as to the concept of *appresentation*: I completely agree with him that appresentations that can be converted into perceptual presentations, and appresentations in which in principle this cannot occur, must be rigorously distinguished. It will not be easy, however, to draw the line of demarcation. On the one hand, there are appresented aspects of perceptual things as, for example, the inside of the earth which cannot, in principle, be converted into perceptual presentations; on the other hand, with his so-called "*perceptual theory of the alter ego,*" Scheler was right insofar as we directly perceive in the smile of the Other his joy; in his folded hands his praying. I would like to modify somewhat Fink's thesis that it is impossible to bring another's appresented inner life to perceptual presence by saying that I can apprehend the Other's inner life only by means of indicative symbols (his gestures, his facial expressions, his language, his actions), that I can apprehend it only by appresentations. Indeed, it is a peculiarity of symbol-relationships in general that the symbol alone is present, whereas that which is symbolized is only appresented. In this sense I said that Husserl's theory of appresentation, especially in its application to the theory of sign and symbol relations, remains indubitably important.

That the constitutions of the transcendental experience of the Other cannot be reduced to appresentation alone is indeed likewise indubitable.

Dr. Fink further mentioned the reciprocal relationship of the ego to the Other as essentially involved in the experience of the alter ego, the relationship in which the Other is experienced by me as being himself oriented to me. He refers to the fact that this reciprocal relation potentially admits of infinite reiterations, and he compares that reciprocal reflection to that of two mirrors placed opposite each other. It may be of interest, in this connection, to mention that this comparison – called the "looking-glass effect" – plays a great role in the theories of the experience of the Other, advanced by some American philosophers (William James, Cooley, G. H. Mead). These writers even found the experience of my Self upon my experience (or anticipation) of the impression or image which the Other has of me. But perhaps the inner reciprocal relation is not infinitely reiterable because, retaining Fink's metaphor, the mirrors cannot of necessity, be placed parallel to each other. On the other hand, it cannot be doubted that this reciprocal relation in the encounter of ego and alter ego is not sufficient to account for the immediacy in which the co-existence with the Other (*Mitdasein*) is apprehended in such a situation.

One must be grateful to Fink for raising, in that same context, the question of the simultaneity of the ego with Others, of the common Now as a presupposition for differentiating a Here and a There. The problem of simultaneity, taken not merely as a common Now in objective time but also as a community of two inner flows of time – "*durée*" in Bergson's sense – seems to me to be of the greatest significance for the problem of intersubjectivity, and that not only in regard to transcendental but also to *mundane* intersubjectivity. In several writings I have called attention to the fact that, in reflective advertence, the ego may grasp only its past experiences or the initial – already completed – phases of still ongoing experiences, while it is capable of grasping the experiences of the alter ego in the simultaneity of Now. This can briefly be illustrated in the communication of language: the speaker builds up his discourse in his conscious, polythetic acts to which the successive acoustical events in the outer world are coordinated in strict simultaneity. These events in the outer world are perceived by the listener and interpreted in his own strictly simultaneous polythetic conscious acts as symbols for events in the consciousness of the speaker. By means of the speech, events in the external world, the two streams of consciousness are synchronized. This makes possible the constitution of a common Now and consequently, of a We. This, to be sure, is only one instance of a universal and essential state of affairs (*Wesensverhalt*). Since I can grasp in simultaneity your conscious processes occurring Now, while I can apprehend reflectively only those of my experiences which are, at best, "just past", the consciousness of the Other can be, indeed, defined as a consciousness whose processes the ego can apprehend in simultaneity. I believe that – if I correctly understand Dr. Fink's observations about the common Now – his question might have been answered by my remarks which show that I completely agree with him.

As far as the co-originariness of the objective world and intersubjectivity is concerned, which Fink interprets as a possible opinion of Husserl, I grant that this view is supported by certain passages which, incidentally,

have been cited in my paper. They are to be found in manuscripts published in *Ideen* II. There can be no doubt, however, that in other passages
the objectivity of the world is founded upon intersubjectivity which, in
turn, is founded upon a "communicative environment" that is simply
taken for granted. Dr. Fink's reference in this connection to the Kantian
derivation of the objectivity of the world-itself profoundly puzzling – is
not completely clear to me. But it would lead too far afield to enter into
this question. Before analyzing it we would have to come, necessarily,
to an agreement about the sense of the Kantian "transcendental apperception" and his distinction between judgments of perception and
judgments of experience. At any event, I find it difficult to accept the
possible co-originariness of intersubjectivity and the objectivity of the
world as a *transcendental* constitutional problem in the frame of Husserl's
thought. I, too, have no doubt, however, that both categories are co-
originary as far as the primary comprehension (*Vorverständnis*) of the
life-world in the natural attitude is concerned.

Of special importance is, it seems to me, Dr. Fink's suggestion that
the transcendental subject must constitute himself and Others as mundane subjects – as to their sense – and that here the finitude of man, the
human fate of death, must be taken into account. Here it clearly appears
that I experience the fact that I am fated to die in a completely different
way from the way in which I experience the fact as concerning Others.
I survive the death of the Other, in his mundane objectivity, and for me
this death is the objective end of the mundane intersubjectivity in which
I was joined with him. My own death is as certain to me as my mundane
finitude. Mundanely I cannot survive – even if I assume (as did Husserl in
his last conversation with me) that the transcendental subject cannot
die. But what about the transcendental subjectivity of the Other
and what about the transcendental intersubjectivity which joins my
transcendental subject to his, when he, the Other, dies? Does not this
consideration alone refute the possibility of a plurality of transcendental
subjects?

I am especially indebted to Dr. Fink for the indication that Husserl
had taken into account in his last manuscripts the aporias pointed out
by me. I am not familiar with those manuscripts and have stayed within
the bounds of published texts, as I expressly noted in my paper. Dr.
Fink's comments are, however, a valuable commentary to Husserl's
somewhat inscrutable references to the "primal ego" in *Krisis* (Par. 54b)
to which I referred at the end of my presentation.

In his observations, Professor Ingarden dealt with the complex
structure of the matters commonly grouped together under the name of
"empathy," and developed five thematic areas, or processes, in the
experience of the psyche of the alter ego. In his theory of sympathy
Scheler had proposed a similar inventory. He tried, however, to establish
internal relationships among these processes, showing which processes
are founded upon which others. This would require further critical
analysis. Professor Ingarden's comments are, unfortunately, much too
condensed to permit a complete understanding of his line of thought.
Above all, it is not clear to me whether or not he assumes a foundational
nexus between the five processes of experience of the Other which he
enumerates; and, if this is the case, why he begins with the immediate
grasping of an autonomous course of action of the Other and ends with

"empathy" in the pregnant sense, i.e., with appresentations which impute to the Other a conscious life. Does not interpretation of some event as an autonomous course of action of the Other presuppose an imputation to the Other of certain conscious processes: the projection of goals, the choice of means and some context of motivation?

Now I turn to Professor Beck's commentary concerning the three egos involved in the performances of the phenomenological reduction as presented by Husserl in *Cartesianische Meditationen* and by Fink in his *Kant-Studien* essay. I would like to note that in this respect I have merely tried to present and immanently criticize Husserl's view. In my paper I have deliberately taken no position on the theory of the three egos. But I do not hesitate to state that I consider them as untenable not only on the grounds of the aporias I have indicated, but also because of other considerations, the presentation of which would lead too far afield. I completely share Professor Beck's view that an ontology of the life-world which is not only a physical world, but also – or perhaps above all – a *social* world, must present the ego as already in a reciprocal relationship with Others. But I do not agree with the speaker that social relationships are founded upon a metaphysical need of the finite ego for the Other. Nor can I agree with his thesis that the performance of the epoché as such, be it the first or the second, must necessarily falsify the situation. Husserl insisted again and again on the thesis (indeed, difficult to understand) that even after the performance of the second epoché my experiences *of* the Other remain as intentional correlates in the sphere that is "properly" of my ego.

Dr. Graumann asked why a constitutive establishment of an ontology of the life-world on the basis of the life-processes of transcendental subjectivity should remain unattainable in principle. As I did in my paper, I again refer to Fink's argumentation in his essay in *Problèmes actuels de la phénoménologie*. I consider Fink's argument there as conclusive. This, however, involves neither that transcendental phenomenology has, in principle, to relinquish the clarification of the sense-structure of intersubjectivity, nor that phenomenology as such has to limit itself to this task. On the contrary, I am of the opinion that Husserl showed the way – even if he did not take it – which a phenomenological analysis of the social world – the ontological status of which is to be accepted – would have to follow. This is not the way of transcendental constitutional analysis, but of a phenomenology of the natural attitude, postulated in the *Nachwort zu meinen "Ideen"*, the goal of which would have to be, among other things, to elucidate the hitherto unclarified foundations of all social sciences.

In this connection I believe I have also answered the most important questions raised by M. Kelkel. I cannot see why the failure of the attempt, on the part of transcendental phenomenology to constitute intersubjectivity in the sense of the creation of a universe of monads, and, thereby, of a creation of an objective world for everyone, could be construed as a general failure of transcendental phenomenology, even as a failure of Husserl's whole philosophy. It can only be said that Husserl, in his claim to found the existence of the social world on constitutive operations of the consciousness of the transcendental ego, made "an extravagant use" – to put it in Kantian terms – of the method of transcendental constitution. As I tried to explain at the end of my paper, the appearance of solipsism comes about only as a result of the artificial exclusion of the hidden intentional processes of *mundane* intersubjectivity as a founding stratum. It comes about in consequence of the reduction which eliminates from my world one of its essential traits: my world as given to me as a world for everyone. In any case, I am for from viewing the Husserlian constitution of intersubjectivity as a *deduction* in the technical sense of the term; against such an interpretation M. Kelkel rightly appeals to some important texts of Husserl. My esteemed critic rests his charge of such a misinterpretation upon two passages in my paper where the word *"déduire"* is used. This is, however, a misunderstanding brought about by the translation – which, incidentally, is a perfectly correct one – in which the neutral German term *"Ableitung"* (deduction, derivation), also used by Husserl in this context, was rendered with *"déduction"*.* The different shades of meaning of the terms in the two languages (a problem which could be fruitfully analyzed by phenomenologists) make such difficulties in communication, to which M. Kelkel alludes at the end of his remarks, practically unavoidable.

I wish to express my deep indebtedness to Professor Maurice de Gandillac. I have the greatest admiration for his efforts, the patience, and the ability, which he devoted to the translation of my lecture.

---

* *"The Problem of Transcendental Intersubjectivity in Husserl* was read as a lecture in French at Royaumont in a translation prepared by Professor Maurice de Gandillac. As in the case of the essay, so in the case of this reply to *Comments on the Essay,* the original German text has been used as a basis for the English translation

TYPE AND EIDOS IN HUSSERL'S
LATE PHILOSOPHY

In a brilliant paper presented to the "Colloque international de phénoménologie à Royaumont 1957"[1] Professor Eugen Fink deals with what he calls the operative concepts in Husserl's phenomenology. He distinguishes in the world of any major philosopher between thematic and operative notions. Whereas the former aim at the fixation and preservation of the fundamental concepts, the latter are used in a vague manner as tools in forming the thematic notions; they are models of thought or intellectual schemata which are not brought to objectifying fixation, but remain opaque and thematically unclarified. According to Fink, the notions of "phenomenon," of "constitution," and "performances" (*Leistungen*), and even those of "epoché" and of "transcendental logic" are used by Husserl as operative concepts. They are not thematically clarified or remain at least operatively adumbrated, and are merely headings for groups of problems open to and requiring further analysis.

The present paper makes the attempt to show that the notion of typicality, which, according to Husserl's later philosophy, characterizes our experiencing of the life-world in the natural attitude on both the predicative and the prepredicative level, and even the notion of ideation, (at least in the sense of eidetic generalization, that is, the grasping of the ideal genera and species of material universals) are also widely used by him as mere operative schemata of a highly equivocal character and are in need of further clarification.

To start with the typicality of our experiences of the life-world

---

[1] E. Fink, "Les Concepts opératoires dans la phénoménologie de Husserl" in *Husserl*, Paris, 1959, pp. 214–230.

so central for Husserl's late philosophy, we find that three groups of problems lead him to a closer investigation of this feature: (1) the horizonal character of our experiences in the natural attitude, and the limiting notion of "world" as the foundation of the qualities of preacquaintedness and familiarity adherent to them; (2) the problem of the genealogy of logical forms, including the constitution of universal objectivities as originating in prepredicative experience; (3) the structure of our experiences of the life-world (*Lebenswelt*), their necessary vagueness, and their determination by our interests. Although it will hardly be possible to handle separately each of the aforementioned problems in its relation to typicality, it is hoped that our analyses of the various approaches (which we propose to perform without trying to embark upon a discussion of the historical development of Husserl's pertinent thought, and without any reference to his so far unpublished writings) will show the reasons for the equivocations involved in Husserl's pertinent views. They are hardly compatible with one another and are of an operative nature. We will close with a few questions referring to the relationship between the typicality of our experiences in everyday life and the possibility of the so-called "free variations" performed in phantasy which are supposed to lead by the process of ideation to the intuition of the eidos.

I. THE PREACQUAINTEDNESS OF THE WORLD AND ITS OBJECTS; INNER AND OUTER HORIZON

We start with a brief analysis of our experience of everyday life as described in Husserl's *Erfahrung und Urteil*.[2] As usual – and sometimes to the great disadvantage of his general theory – Husserl takes as the paradigm of our experiencing the perceiving of concrete objects of the external world given to our actual or potential sensory apperception. To the naive attitude of our everyday life objects are simply pregiven as assumedly being and being in such and such a way. They are pregiven to us in the

---

[2] *Erfahrung und Urteil: Untersuchungen zur Genealogie der Logik*, redigiert und herausgegeben von Ludwig Landgrebe, 2. unveraenderte Auflage, Hamburg, 1954; see for the present section of this paper especially the Introduction and Part I, but also the very important Sections 82 and 83.

unquestioned (although always questionable) assurance of an uncontested belief, and thus not on the ground of a particular act of positing, and still less on the ground of an existential judgment. But our experience of these given objects shows two characteristics: in the first place, all objects of our experience have from the outset the character of typical familiarity; in the second place, the process of our apperceiving these objects by originary intuition is always permeated by anticipations of not actually apperceived but cointended features. Both characteristics are closely connected with each other and with the typicality of our experiences, as we shall show.

According to Husserl, the world and the individual objects in it are always experienced by us as having been preorganized by previous experiencing acts of the most various kinds. In any experience, even that of an objectivity apperceived for the first time, a preknowledge of as yet unapperceived properties of the object is involved, a preknowledge which might be undetermined or incompletely determined as to its content, but which will never be entirely empty. In other words, any experience carries along an experiential horizon which refers to the possibility (in subjective terms, to the faculty) not merely to explicate step by step the objectivity as it is given in actual apperception, but also to obtain by additional experiencing acts ever new additional determinations of the same objectivity. This infinite open horizon of the actual experience functions in its indeterminateness from the outset as the scope of anticipated possibilities of further determination; yet in spite of their undetermined generality these anticipations are, according to Husserl, nevertheless *typically* determined by their *typical* prefamiliarity, as *typically* belonging, that is, to the total horizon of the same and identifiable objectivity, the actually apperceived properties of which show the same general *type*.

Thus, it is the horizonal anticipations which predelineate the typical preacquaintedness and familiarity of the objectivity given to our apperception. First of all, the object is within that universal horizon of all horizons to which we refer in the natural attitude by the term "world." The world is the total horizon of all possible experiences. Any object is an object *within* the world which, in the natural attitude, does not become thematic itself, but is just taken for granted. For example, any single real object of the outer world is apperceived as a valid existent within the general horizon of the world, and this means, among other things, that it is apperceived as an identical and as "always the same" identifiable element of the world, and having as such its position within universal space and universal time. But the world as the unquestioned horizonal background of all possible experiences of existents within it has merely *in general* the subjective character of familiarity without being known in its *individual particularities*. Each individual existent which is apperceived as such has, in addition, its particular horizonal structure within which all further distinctions of acquaintedness and unacquaintedness originate. The object is given to the apperceiving consciousness not merely as an objectivity as such, but as an existent of a particular type: as a thing of the outer world, as a plant, an animal, a human being, a human product, and so on. Even more: it is apperceived as pertaining to further and further differentiated "genera" with their subordinated "species" – provided that we are permitted to use analogically these technical terms for the prepredicative and preconceptual forms of simple apperceptual experiences now under scrutiny. Accordingly, to Husserl structurization by preacquaintedness and unacquaintedness is a fundamental feature of our consciousness of the world. This structurization is permeated by the relative distinction between undetermined generality and determined specificity. If we call the open frame of further determinability of the apperceived object the *inner horizon* of this object, then we may say that the further determination occurs by explicating the preindicated horizonal implicata and, correlatively, the adherent open possibilities of anticipated activities of the mode "I can" (I can examine the object more closely; I can make its unseen back side visible by turning it around or by locomotions of my body, etc.). The inner horizon can thus be characterized as the empty frame of the undetermined determinability, indicating and prescribing both the particular style of any further explication and a particular typicality of the anticipated explicata so to be obtained. That is why Husserl comes to the conclusion that all particular apperceptions are fulfillments of that which has been meant in advance.

Now it has to be emphasized that the horizon is continually in flux. With any new intuitive apperception new determinations or rectifications of previous determinations modify the possible anticipations and therewith the horizon. No apperception is merely instantaneous and transient; any apperception becomes a part of habitual knowledge as a permanent result. Sometimes Husserl speaks of the "sedimentations" of preceding experiences. To be sure, these habitual possessions are latent, but this implies that they may be "wakened" or "called forth." This occurs by way of a passive synthesis of congruence (*Deckungssynthese*), based on similarity of dissimilarity, a synthesis for which Husserl uses the traditional term of "association," hastening to warn us that its meaning as used by him is a different one. To Husserl "association" designates a general form of immanent genesis inherent to consciousness. It means exclusively the purely immanent relation of "something recalls something else," "something refers to something else." Thus a *pair* is constituted, one member of which "wakens" the other. Similar experiences are called forth by similar ones and contrast with the dissimilar. It seems that Husserl changed the terminology later on [3] and handled the problem of association as a special case of "pairing" or "appresentation."[*]

Thus the apperception of an objectivity in its horizon calls forth the recollection of other objectivities similar to or even like the former, and constitutes therewith a typicality on the ground of which by apperceptive transference (*Apperzeptive Uebertragung*) other objectivities of a similar kind are also apperceived from the outset as objectivities of the same type, that is, of a pregiven more or less specific familiarity. It can be easily seen that with any step of originary apperceiving and explicating not only the objectivity under scrutiny becomes further determined, but concomitantly a modification of the horizon of all possible experiences as a whole occurs. New typical determinations and familiarities are constituted and predelineate the direction of apperceptive expectations which attach themselves to the givenness of newly encountered objectivities. The extension of the typi-

---

[3] *Cartesianische Meditationen und Pariser Vorträge*, herausgegeben und eingeleitet von S. Strasser, *Husserliana* I, Den Haag, 1950; cf. IV. Mediation, Sections 38, 39; V. Meditation, Sections 50–52.

[*] See *Collected Papers*, Vol. I, p. 125.

cality thus constituted might widely vary depending upon the manner in which the objectivity is anticipatorily appresented. This extension – always according to Husserl – discloses itself merely in the fulfillments of the anticipations and can be conceptualized by particular intentional acts in hindsight only.

We shall return very soon to the problem of conceptualization, especially in its relationship to typicality. At this juncture an example of the typicality of the natural experiential apperception given by Husserl in another context[4] might be a welcome illustration of the preceding. He points out that in the natural attitude things in the factual world are from the outset experienced as types, namely, as trees, animals, snakes, birds, and in particular, as fir, maple, dog, adder, swallow, sparrow, etc. That which is apperceived as a type recalls similar things in the past and is to that extent familiar. Moreover, what is typically apperceived carries along a horizon of possible further experiences in the form of a predelineation of a typicality of still unexperienced but expected characteristics of the object. If we see a dog we anticipate immediately his future behavior, his typical way of eating, playing, running, jumping, etc. Actually, we do not see his teeth, but even if we have never seen this particular dog, we know in advance what his teeth will look like – not in their individual determination, but in a typical way, since we have long ago and frequently experienced that "suchlike" animals ("dogs") have something like teeth of this and that typical kind.

But why are certain characteristics of the object paired with characteristics of other objects as typically similar, while others, – at least for the time being – are disregarded? William James and Bergson have developed their theory of the selectivity of consciousness in order to answer this question, which is directly related to the constitution of typicality. Husserl, too, acknowledges that the explicating activity by which the object is apperceived as a unity of characteristics is not evenly distributed over all the particularities which detach themselves, but that "our glance is directed toward specifally impressive properties of the object by which the object of this particular typicality or this individual object distinguishes itself from objects of equal or similar typicality."[5]

---

[4] *Erfahrung und Urteil*, Section 83.
[5] *Ibid.*, p. 139.

What is, however, the factor that makes certain traits of the object "specifically impressive"? According to Husserl, it is our *interest*. He distinguishes two kinds of interest: first, the object, which is passively pregiven to us, affects our receptivity and wakens in us the more or less intense tendency to follow the stimulus emanating from and imposed upon us by the object, and to advert to it. That is why Husserl interprets receptivity as the lowest form of ego-activity. The adversion evokes an interest in the object surpassing those of its features which are merely pregiven in the mode of actuality and striving to ever new apprehension. (This first notion of interest recalls Leibniz's definition of consciousness as the tendency to proceed to ever new experiences.) The second and broader notion of interest does not originate in the simple adversion toward the object, but in making it *thematic*. Theme (in the precise sense) and object do not always coincide, as for example in a situation in which I am occupied with a scientific work as my theme, but am "interrupted" by a noise in the street. Even then I have not dropped my theme, to which I return after the interruption has passed. Acts of interest in this broader sense surpass, then, the mere being adverted to the object, say by perceiving it or even searchingly examining it: they involve "taking part" in this activity ("*Dabei-sein*"), an "*inter-esse*" in the literal sense of this word.[6]

Husserl, in the texts published so far, does not continue this analysis beyond these fugitive remarks. But it is quite clear that it is the interest, or, perhaps better, the system of interests which codetermines typicality.

So far we have spoken merely of the inner horizon of the object and its explication. But any object adverted to stands out from a background, a field, which is not adverted to, but is just "there." We may say that the object has an open, endless horizon of coexisting objects, hence a horizon of a second level which is related to the horizon of the first one. We call this horizon the *outer horizon* of coexisting objects to which I may at any time turn as to objects being either different from or typically similar to the object I am actually adverted to. In a certain sense the meaning of the latter is codetermined by its outer horizon as the totality of my potential experiences of coexistent objects and

---

[6] *Ibid.*, Section 20.

their relations to the actually apperceived one. But this is not all: the meaning of the object which is in immediacy given to our actual intuition refers also to its – mostly hidden – relations to objects which were given to us once in the past, and might now be represented in terms of recollections of various kinds, and even to objectivities of our free phantasying, provided that a relationship of similarity between them and the actually given object prevails at all. The unity between the related elements might be experienced merely passively as pregiven in the unity of our consciousness. But – in contradistinction to the process of explicating the implicata hidden in the inner horizon – all these relations can be made thematic. The activity by which this is done is called by Husserl "relating contemplation" (*beziehendes Betrachten*). However, it has to be emphasized that a mere addition of further objects to the actually given object is as such not a relating contemplation. The latter requires a specific interest in the broader sense which makes the object taken as the point of departure the main theme. If, for example, my fountain pen is the main theme, then the table upon which it lies is not the main theme, but a theme merely with respect to the fountain pen. Which object, in such a case, becomes the main theme depends again upon the direction of the then prevailing interest, and the relating contemplation may reveal different determinations of either of the related object such as: $A > B$, $B < A$; A lies upon B, B beneath A.

It goes without saying that everything stated before about the inner horizon as to the habitual sedimentation of once obtained knowledge and as to its functions in the renewed or entirely new determination of objectivities – and therewith in the ascertainment of their typicality – is also valid for habitualities originating in relating contemplations.

II. EMPIRICAL TYPES AND UNIVERSALS

So far our analysis has been restricted to the prepredicative level. We have seen how empirical types are, according to Husserl, preconstituted in passivity, which he considers as the lowest form of the constitution of universals. Of particular interest to him is now the transition from the empirical types to the

predicative judgments dealing with generic concepts, and further
to the constitution of universal objectivities of the highest level
and the forms of all-or-none judgments. Let us first follow this
development in terms of the typicality of the apperceived objects.[7]
Anything apperceived in its typicality *may* lead up to the universal concept of the type under which we apprehend it. But we
need not be directed in such a manner toward the generic; we
need not apperceive thematically this concrete individual dog
as a singularization of the general notion "dog." "*In general*"
one dog is like any other dog. If, however, we remain directed
toward the dog as an individual, then the passively preconstituted relation of this individual dog to the type under which he
was apperceived from the outset remains unthematized. This
typicality will not exhaust all similarities of the concrete object
which will be revealed in the progress of our experiencing it.
To the type "dog," for example, belongs a set of typical properties with an open horizon of anticipations of further typical
characteristics. If we proceeded in our experiencing of this or
that individual dog, we would find ever new characteristics which
do not belong just to this individual dog, but to dogs in general,
characteristics which are predelineated by the properties ap-
propriated by us as typical for dogs in accordance with the
incomplete and fugitive experiences we had had of them until
now. This is the origin of a *presumptive idea of a universal* which
surpasses the *concept* of *real* dogs as it originated in *real* experiences. Husserl calls this idea a presumptive one because we live
continually in the empirical certainty – a certainty good until
further notice – that what proves to be on the ground of known
properties an object of a particular type will also have all the
further characteristics regularly discovered in other objects of
this type by regular induction, and so on. In this manner the
empirical concepts undergo continual change caused by the
resorption of new characteristics under the guidance of the
empirical idea of an open and always rectifiable concept, an idea
which is at the foundation of our empirical faith in the continuity
of our real experiences.

To be sure, the prevailing assumption that always new typical
moments can be grasped in the process of experiencing may be

[7] See *Ibid.*, Sections 82 ff., esp. 83 and 84.

disappointed. Immediate experience frequently distinguishes things in accordance with certain striking relations which might obfuscate factual inner relations. The appertaining of the whale (in German: *der Walfisch*) to the class of the mammals is, for example, hidden by the exterior analogy to the way of life which this animal shares with the fishes. In such cases we speak of nonessential types (*ausserwesentliche Typen*). In the comprehensive experience of concrete Nature the individuals are more and more grouped under essential types (*wesentliche Typen*) of various degrees of universality. It is this state of affairs upon which scientific empirical research into Nature and its history is founded. By necessity it refers to prescientific and in many cases unessential types of the natural experiential apperception. Scientific concepts of species aim at the determination of essential types by systematic and methodical experiences, but they too carry along an open infinite horizon of – at the outset still unknown – typical characteristics to be determined by further research. The typical refers in this case also to causality: the causality of the "life" of the animals or plants of the particular types (species) under particular conditions, their development, procreation, etc.

III. CONSTITUTION OF UNIVERSAL OBJECTIVITIES IN THE PREDICATIVE SPHERE [8]

Yet our presentation of the transition from the prepredicative type to the empirical presumptive idea did not deal with an important intermediary step, namely, the constitution of the typically generic and finally universal objectivities in the predicative sphere. The prepredicative receptive experience is guided by the interest in perceiving, that is, the tendency to bring the given objectivity in all its aspects and perspectives to our intuition. But this is merely a preliminary level of the interest in knowing (*Erkenntnisinteresse*) the objectivity, and in preserving the knowledge once attained. This is done by a cognitive activity of the I, the outcome of which is predication. Husserl speaks also of the predicative spontaneity as opposed to the receptive experience. It is important for the understanding of

[8] *Ibid.*, Parts II and III.

the process of predication to see that any predicative judgment includes a form of universality (*Allgemeinheitsform*), a determination of the object *"as"* being this and that. This is the counterpart of grasping from the outset an object in pure receptivity as being of a somehow familiar type. If, for example, we determine this particular perceptual object as being red and form the perceptual judgment, "S is p," then by reason of the universality of the determination "red" the relation to the universal "redness" is already implicitly contained in this "determining-as-being-red." To be sure, this relation has so far not become thematic, as it would be in the form: "this is *one* red object." But only in the latter case could we speak of conceptual thinking in the proper sense.

The simple predication "S is p" corresponds to the explication of an object perceived. But whereas the explication of a substratum S consists in a passive synthesis of congruence between S and its determinant moment p, the positing of S as the subject (in the logical sense) of the predicative judgment "S is p" requires a new form of activity which is motivated by the supervening interest (in the broader sense) in actively determining S as the thematic *terminus a quo* and p as the *terminus ad quem*. In other words, an *active* intention aims now at grasping that which was previously given in *passive* congruence. This activity is not only synthetic activity in general but at the same time the activity of synthesizing. We become aware that S is determined by p in the form "S is p." This process occurs in polythetic steps.

But "S is p" is merely the archetype of predication. The determining process may go on from p to q to r, which may lead to judgments of the form "S is p *and* q *and* r," if the cognitive interest is equally distributed among all members, or to (linguistically) subordinate clauses, that is, to judgments of the form "S, which is p, is q," etc. In his studies dedicated to the genesis of predicative judgments Husserl analyzed a great number of such forms, the description of which would surpass by far the limits of this paper. We turn instead immediately to his theory of the constitution of universals in productive spontaneity. It is precisely here that the notion of typicality receives a modified meaning. Husserl recalls to us that the relation of a single object to the typically general prevails already in any apperception of the individual on the ground of the horizon of familiarity. The decisive point is, however, whether or not this relation becomes thematic in a process of judging. If it does, the characters of familiarity may lead to the active, spontaneous constitution of a new kind of objectivities, namely, to *the typically generic itself*, as whose "representative" the individual object is apperceived, that is, as an *objectivity of this kind, of this type*. The universals constituted in these supervening acts of free spontaneity – the types, species, genera, etc. – may be of various levels of generality. The generality of the empirical presumptive type is merely one among them and a relatively low one; at the highest level are the pure or eidetic universals and, based upon them, judgments which no longer originate in the thematization of the relations of the objectivities to their empirical types of familiarity, but in the thematization of their relations to pure essences.

Let us very briefly illustrate the constitution of universals in productive spontaneity by an example. Suppose we found in concentration upon S the moment p as standing out in the form S is p. Our interest shifts now to S', S", S''' which coaffect us because they too show the same moment p as *their* outstanding individual moment. In this case we have to distinguish two series of judgments: the first one in which the individual moment is predicated to each substratum: "S' is p'," "S" is p''," "S''' is p''' "; and a second series in which everywhere the same p (without prime) is predicated to each substratum as the universal identical unity of the species constituted passively in the congruence of likeness of p', p'', p'''. Then we arrive at judgments such as "S' is p," "S" is p," etc., whereby p is no longer a predicative individual kernel, but a general one. In the judgment "S' is p'," the p' designates the *individual* moment in the *individual* object S', whereby the substratum S' and its individual moment are identified. We call such a judgment an individual judgment. In the judgment "S' is p" universals appear at least on one side, since p designates the universal (*das Allgemeine*). We call such a judgment a generic judgment (*generelles Urteil*). This is a new form of judgment because the difference of the kernels leads to a modified form of the synthesis of identity as compared with the simple explicative synthesis which we considered to be the basic form of our categorical judgment "S is p," although the former is founded on the latter.

IV. THE ENLARGEMENT OF THE NOTION OF TYPICALITY IN HUSSERL'S "KRISIS" [9]

We now have to study the nature of pure universals as they are revealed by the eidetic method. Before doing so, however, we want to follow the analysis of typicality which Husserl has reassumed in his last work, the "Krisis," supplementing and, as it seems to me, considerably modifying, his theory. As usual, Husserl takes as his paradigm the apperception of concrete objects of the external world given to our actual or potential sensory experience. To the nature of the experiential givenness of such objects belongs also a typical regularity in their changeability both as to their position in space and time and as to their qualities in form or content. None of these changes is contingent or arbitrary, but all of them, in their sensory typical mode, are empirically interdependent. These interrelations are themselves moments of the experiential intuition of everyday life; they are experienced as that which makes objects coexisting in simultaneity or succession belong together. The objects in the intuitive environment (always taken as they are given to us intuitively in the experience of everyday life, and accepted as real in the natural attitude) have, as it were, their "habits" of behaving similarly under typically similar circumstances. And even if we take the world as a whole in its fluctuant actuality ("strömende Jeweiligkeit") in which it is to us simply there, this world as a whole, too, has its "habit" of continuing to be as it has been so far. Thus, our empirically intuitive environment has its empirically all-encompassing style; and this remains invariant in whatever manner we imagine this world as modified or in whatever form we represent it in the style in which we have the world now, and in which we have had it so far. Of this fact we may become conscious in reflection, and by performing free variations of these possibilities, we may make thematic the invariant general style

[9] *Die Krisis der europäischen Wissenschaften und die transzendentale Phänomenologie: Eine Einleitung in die phänomenologische Philosophie*, herausgegeben von Walter Biemel, *Husserliana* VI, Den Haag, 1954.

in which this intuitive world persists in the flux of the total experience. Then we understand that, in general, things and events do not occur and take this course in a haphazard way, but that they are *a priori* bound to this style as the invariant form of the intuitive world; in other words, that by a universal causal regularity everything that coexists in the world has the character of belonging together, on the ground of which the world is not merely a totality (*Allheit*) but a total unity (*Alleinheit*), a (to be sure, infinite) whole. It is this universal causal style of the intuitive environment which makes hypotheses, inductions, predictions concerning the unknown features of the present, the past, and the future possible. But in the prescientific (and, if we understand Husserl correctly, we have to add: *a fortiori* in the prepredicative) cognitive life we remain with all this in the approximation of typicality.[10]

In the *Krisis* and the related manuscripts Husserl emphasizes again and again that things in the intuitive environment and all their properties vacillate in their mere typicality; their identity with themselves and their being like other things is just an approximation. In all these relations there prevails a gradation of perfection, the degree being dependent upon the specific practical interest to be satisfied. With a change of interest a formerly satisfactory degree of perfection might no longer satisfy the new interest.[11] In another passage of the *Krisis*[12] Husserl points out that although this typicality makes scientific description and phenomenological-transcendental truth possible, it pervades the unity of the life-world and the universe of objects in it in spite of and beyond all its relativities. It would be possible to make this typicality (without any transcendental interest, that is, in the naive attitude before performing the *epoché*) the theme of a particular science, namely, of an ontology of the life-world as the world of our actual and potential experiential intuitions. To be sure, the life-world, which includes all practical objectivities, even the objectivities of the sciences as cultural facts, refers in the continual change of its relativities to subjectivity. Yet in spite of all these changes and in spite of all rectifi-

---

[10] *Krisis*, Section 9b.
[11] *Ibid.*, Section 9a, pp. 22 f.
[12] *Ibid.*, Section 51, p. 176.

cations it follows its essential typicality, to which all life, and therewith all sciences of which it is the foundation, remain subjected. This ontology of the life-world can be revealed in pure evidence. In a supplementary text, eliminated by the editors as a mere repetition,[13] Husserl wonders why the *"Geisteswissen- schaften"* have so far failed to develop such an ontology of the life-world in their search for the *a priori* peculiar to their field. It would reveal, for example, the types of sociality (family, tribe, state, etc.) or of objects of culture as well as the types of particular historical or cultural environment (of the Egyptians, the ancient Greeks, the so-called primitives, etc.). And on occasion Husserl emphasizes that this typicality of the life-world is by no means my private affair, but that of the "socialized" subjectiv- ity (*vergemeinschaftete Subjektivität*): the concrete typicality of the life-world is that of the world valid for all of us. Not only my own life but also that of each of us in the unity of its actual flux is continually surrounded by the actual horizons of our practical power (*Vermöglichkeit*) to guide, direct, and influence actual occurrences by an interference of our Self. But although I am always certain of such a power, I am, like everyone, bound to the essential typicality which pervades all actualities and potenti- alities. This is so because all horizons in their modifications form one universal horizon, first my own, and then, in the general interconnectedness of all subjects, the trans-subjective universal horizon. This problem leads again to the preacquaintedness of the life-world as a whole and the concrete objects in it.

At the end of the *Krisis* [14] Husserl considerably enlarges the notion of the typicality of the life-world. Things, he says, have their particular concrete typicality, expressed by the "nouns" of the particular vernacular. But all specific typicality is en- compassed by the most general one, the "regional" typicality, such as the region of inanimate and animate things, among the latter, man, etc. This typicality in its continual factual generality determines practice in everyday life; as essentially necessary it can be revealed only by an eidetic method.

---

[13] *Ibid.*, pp. 529 ff.; refers to Section 51, p. 176.
[14] *Ibid.*, Section 63, pp. 229 ff.

V. TYPE AND EIDOS

The last part of *Erfahrung und Urteil* [15] deals with the nature of pure universals as obtained by the eidetic method. Husserl here describes this method in a way similar to his description in *Ideas* I and III. An experienced or phantasied objectivity is interpreted as an example of the universal, and at the same time as a prototype (*Vorbild*) for modifications by a series of free variations in phantasy. All of these variations have concrete similarities with the same prototype, and the manifold of new images produced in phantasy is permeated by an invariant identical content in terms of which all the arbitrarily performed variations come to congruence, whereas their differences remain irrelevant. This invariant element prescribes their limits to all possible variations of the same prototype; it is that element without which an objectivity of this kind can neither be thought nor intuitively phantasied. Upon the manifold of the variants produced in the process of arbitrary variations the intuition proper of the universal as eidos is founded and can now be grasped purely as such. This intuition of the eidos consists in the active apprehension of that which was passively preconstituted: the exemplar chosen as point of departure guides us as prototype to ever new images created by association and passive phantasy or by fictitious transformation in active phantasying.

Yet there are important differences between empirical universals and eidetic ones. The former are not only contingent in the sense that their formation starts from a particular given contingently in factual experience, but also in the sense that the conceptualization proceeds on the ground of comparison with likewise contingently given similarities. In the natural attitude the experienced world is given to us as the universal persistent ground of being and as the universal field of all of our activities, whatever interest we follow. The formation of pure concepts, however, must not depend on these contingencies of the factually given but must be capable of prescribing rules for the experiencing of all empirical particulars. By the process of ideation we put out of play the relationship of our experience with the world and

[15] Part III., esp. Ch. II.

liberate the environmental horizon of the variants from any attachment to any experiential activity. By doing so we place ourselves in a world of pure phantasy, of pure possibilities. Each of them may now become the central member of a set of possible pure variations in the mode of arbitrariness; from each of them we may arrive at an absolute pure eidos – provided that the sequences of variations can be connected to a single one. Thus we obtain a different eidos for colors and sounds; they are of different kinds with respect to that which is purely intuited in them.

Any eidetic concrete possibility permits specifications of the highest freely formed universals. Still directed toward pure possibilities, we may introduce limiting preconditions for the activities of pure phantasying, for example, by postulating that the universal "geometrical figure" should be limited by three sides. Then we may investigate the essential properties of such a formation, the eidos of the triangle. Of course, such a specification of eidetic universals should not be confounded with concrete concepts such as tree, dog, etc. Empirical concepts are not genuine specifications of pure universals; they mean typical generalizations, scopes of anticipations of experiences delineated by actual experiences. On the other hand, the eidetic universality can be related to appearing realities at any time. Any actually emergent color is at the same time possible in the pure sense; any one can be taken as an example or prototype and be transformed into a variant. Thus we may transpose all actualities to the level of pure possibilities, the realm of arbitrariness.

But if we do so, it turns out that even this free arbitrariness has its particular limitations. That which can be varied in arbitrary phantasying has necessarily an inner structure, an eidos, and therewith laws of necessity which determine the characteristics an objectivity must have in order to be of this or that particular kind. There is, however, another text clarifying the relationship between typicality and eidos which is of particular importance, since it represents a later version than that of *Erfahrung und Urteil*. We find it in the second and fourth Cartesian Meditation [16] in connection with the description of the

---

[16] *Cartesianische Meditationen*, Sections 20–22, 34.

characteristics of intentional analysis after the performance of
epoché. Husserl points out that the flux of intentional synthesis
which noetically and noematically constitutes the unity of the
meaning of an objectivity is necessarily regulated in accordance
with an essential typicality. (Of course, this term is used here in
a new sense.) The most general typicality, which includes all
specifications, is the general scheme *ego-cogito-cogitatum*. In the
specifications of this typicality the intentional objectivity of the
cogitatum plays the role of a transcendental clue for the disclosure of the typical manifoldness of cogitations which in
possible syntheses refer to it as having the same meaning. Possible perception, retention, recollection, anticipation, signification,
analogical intuition are examples of such specified types of
intentionality which refer to any thinkable objectivity. These
specifications may be of a formal-logical (formal-ontological)
kind, such as the modes of "something in general" (*Etwas überhaupt*), the singular and concrete individual, the generic, the
plurality, the whole, the relation, etc. It is precisely here that the
radical distinction between real objects in the broadest sense and
categorial objectivities becomes apparent, the latter referring to
their origin in *operations* of a polythetic activity of the I, the former
being the outcome of a mere passive synthesis. On the other
hand, there are material-ontological specifications attached to
the concept of the real individual, which is subdivided in its real
regions, for example, (mere) spatial corporeal thing, animal, etc.,
a subdivision leading to corresponding specifications of the pertinent formal-logical modes (real quality, real plurality, real relation, etc.). If we hold fast to any objectivity in its form or
category and if we continue to keep in evidence its identity
subsisting in all the changes of its modes of consciousness, then
we discover that the latter are by no means arbitrary ones,
however fluctuant they may be. They remain always bound to a
structural typicality which continues to be indestructibly the
same as long as consciousness continues to grasp the objectivity
as being of such and such a kind and as long as it is held in the
evidence of identity through all the changes of its modes of
consciousness. And Husserl adds to this important passage that
it is the task of the transcendental theories to explain systematically this structural typicality and its constitution by ana-

lyzing the system of possible objectivities and their inner and outer horizon. One of the basic forms of specific transcendental methods is the eidetic intuition. Taking an empirical fact as our point of departure, we transpose the factual experiences to the realm of "irrealities," of the "as if," which confronts us with the *pure* possibilities, purified, that is, of everything bound to the particular fact and any fact at all. Thus we obtain the eidos as the intuited or intuitable pure universal which, not conditioned by any fact, precedes all conceptualizations in the sense of "meanings of words"; on the contrary, all pure concepts have to be formed as adjusted to the eidos. In the *Cartesian Meditations* Husserl uses the eidetic method not only for the description of the various types of cogitations, such as perception, retention, assertion, being fond of something, etc., but also for the transformation of the factual ego into an eidos "transcendental ego," of which the former is merely a possible modification.

VI. SOME CRITICAL REMARKS

At the beginning of this paper we maintained that the notion of typicality, so central in the later philosophy of Husserl, is an operative and not a thematic one. It is hoped that the preceding presentation has corroborated this statement and has shown that this notion is fraught with manifold equivocations and used by Husserl with different meanings in different contexts. In terms of *Erfahrung und Urteil* typicality is genetically pre-constituted in previous experiences which form latent habitual possessions and are called forth or awakened by a passive synthesis of congruence if we apperceive actually a similar object. At the same time, by apperceptive transference a set of anticipations is created which attach themselves to the givenness of a newly encountered objectivity of the same type. Thus typicality is the origin of the preacquaintedness and the familiarity of the objectivities within the world. A text published by Husserl himself as Appendix 2 to *Formale und transzendentale Logik* [17] explains this process rather graphically. Each mode of givenness, we read here, has a double after-effect: first, the recognition of

---

[17] *Formale und transzendentale Logik: Versuch einer Kritik der logischen Vernunft,* Halle, 1929, Beilage II, Sections 2a and b, pp. 276–279.

similar objects in the congruence of a passive synthesis with objects recollected becomes possible; second, there is what Husserl calls in this text the "apperceptive after-effect" on the ground of which the preconstituted objectivity is apperceived in a similar situation in a similar way. These are, according to Husserl, essential intentional structures of empirical experience (although not empirical facts).

The notion of typicality as used in the *Krisis* is the form in which the objects within our intuitive environment – the *Lebenswelt* – together with their properties and their changes are given to our natural attitude. This form is that of a vacillating approximation. All regularities, even the causal ones, belong to the typical "habit" in which things behave, as it were, under typical similar circumstances. A gradation of perfection, which, in turn, depends upon our actual practical interest to be satisfied, prevails in all these relations. On the other hand, however, this typicality, in its continual factual generality, determines practice. Its essential necessity can be revealed only by the eidetic method. This essential typicality is characterized in the pertinent passages of the *Cartesian Meditations* dealing with the eidetic reduction. Here we learn that it is the flux of intentional synthesis which shows, after the performance of the *epoché*, an essential typicality; first, the most general one of *ego-cogito-cogitatum*, then more specific types of cogitations for the disclosure of which the *cogitatum* serves as a transcendental clue. These specifications may be of a formal-ontological kind and then lead either to real objects as the outcome of passive synthesis or to categorical objectivities as results of operations of the I; or, they may be material-ontological specifications in accordance with the real regions. The relationship between typicality and eidos is here obviously conceived in a different way from that of the final chapters of *Erfahrung und Urteil* referred to before. The operative use of the notion of typicality gives rise to a series of questions which remain unclarified in Husserl's published writings.

(I) *Erfahrung und Urteil* connects the notion of typicality with a set of other operative notions which never become thematic for a philosophical analysis and are equivocal in respect of their relation both to one another and to the notion of typicality. These are the concepts of "similarity," "synthesis by congruence," "association," "impressive aspects," "interest." Is it Husserl's view that typicality is founded upon the preconstitution of similarity by association? Or have we to assume that similarity itself presupposes an experience of typicality, namely, that of the typically similar? And what is typically similar? The "impressive" aspect of the actually perceived object. What makes this aspect impressive? Our prevailing interest in the broader or narrower sense. Moreover, what sets the passive synthesis of congruence going by which the actually apperceived object is paired with a recollected element that is just a latent habitual possession "called forth" as a similar or dissimilar one? Is it indeed the same passive synthesis of congruence which creates by apperceptive transference a set of anticipations that attach themselves to the givenness of a newly encountered objectivity of the same type, and thus brings about the character of preacquaintedness and familiarity of our experiencing of the life-world in the natural attitude?

(2) Does not the equivocal description Husserl gives of the awareness of similarity, of the impressive aspects of the typical due to our interest, and of the synthesis of congruence originate in the fact that he takes as his model of all his pertinent investigations the perception of an object in the outer world and, even more precisely, the visual perception of such an object? If we take as an example a musical theme with its transposition in other keys, its inversion, enlargement, diminution, variations of all kinds, does then the "similarity" of all these modifications not already presuppose a similarity of specific typical characteristics? And if we turn to objectivities which are not perceptual objects of the outer world, say mathematical functions which are recognized as being "similar," does this "similarity" not refer to particular typical characteristics of these functions?

(3) Husserl develops in *Erfahrung und Urteil* the important distinction between essential and nonessential types. The question arises, however: On what level does this distinction become visible? Are not all the types in terms of which we experience the life-world in the naive attitude equally essential? Are not all of them the outcome of similar elements paired by passive synthesis of congruence? Or does a distinction between

the merely seemingly similar and similarity based on inner relations prevail even on this prepredicative level?

(4) The nature of the typicality of the life-world and the meaning of its preacquaintedness becomes especially complicated if we accept Husserl's statement that this typicality is by no means my private affair, but that of the "socialized" subjectivity. It is the concrete typicality of the world valid for all of us. This is without any doubt the case. But where is the origin or the foundation of this intersubjective or transsubjective validity? Is there such a thing as a transsubjective passive synthesis of congruence by wakening a preconstituted and latent (as an habitual possession) element of the pair? We submit that all the operative notions of phenomenology lead to insoluble difficulties when applied to problems of transsubjectivity.

(5) The distinction between activity and passivity of the conscious life is highly unclarified, and created many difficulties for such eminent students of phenomenology as R. Ingarden,[18] Jean Wahl,[19] and L. Landgrebe.[20] In the context of our problem we found texts in which a sharp distinction is made between passive receptivity and predicative spontaneity, and others which interpret receptivity and the "adverting" to the object as the lowest form of spontaneity. We met the notion of an active performance of consciousness in our study of *Erfahrung und Urteil*, first in the distinction between explicating the inner horizon and the possibility of making the outer horizon thematic by the particular activity of the I which Husserl calls "relating contemplation." We then found that particular activities make the transition possible which leads from empirical types to predicative judgments dealing with generic concepts, and finally to the constitution of universals of the highest level and the form of all-or-none judgments. To be sure, according to Husserl, the type leads to the presumptive idea of a universal. A relation of a single object to the typically general already prevails in any apperception of the individual in its horizon of familiarity. But all predication presupposes a cognitive activity of the mind, an

[18] *Cartesianische Meditationen*, p. 214.
[19] J. Wahl, "Notes sur la première partie de Erfahrung und Urteil de Husserl," *Phénoménologie et Existence*, Paris, 1953, p. 100.
[20] Lettre de L. Landgrebe sur un Article de M. Jean Wahl, ib. p. 206.

active intuition which aims at grasping thematically that which was previously given in passive congruence. The question arises, however, whether the formation of the basic empirical type does not presuppose an activity of the I. In a masterful manner Husserl has described for the realm of predication the way in which undivided judgments of the form "S' is p'," "S" is p" ..." are transformed into generic judgments of the form "S' is p," "S" is p ..." which is possible on the foundation of a passive congruence of likeness of p', p'' ... considered as instances of p. But, as we once suggested,[21] does not typification, even in the prepredicative sphere, consist in the "suppression of the primes" adhering to the apperceived individual object? In other words, is the distinction between passivity and activity of the conscious life indeed valid, and if valid, a suitable criterion for the determination of the "degree of generality?"

(6) Yet in spite of the texts referred to in the preceding paragraph, the whole work of Husserl clearly shows that there is a decisive difference between the formation of generic judgments of any level of generality and the intuitions of the eidos. Whereas empirical universals are contingent, ideation puts out of play the relationship of experience with the world by taking the concrete individual merely as an exemplar, a prototype, a point of departure for a series of free variations arbitrarily performed in phantasy: the empirical factuality is thus replaced by pure possibilities. (We want to speak merely of material universals arrived at by eidetic generalization, thus disregarding in this connection the formal universals arrived at by eidetic formalization.) The question of first importance which presents itself is whether the "free variations" to be performed in phantasy, starting from the individual object as example or prototype, are indeed as free as they seem, that is, whether the arbitrariness of transforming the empirically given into a special case of general possibilities does not have well-defined limits. To be sure, Husserl himself recognizes such limits when he speaks of regional ontologies or, in a terminology used by him in earlier writings, of spheres of incompatibility (*Unverträglichkeitssphären*). The freedom of variations in phantasy will not permit us to arrive,

---

[21] "Common-Sense and Scientific Interpretation of Human Action," *Collected Papers*, Vol. I, p. 21.

starting from the prototype of a colored object, at the eidos of sound. It is doubtless possible to grasp eidetically material realms or regions of being, but these regions are not constituted by performances of our consciousness: they are indeed ontological regions of the world and, as such, given to our experience or, as we may say, imposed upon us. But we have to drive the questioning even farther. Is it possible, by means of free variations in phantasy, to grasp the eidos of a concrete species or genus, unless these variations are limited by the frame of the type in terms of which we have experienced, in the natural attitude, the object from which the process of ideation starts as a familiar one, as such and such an object within the life-world? Can these free variations in phantasy reveal anything else but the limits established by such typification? If these questions have to be answered in the negative, then there is indeed merely a difference of degree between type and eidos. Ideation can reveal nothing that was not preconstituted by the type.

It is impossible to investigate this question within the frame of this paper. But even our fugitive remarks have shown that the notion of eidetic reduction is at least partially an operative one.

SOME STRUCTURES OF THE LIFE-WORLD *

The following considerations concern the structure of what Husserl calls the "life-world" (*Lebenswelt*) in which, in the natural attitude, we, as human beings among fellow-beings, experience culture and society, take a stand with regard to their objects, are influenced by them and act upon them. In this attitude the existence of the life-world and the typicality of its contents are accepted as unquestionably given until further notice. As Husserl has shown, our thinking stands under the idealities of the "and so forth" and "I can do it again."** The first leads to the assumption that what has proved valid thus far in our experience will remain valid in the future; the latter to the expectancy that what thus far I have been able to accomplish in the world by acting upon it I shall be able to accomplish again and again in the future. Therefore we can speak of fundamental assumptions characteristic of the natural attitude in the life-world, which themselves are accepted as unquestionably given; namely the assumptions of the constancy of the structure of the world, of the constancy of the validity of our experience of the world, and of the constancy of our ability (*Vermöglichkeit*) to act upon the world and within the world.

What is given as unquestionable is in first approximation to be designated as that which we take for granted as familiar; as such it is the form of the understanding which we have in the natural attitude of both the world and ourselves. But it belongs to the nature of what we accept as unquestionably given that at any moment it can be put in question, just as that which all along we have taken for granted might at any moment prove

* Translated from the German by Aron Gurwitsch.
** See *Collected Papers*, Vol. I, p. 224 f.

unintelligible (*unverständlich*). Even the assumptions of constancy are valid only until further notice: Expectancies based on the constancy of the structure of the world may be disconfirmed (*explodieren*), what has been valid may become doubtful, what has appeared as feasible (*vermöglich*) may prove unrealizable. What had been accepted as unquestionably given then becomes a problem, a theoretical, practical or emotional problem, which must be formulated, analyzed and solved. All problems arise on the background of what had been given as unquestionable (it is the latter which in the proper sense of the word becomes questionable ("*fragwürdig*") and all solutions of problems consist in transforming, by the very process of questioning, that which has become questionable into something new which now in turn appears as unquestionable. Already that which without being questioned is accepted as a matter of course has its open horizons, both inner and outer horizons, which in the natural attitude are given to us as susceptible of possible exploration. To solve the problem, whether of a practical or theoretical nature, which results from the fact that that which thus far had been taken for granted has become questionable, we have to enter into its horizons in order to explicate them. As soon as we have attained knowledge we deem sufficient of that which has become questionable, we discontinue that endless task and by an arbitrary decree consider the problem as solved in a way sufficient for our purposes. How does it happen that a problem arises at all, that is to say, how does it happen that that which has become questionable for us appears as worth being questioned? What is relevant for the solution of a problem? When does it appear to us as "sufficiently solved" as far as our purposes are concerned so that we discontinue further investigations?

All these questions point to different meanings of the concept of relevancy, some of which will be analyzed in the following. First of all, we have to consider succinctly some fundamental structures of the life-world accepted as unquestionably given. This unquestionedness and familiarity are by no means homogeneous. Our knowledge about it and our ability (*Vermöglichkeit*) to act in it and upon it exhibit manifold stratifications.

Let us consider the stratification of the life-world in a spatiotemporal respect. There is, to begin with, a stratum of the life-world experienced or experienceable which is now within my actual reach, (reach of hearings, seeing, manipulation etc.), a world of which I have or can have direct perception with or without the aid of instruments of all sorts, of which I know that it acts upon me immediately, and upon which I can act immediately – with or without the aid of instruments. I also know of the world which formerly was, but no longer is, within my reach. Here we still have to distinguish as to whether my experience of that world includes the expectancy that, at least in principle, I can bring it back within my actual reach, or whether this is not the case. If it is within my ability to restore my previous reach, e.g., by returning to the point from which I had taken my departure, then with reference to the idealizing assumptions of the "and so forth" and "I can do it again," I accepted as unquestionable that within the restored reach I shall on principle find again the same world which I had experienced previously, when it had been within my actual reach, perhaps with the modification "the same but altered." The third zone is the segment of the world which neither is nor was within my actual reach, which, however, I might bring within my actual reach. This zone too has its peculiar degree of familiarity. In the first place, I take it as unquestionable that its typical structures will be the same as the regions which I actually experience or have experienced. In the second place, the problem of the structure of the social world intervenes here in so far as I take it for granted that the world within your actual or restorable reach is, in principle, the world within my potential reach although, on account of my biographical situation, my experiences of it will differ from yours, which correspond to your biographical situation.

The stratification of the world into zones of actual, restorable and obtainable reach already refers to the structure of the life-world according to dimensions of objective temporality and their subjective correlates, the phenomena of retention and protention, recall and expectancy, and to the peculiar differentiations of the experience of time which correspond to the manifold dimensions of reality. Here we can not deal with these highly intricate problems.

One word must be added as far as the structuring of the social world is concerned. The social life-world within our reach will be called the domain of direct social experience and the subjects encountered in it, our fellow-men. In this domain we share with our fellow-men a common span of time; moreover, a sector of the spatial world is within our common reach. Hence the body of my fellow-man is within my reach and vice versa. This central domain is surrounded, as it were, by the world of my contemporaries whose subjects coexist with me in time without, however, being with me in reciprocal spatial reach. Contemporaries know about one another in multifariously articulated typified ways which admit of all degrees of fulfillment and emptiness, intimacy and anonymity, and whose description is the task of a philosophical sociology. Notwithstanding all social distance, contemporaries are in principle able to act on one another. The world of contemporaries contains, of course, regions which consist of former fellow-men – whether these may or may not again become fellow-men for me – and potential fellow-men. Furthermore, there is the world of our predecessors which acts upon us while itself being beyond the reach of our action, and the world of our successors upon which we can act but which cannot act upon us. The former is given to us as a problem, to be interpreted by means of more or less specific and concrete typifications, the latter is in principle a region of complete anonymity.

All these stratifications belong as unquestionably given to our naive experience of the socialized world. Even the typifications and symbolizations on terms of which we distinguish the several strata of our social world, construe and interpret their contents, determine our action in it and upon it and its action upon us according to all degrees of ability, are predefined as unquestionably given by virtue of the socially conditioned schemata of expression and interpretation prevailing in the group to which we belong and which we used to call the "culture" of our group. It too, above all, is part of our life-world which we take for granted. It co-determines what within our culture is accepted as unquestionable, what can become questionable and what appears as worthy of questioning; it also co-determines the delimitation of the horizon to be explicated, that is, the conditions under which for purposes of social life an emerging problem can be considered as solved.

This is so because only to a very small extent does the

knowledge of each individual originate from his personal experience. The overwhelming bulk of this knowledge is socially
derived and transmitted to the individual in the long process of
education by parents, teachers, teachers of teachers, by relations
of all kinds, involving fellow-men, contemporaries and predecessors. It is transmitted in the form of insight, beliefs, more or
less well founded or blind, maxims, instructions for use, recipes
for the solution of typical problems, i.e., for the attainment of
typical results by the typical application of typical means. All the
socially derived knowledge is, to begin with, accepted by the individual member of the cultural group as unquestionably given, because it is transmitted to him as unquestionably accepted by the
group and as valid and tested. Thus it becomes an element of the
form of social life, and as such forms both a common schema of
interpretation of the common world and a means of mutual
agreement and understanding. This leads us to the next step,
namely the question of the structuring of all knowledge about
our life-world in its multiple articulations.

As William James has already seen, in the naive attitude of
our daily living there corresponds to the afore-mentioned
structuring of the spatial-temporal and social-cultural world,
partly overlapping it, a differentiation of our knowledge about it.

He made the fundamental distinction between "knowledge of
acquaintance" and "knowledge about." "Knowledge about"
refers to that comparatively very small sector of which everyone
of us has thorough, clear, distinct, and consistent knowledge, not
only as to the what and how, but also as to the understanding of
the why, regarding a sector of which he is a "competent expert."
"Knowledge of acquaintance" merely concerns the what and leaves
the how unquestioned. What happens when we operate the dial of
the telephone is unknown to the non-expert, it is incomprehensible
to him and even immaterial; it suffices that the partner to whom
he wants to speak answers the telephone. We assume that the
apparatus, the procedure, the recipe, the maxim of our practical
conduct will, in the normal course of things, stand its test in the
future as this has thus far been the case, without our knowing
why this is so and upon what this confidence of ours is based.
The zones of our "knowledge about" and "knowledge of acquaintance" are surrounded by dimensions of mere belief which

in turn are graded in multiple ways as to well-founded-
ness, plausibility, likelihood, reliance upon authority, blind
acceptance, down to complete ignorance. Among all these spheres
of knowledge it is only the "knowledge about" that stands under
the postulate of clarity, determinateness and consistency. All
other spheres, notwithstanding their inner contradictions and
incompatibilities by which they are affected, belong to the realm
of what is not questioned (*unbefragt*) and, therefore, unquestionably accepted, briefly to the realm of what "is taken for granted,"
as long, at least, as such knowledge suffices to find through its
aid one's way in the life-world. It must be noted that these forms
of our knowledge concerning the life-world, whose "ideal types"
we have sketched rather roughly, are differentiated in manifold
ways and that they perpetually change for the individual, from
individual to individual, from individual to the social group, for the
group itself, and finally from one group to the other. The content of
what is known, familiar, believed and unknown, is therefore relative: for the individual relative to his biographical situation, for the
group to its historical situation. A further fundamental category of
social life is the inequality of the distribution of knowledge in
its various forms among the individuals belonging to the group
and also among the groups themselves. This fundamental category deserves to be made the central theme of a sociology of
knowledge which is aware of its true task.

Now, what determines this differentiation of knowledge in its
several forms? The answer to this question immediately leads
us to the theme of relevancy.

Let us call the knowledge which at a certain moment of time
the individual has at his disposal in the way described above his
stock of knowledge, and its several gradations, its degrees of
familiarity. If we briefly examine how the individual experiences
its structure, we discover as subjective correlates of the several
forms of knowledge corresponding zones of interests by which
the individual is motivated. The individual finds himself perceiving, thinking, acting in the world which he, as a spontaneous
being, apperceives. Leibniz has rightly defined spontaneity
as the capacity to proceed from apperception to ever new apperceptions. If, however, the individual lives naively, it is not that
the world of nature, culture and society is given to him in its

entirety, for him to find his way in it, to master it by action or thought. The articulation of the world, as sketched in the beginning, into strata of different reaches implies that the individual living in the world always experiences himself as being within a certain situation which he has to define. Closer analysis shows that the concept of a situation to be defined contains two principal components: The one originates from the ontological structure of the pregiven world. To make a glass of sugared water, Bergson says, I must wait until the sugar has dissolved. The other component which makes it possible to define certain elements by singling them out of the ontologically pre-given structure of the world originates from the actual biographical state of the individual, a state which includes his stock of knowledge in its actual articulation. What belongs to the former, the ontological component of the situation, is experienced by the individual as imposed upon, and occurring to him, as a condition imposed from without upon all possible free manifestations of spontaneity. The biographical state determines the spontaneous definition of the situation within the imposed ontological framework.

To the experiencing subject's mind, the elements singled out of the pregiven structure of the world always stand in sense-connections, connections of orientation as well as of mastery of thought or action. The causal relations of the objective world are subjectively experienced as means and ends, as hindrances or aids, of the spontaneous activity of thought or action. They manifest themselves as complexes of interest, complexes of problems, as systems of projects, and feasibilities inherent in the systems of projects. The system of these complexes, which are interwoven in manifold ways, is subjectively experienced by the individual as a system of his plans for the hour or the day, for work and leisure; all these particular plans being integrated into one supreme system which, without being free from contradictions, encompasses all the other plans. We shall call the supreme system the "life-plan." Be it noted that we use the world "plan" in an enlarged sense which does not necessarily involve the element of deliberateness (*Absichtlichkeit*). There also exist plans which are imposed.

The life-plan thus determines the particular plans which, in turn determine the current interests. The interest prevailing at the moment determines the elements which the individual singles out of the surrounding objective world (whose articulation has previously been described) so as to define his situation. It is by virtue of the same interest that out of the pregiven stock of knowledge those elements are selected as are required for the definition of the situation. In other words, the interest determines which elements of both the ontological structure of the pregiven world and the actual stock of knowledge are *relevant* for the individual to define his situation thinkingly, actingly, emotionally, to find his way in it, and to come to terms with it. This form of relevancy will be called *"motivational relevancy"* because it is subjectively experienced as a motive for the definition of the situation.

Motivational relevancy may be experienced as imposed from without or else as a manifestation of inner spontaneity of any form (from a dark urge up to a rational project). It can be experienced in all degrees of evidentness or else, it can be unconscious in the sense of Leibniz's *"petites perceptions"* and even in that of modern depth psychology. The degree of clarity of the insight in which motivational relevancy is experienced depends upon the structure of the actual stock of knowledge from which the elements required for the definition of the situation are selected.

The actual stock of knowledge is nothing but the sedimentation of all our experiences of former definitions of previous situations, experiences which might refer to our own world in previously actual, restorable, or obtainable reach or else to fellow-men, contemporaries, or predecessors. In the light of our foreknowledge the situation to be defined may appear as typically alike, typically similar to a situation previously defined, as a modification or variation of the latter or else as entirely novel, and all this in what Husserl has called synthesis of recognition in all its species. The reference of the situation to be defined to the stock of knowledge may concern elements of the "knowledge about," "knowledge of acquaintance," mere belief or ignorance. If the elements of our stock of knowledge, which are at our disposal in the mentioned gradations, suffice for the definition of the situation, as far as motivational relevancy is concerned, then the definition takes place as a matter of course in the form of the unquestionably given. Such will be the case in all affairs of routine. However, it may happen that not all motivationally relevant elements foreknown in sufficient degrees of familiarity are adequate, or that the situation proves to be one which cannot be referred by synthesis of recognition to a previous situation typically alike, similar, etc., because it is radically new. In such a case it becomes necessary to "know more about" these elements, be it that new knowledge must be acquired, be it that the knowledge at hand must be transformed into higher degrees of familiarity. Such an element will become relevant for further acquiring of knowledge and hence, relevant also for the definition of the situation. This relevancy, so founded upon motivational relevancy, still differs totally from it. Now the relevant element is no longer given as unquestionable and has to be taken for granted: on the contrary, it is questionable but also worth questioning, and for that very reason it has acquired relevancy. That relevancy will be called *"thematic relevancy"* because the relevant element now becomes a theme for our knowing consciousness, a process which in traditional psychology has usually been treated under the heading of "attention."

What makes the theme to be a theme is determined by motivationally relevant interest-situations and spheres of problems. The theme which thus has become relevant has now, however, become a problem to which a solution, practical, theoretical or emotional, must be given. We now turn to the thematically relevant problem which, though it may genetically have been motivated by more encompassing problems, interests and plans, after it has been constituted as thematically relevant, is detached from its context of motivation and becomes interesting and therefore worth questioning in its own right, so to speak. Yet this way of expression is not sufficiently precise. The motivationally relevant contexts continue remaining as outer horizons of what has become thematically relevant: We can turn to them again, we can question and explicate them, and we do so in fact to find the point at which we have to abandon any further investigation of the thematically relevant, because our knowledge of it has become sufficiently clear and familiar for the thematic problem at hand to be considered as solved with regard to the encompassing context. The total motivationally relevant interest-situation determines when our "curiosity" to scrutinize the thematically relevant has to be considered as satisfied. In a different respect, however, the total situation merely forms the background or the margin of the actually relevant theme. The theme alone, as we say, is in the focus of our interest: the problem involved in it must be solved before we can turn to other things. We say "first things first" – "the most important first" – giving thus in colloquial language an excellent definition of the thematically relevant.

The thematically relevant is the problem and, as we said, as such it is worth questioning and is also (for reasons of motivational relevancy) questionable. It solicits us to penetrate into its inner and outer horizons, to bring it, in a synthesis of recognition, to coincidence with elements contained in our stock of knowledge and, first of all, to discover its typical pertinence to preconstituted and therefore typically familiar world phenomena. There arises here a series of important connections with other domains of phenomenological research which we can not study more closely within the present context. We merely want to point out briefly three spheres of research: (1) Husserl has shown that, from the outset, the prepredicative experience of the life-world is fundamentally articulated according to types. We do not experience the world as a sum of sense data, nor as an aggregate of individual things isolated from and standing in no relations to one another. We do not see colored spots and contours, but rather mountains, trees, animals, in particular birds, fish, dogs, etc. What Husserl has not explained in his published writings, however, is that this typification takes place according to particular structures of relevancy. In prepredicative typification I can perceive my dog Fido in his typical behavior as healthy or sick, as an individual, a German shepherd dog, a typical dog in general, a mammal, a living creature, a thing of the external world, a "something at large." Which typical structure I choose depends upon the thematic relevancy which this object has for me. Contexts of a similar kind appear in the sphere of predicative judgment, at least in everyday thinking. Every judgment of the form "S is p" is by necessity elliptical, since "S" is never exclusively "p," but besides many other things like "q" and "r," "s," "t" ... it is also "p." In the biographical moment under consideration in which I pronounce the judgment "S is p," "S-being-p" is thematically relevant for me, because it is thus constituted by the motivational relevancies which in their totality are referred to in abbreviated form by the expression "in the biographical moment under consideration."

(2) How in the field of transcendental subjective consciousness – after the performance of the phenomenological reduction – the relations between theme, horizon and margin are arranged, how they condition one another and how they shift, has been excellently analyzed by Aron Gurwitsch in his book: *Théorie du champ de la conscience*.* Though Gurwitsch believes that his use of his term "Relevancy" differs from mine, I fully endorse his analysis. It seems to me that his concept of "relevancy" is a special case of my concept of "thematic relevancy," mine being more encompassing in so far as I am concerned with a phenomenology of the life-world, with which man in the natural attitude has to come to terms not only in thought but also emotionally and in action, whereas Gurwitsch's analyses only deal with transcendental consciousness after the reduction has been performed and hence the "world has been bracketed."

(3) Furthermore, Husserl has established the important distinction between open and problematic possibilities. After the thematically relevant has become a problem it can be considered both within the general framework of the ontologically pretraced spheres of incompatibility and with respect to alternatives between which a choice has to be made, that is – in Husserl's language – as a problematic possibility. In the latter case a choice can be made between but a finite and comparatively small number of possible solutions, each one of which carries its own weight. The thematically relevant problem is solved as soon as it can be decided under which of the available alternatives it has to be subsumed, a process which, in turn, is determined by the more encompassing system of motivational relevancies.

Under all circumstances the solution of the thematically relevant problem involves the reference to the actually present stock of knowledge, as ordered beforehand according to degrees

* Duquesne University Press has published an English translation: *The Field of Consciousness*, Pittsburgh, 1964.

of acquaintance, of familiarity, of belief in the manner already described. However, not all the elements of the stock of knowledge are equally "relevant" for the solution of the problem involved in the theme. The bulk of our foreknowledge is without bearing upon the theme and, therefore, immaterial for its being grasped and elaborated. Obviously, in the present context the term "relevant" is used in a new sense – a third one – which shall be called "*interpretational relevancy*."

In associationist psychology the complex mechanism of the interpretational relevancies and their relationship to motivational and thematic relevancies is simply posited as unquestionably given and, on this unclarified basis, the well-known principles of spatial and temporal contiguity, of similarity and difference are established. But how the associative combination of the acquired knowledge with what is thematically relevant comes about remains unclarified. The insight into the previously sketched structure of our stock of knowledge according to degrees of familiarity may be of help. If we ask, first of all, how the structuring came about, we find that our foreknowledge consists in material that was previously of thematic relevancy, material which, now given in the form of the unquestioned, is no longer given as a theme but merely as a horizon and, more particularly, in the form of a habitual acquisition. The transformation of the thematic-problematic into what henceforth will be possessed as unquestioned has genetically taken place by virtue of motivational relevancies conditioned by factors of biography and situation, motivational relevancies which determine the condition under which the problem involved in the theme could be considered as solved: that is, the point at which further investigation has become thematically irrelevant, because the knowledge obtained was sufficient for the definition of the previous thematic situation. As we have briefly shown before, our knowledge of the life-world, whether pre-predicatively given or formulable in predicative judgments, is knowledge of the *typicality* of the objects and events in the life-world. The typicality, in turn, is determined by the exigencies of the previous thematic situation which had to be defined so as to come "to terms with it." The same exigencies also determine the degree of familiarity of the elements of knowledge which by the ac-

complished solution of the thematic problems have been transformed into habitual acquisitions. This acquired knowledge of the
typicality of the life-world has its proper style in every degree
of familiarity. All typification is relative to some problem: there
is no type at large but only types which carry an "index"
pointing to a problem. If, by syntheses of recognition, an actually relevant theme is brought to coincidence as typically known,
typically familiar, typically alike, with a type which pertains
as habitual to the horizonally given stock of experience and
displays the same degree of familiarity, then this foreknown
type becomes interpretationally relevant with respect to the
actual theme. We then say with reference to that theme that
we have already experienced "something of that sort" or heard
about it, or that we know in a casual way what is in question.
We say, furthermore, that we have reason to assume, that we
believe, suppose, deem it probable or possible, hope, fear that the
situation now to be defined has typical familiarity with the one
experienced before: the present situation, to be sure, is *"atypical"*
in some respect or other, yet by and large it has the same typical
style. The term "atypical" is ambiguous: it may mean that the
"atypical" condition as experienced in the present situation is
incompatible with the previously experienced typifications of
situations with which the present one is compared, or that it
could be, or could be made, compatible with them if one of the
two types were brought to a higher level of familiarity, or finally,
that what is now thematically relevant displays completely
novel features which cannot be brought into coincidence with
any elements of the previously acquired stock of knowledge.

The elements of the horizonally given stock of experience
which are interpretationally relevant are brought to bear upon
the solution of the thematic problem, prove to be knowledge
organized beforehand in several degrees of familiarity and according to different styles of typification, knowledge which
derives from the fact that material which had previously been
thematically relevant has been transformed into acquired
knowledge now accepted as unquestioned. Because of this
previous ordering, moreover, the elements that are interpretationally relevant at a particular time stand in a specific sense-
connection with one another which is conditioned both bio-

graphically and ontologically and has its origin in motivational relevancies which are the same as the ones in which the now thematically relevant originates. Just this common origin in motivational relevancy seems to us to explain the enigmatic possibility of "effective coincidence by synthesis of recognition." We may assume that further analysis of the context will throw some light upon the secret of association. Perhaps Kant had something similar in view when, in the first edition of the *Critique of Pure Reason*, he distinguished the threefold synthesis of apprehension in intuition, of reproduction in imagination and of recognition in the concept, a tripartition, which in the second edition is unified in the synthesis of apperception.

The "effecting of coincidence" between the actually thematic and the horizonally given elements of the stock of experience, which hereby become interpretationally relevant, is by no means always, nor even preponderantly, a passive process. To a large extent, the selection of the material which at a given moment of time becomes interpretationally relevant is a result of learning. As early as in childhood we have to learn what we have to pay attention to and what we have to bring in connection, so as to define the world and our situation within it. The selection and application of interpretationally relevant material, even after it is once learned, and has become a habitual possession and a matter of routine, still remains biographically, culturally and socially conditioned. The same life-world lends itself to a magic interpretation by primitive people, a theological one by the missionary, and a scientific one by the technologist. It could also be shown to what extent the system of interpretational relevancies depends upon the structuring of the world into zones of reach and into the different dimensions of social experience. The systematic investigation of this wide domain is still lacking. We still do not possess the high art Leibniz has demanded, which would teach us to avail ourselves of what we know (*l'art de s'aviser de ce qu'on sait*).

What has been said thus far needs some important supplementation in order to prevent possible misunderstandings. First of all, the relationship between typification and interpretational relevancy must still be clarified. What we find in our stock of knowledge as typified experience is nothing but material which had previously been sufficient to transform, with the help of tested and interpretationally verified foreknowledge, thematically relevant problems into unquestionedness. This process of acquisition of experience had led to the sedimentation of the stock of knowledge prearranged according to types and degrees of familiarity. One might also say that, after the thematic problem has been solved, the typifications related to it and already inserted into the stock of knowledge form the line of demarcation between those horizons of the previously thematic problem as are explicated and those as remain unexplicated. But this way of putting it is still inaccurate, since no allowance is made for the fact that no particular problem is ever isolated: all problems are connected with one another, all thematic relevancies form systems, because all motivational relevancies are subjectively experienced as systems of plans subordinate to the life-plan of the individual in question. Because these systems of motivational relevancies determine not only the systems of thematic relevancies but also the corresponding interpretational relevancies, the latter also stand in a systematic context, and the same holds for the typifications originating here from and for the corresponding degrees of familiarity of our stock of knowledge.

These questions are obviously related to the genesis of the stock of knowledge and its specific individual structure. And every moment of our life, the stock of knowledge in all its stratifications as to systems of relevancy, typifications, degrees of familiarity exists and is available within certain limits. As such it is an element of the biographical situation at the moment in question. It forms the unquestionably given background and basis for the definition and mastery of the surrounding worlds – articulated as to zones of reach – of nature, culture, and society. This world as a whole is, in principle opaque, as a whole it is neither understood nor understandable. By virtue of the systems of relevancy and their structures, sense-connections, which to a certain extent can be made transparent, are established between partial contents of the world. For the business of life it means a great deal to see problems even if they cannot be transformed into unquestionableness. Here originate the aporetic categories of that which is unknown but knowable, of that which is known

to be unknowable. The former leads to the possibilities — prede-
termined as to type — of filling empty places in our stock of
knowledge; the second leads to several domains of reality,
superposed upon that of the life-world, which by means of
symbols are referred to the life-world and interpreted within it.

A further necessary supplement to what has previously been
said concerns motivational, thematic, and interpretational
relevancies. As long as in the natural attitude man experiences
his life-world and unreflectingly directs himself to it in his
actions, thoughts or feelings, the differentiation into several
systems of relevancy does not come within his view at all. As
Husserl expresses it: he lives in his acts, directed to things and
events, and in so doing he, so to speak, has the relevancies "in
his grasp." He lives not only in his acts, directed to their objects,
but also lives "in" the corresponding relevancies in terms of
which the questionable is distinguished from the unquestionably
given. A reflective turn is required to see the relevancies themselves and their differentiation into several systematic connections. This turn, however, does not call for the disinterested
attitude of the onlooking observer, not to speak of the scientist
or the philosopher. Every consequential decision in the life-world
brings man face to face with a series of thematic relevancies of
hypothetical nature, which have to be interpreted and questioned
as to their motivational insertion into the life-plan. A theory of
projected action and decision in the life-world requires an
analysis of the underlying systems of relevancy. Without such a
theory no foundation of a science of human action is possible.
The theory of relevancies is therefore of fundamental importance
for the theory of the social sciences.

It is also essential from other and still more important points
of view. In the first place, it is a task of the social sciences to
investigate to what extent the different forms of systems of
relevancy in the life-world – motivational, thematical, and, most
of all, interpretational systems – are socially and culturally
conditioned. Already the typification of acquired knowledge,
that is of the conditions under which problems can be considered
as sufficiently solved and the horizons as sufficiently explicated,
is to some extent socio-culturally co-determined. Not only the
vocabulary but also the syntactical structure of common col-

loquial language, the "inner form of speech" ("*innere Sprachform*")
as Wilhelm von Humboldt has called it, contains the system of
typifications and hence interpretational relevancies which by
the linguistic community are considered as tested and verified,
consequently as given beyond question, as approved and valid
until further notice, and which, in the process of education and
learning, are therefore transmitted to new members of the group.
The same holds for the several means which every culture makes
available for the typical orientation in, and the mastery of, the
life-world, such as tools, procedures, social institutions, customs,
usages, symbolic systems. All knowledge concerning those means
determines motivational, thematic, and interpretational relevancies which the individual member of the given social group
inserts into his stock of knowledge as an unquestionably given
background – imposed upon him or lying within his ability – for
his individual definition of his situation in the life-world.

In the second place, every communication with other men in
the life-world presupposes a similar structure of at least the
thematic and interpretational relevancies. This similar structure
will occupy a privileged position within the social domain
involving fellow-men in face-to-face situations because the
sector of the spatial life-world, common to the partners, by
necessity makes some elements to be of equal thematic relevancy
for both partners, and furthermore because the body of the
partner with his field of physiognomic expression, his gestures,
his actions and reactions discloses an interpretationally relevant field which otherwise would not be accessible to the
same extent. It is the task of a philosophical sociology to study
the modifications which these common or similar systems of
relevancy pertaining to fellow-men in face-to-face situations
undergo in the interpretations of the world of predecessors and
anticipations of the world of successors. For such a philosophical
sociology the phenomenological analysis of the structures of the
life-world has to secure the necessary preconditions.

MAX SCHELER'S PHILOSOPHY

When Max Scheler suddenly passed away in 1928 at the age of barely fifty-four, his friend Ortega y Gasset dedicated to him a beautiful eulogy. He was the first genius, the Adam in the new paradise of eidetic intuition which Husserl's phenomenology had made accessible, the first to whom all things, even the most familiar ones, revealed their essence and their meaning. They appeared to him in a new light with unambiguous outlines like mountain peaks in the early morning. Thus he was overwhelmed by a wealth of new discoveries. And he had to proclaim so many lucid notions that he staggered, bewildered by cognition, drunk with clarity, inebriated by truth. He was in the true Platonic sense, an "enthusiastic" philosopher. But he lived in continual mental haste, and for this very reason his writings are characterized by both clarity and disorder; without organization and structure, they are full of inconsistencies, and it will be the task of future generations to supply his thought with the missing architecture and order.

Nicolai Hartmann characterized Scheler in a similar way. Life was not the theme of his philosophizing, but his philosophy arose from the fullness of his life. He did not aim at visualizing life in an artificially unified perspective of the kind which the construction of a philosophical system might offer. He took up each problem he discovered in its particular dynamics, analyzing its particular logic, revealing its particular implications and following up all these particularities to their origin, unconcerned with the utopian postulate of systematic unification. He thus accepted the world as he found it, with all its inherent inconsistencies, and permitted them to come to the fore in their own right. As a man as well as a thinker Scheler always was prepared to restart and to relearn.

The evaluation of Max Scheler's work by these two eminent contemporaries becomes understandable if we look at the variety of the topics studied by this seminal mind. The edition in progress of his collected works will consist of thirteen large volumes, of which four will contain the author's posthumous papers. The range of his preoccupations is unique in our time. He deals with problems of theoretical biology, psychology, and physics. During his most creative years epistemology, ethics, philosophy of religion, and the phenomenology of the emotional life were at the center of his interest. But later he became more and more involved in the ontological problems of society and reality: he laid the foundations of a new sociology of knowledge, that is, of knowledge in its relationship to the factors governing the material and spiritual life of humanity. At the end of his career Scheler planned to sum up his thought in two books, one on metaphysics, the other on philosophical anthropology. Only the introductory chapter to the latter, dealing with the place of man in the cosmos, was published during his lifetime.*

Most commentators on Scheler's thought distinguish several stages in his development. He started as a personal student of Rudolf Eucken, the philosopher of the life of the spirit, who imbued his disciple with his admiration for St. Augustine and Pascal, Nietzsche, Dilthey, Bergson and, above all, Husserl influenced him deeply. The latter's theory of categorical intuition, his eidetic method, his doctrine of ideal objects – although in a rather unorthodox interpretation – became in Scheler's hands excellent instruments for the exploration of the realms of emotion and value. Converted to Catholicism Scheler became, as a convinced Christian, both a personalist and a theist. But his book on the philosophy of religion had hardly been published when his concept of God and his attitude toward religion underwent a complete change, which has bewildered all his interpreters and induced W. Stark to speak of Scheler's defection. This change was not merely the result of personal experience or, as Jacques Maritain believes, of a crisis of faith. It was rather the outcome of a life-long conflict between his sociological insight into the relativistic structure of the human condition and his faith in the ex-

---

* Beacon Press has published an English translation: Max Scheler, *Man's Place in Nature*, translated with an introduction by Hans Meyerhoff, Boston, 1961.

istence of absolute values, including that of a personal God who reveals Himself in His acts. In this last, pantheistic period Scheler conceived the development of world history as the progression from the illogical and blind vital urges to the fulfillment of the destiny of humanity in the realms of value and spiritual existence. This process now meant to him the manifestation of the divine force, the becoming of God within the world.

In the following brief and all too incomplete outline of some major motives of Scheler's thought, I have had to forego the temptation to follow step by step the development of this extraordinary mind. It is rather my aim to present a few of his basic theories, which I believe are less inconsistent than his contemporaries found them to be. In doing so I have to acknowledge my debt to the writings of Scheler's most gifted personal student, the late Paul L. Landsberg, still unforgotten in France, and the interpretations offered by the eminent German Catholic philosopher Alois Dempf in his two remarkable books *Philosophical Anthropology* and *The Unity of Science*. The studies of these scholars have at least partially fulfilled Ortega y Gasset's hope that future generations will reveal the inner order and architecture of Scheler's philosophy. The procedure I have chosen necessitates, unfortunately, the omission of some of his most outstanding achievements, such as his analyses of resentment, of repentance, humility, and the sense of shame, of the pragmatic motive of our knowledge, and, above all, his philosophy of religious experience during his theistic period.

Scheler's central problem is that of human existence and the place of man within the cosmos. Man finds himself in the midst of an immense world, not as a mere spectator but as being in the world and encountering the world. In accordance with the findings of theoretical biology as developed by Uexküll and Driesch, which influenced Scheler very much, each species has its own particular form for organizing its experiences of its environment (*milieu*). Scheler's problem was twofold: First, he wanted to show that man is just one species within the totality of organic life, experiencing the world in an organizational form peculiar to him, and thus to explain human existence in terms of the accepted biological theories of evolution; second, he wanted to demonstrate that man, in contradistinction to all the other living beings, is to a certain extent independent of his environment and capable of transforming it into a "world." Scheler distinguishes five interrelated levels of psychical existence:

(1) The vegetative life of the plant, on the level of emotional impulse without consciousness and even without sensations and perceptions. (2) The level of instinctive behavior, characteristic of the lower animals, which is meaningful since it is oriented towards an end, that is, directed towards specific elements of the environment. It is independent of the number of attempts that have to be made in order to succeed: it is, so to speak, ready-made from the beginning. (3) The level of associative memory, of conditioned reflexes, to which corresponds behavior tested in an increasing number of attempts, performed in accordance with the principle of success and failure and the faculty of forming habits and traditions. (4) The level of practical intelligence, of spontaneous and appropriate action in new situations, independent of the number of previous attempts. Such behavior presupposes insight into the interconnectedness of the environment and its elements and, therefore, productive (not merely reproductive) thinking, which is capable of anticipating a state of affairs never before experienced and of grasping relations such as "similar," "analogous," "means for obtaining something," etc. In so far as human nature pertains to the sphere of vitality, in so far as its psychical life shows impulses, instincts, associative memory, intelligence, and choice, it participates in all four realms of organic life thus far enumerated. (5) But man is also something else. He is not only psyche but spirit. Spirit is not a phenomenon of life and not derived from evolution; it rather stands over against life and its manifestations. Spirit (*Geist*) not only includes "reason" and this means the faculty of thinking in ideas, but also the power of intuiting essences (*Wesensgehalten*) and certain classes of volitive and emotional acts, such as those of kindness, love, repentance, etc. The center of activity correlated with the level of mind or spirit is called by Scheler the Person and has to be distinguished from the other centers of vitality which he calls "psychical centers."

The realm of the mind is the realm of freedom: freedom from dependence on the organic life, freedom from the bondage of impulses, freedom also from an environment in which the animal is immersed. Man can say "No" to life and its vital urges. He can steer them into certain directions and guide them. Whereas the animal experiences its environment as a system of centers of resistances and reactions, whose structure it carries along as the snail does its shell wherever it moves, the Mind and therefore the Person has the faculty of transforming these environmental centers of resistance into "objects" and the closed "environment" itself into the open "world." Unlike the animal, man may also objectify his own physical and psychical experiences. The animal hears and sees, but without knowing that it does so, and it experiences even its impulses just as attractions and repulsions emanating from things in its environment. Thus, the animal has consciousness, but not self-consciousness; it is not master of itself. Man, however, is the only being that is able to be a Self and to place itself not only above the world but even above itself. He can do so because he is not only a soul (*anima*) but a Person – "*persona cogitans*" in the sense of Kant's doctrine of the transcendental apperception, the "*cogitare*" being the condition for all possible inner and outer experience. Yet this also implies that the mind and its correlate, the person, are essentially not objectifiable.

According to Scheler, Person and act belong indissolubly together. The person is not an empty starting point of acts; it exists and lives only in the fulfillment of intentional acts. Among these acts are those of feeling, preference, love, hate, admiration, approval, rejection, etc., which are related to values. These acts, however, are not only value-feeling but value-disclosing acts. Husserl had shown that there are ideal objects of knowledge which are just as independent of the knowing subject as real objects are. Scheler used this insight for a new approach to a field inaccessible to both Nietzsche's relativism and Kant's formalism, that is, to the disclosure of the realm of concrete values. Values are to Scheler the intentional objects of feeling (*intentionale Gegenstände des Fühlens*) but, as such, totally different from the states of feeling themselves. They are *a priori*, objective, eternal, and immutable. They are given to us in and through visual perception. The mode of perception whose objects are the values and the eternal order among them are beyond the grasp of the intellect, which is as blind to them as the ear is to color. The emotional aspects of the mind are not founded upon ratiocination and have to be accepted by ethics quite independently of logic. Scheler assumes, following Pascal, an inborn aprioristic *ordre du cœur* or *logique du cœur*.

Scheler characterizes his basic position as an ethical absolutism and objectivism, emphasizing that it also could be qualified as an emotional intuitivism and a concrete apriorism (*materialer Apriorismus*). At any rate, it is a strictly personalistic theory. This view is in contradiction to Kant's formalism in ethics, but it is unfortunately impossible to discuss Scheler's objections to Kant within the frame of the present paper.* Nor can we enter into Scheler's criticism of the relativistic theories of value. Scheler admits that the realm of eternal and immutable values appears to each society and to each historical period only in a timebound perspective. This is so because only one particular sector of the cosmos of values becomes visible from a particular vantagepoint. Thus we should not speak of a relativism but rather of a perspectivism of values.

Scheler's doctrine of the order of the modes of values, which again is objective and discernible, is of decisive importance for his philosophical approach. At the lowest level are the pleasure-values of the agreeable, of what is useful in terms of our activity. Next in rank are the life-values, the values of the noble and of health, which originate in the struggle between sensuality and mind, between flesh and spirit; then follow the spiritual values, comprising goodness and beauty; the sacred values of holiness, reverence, and humility occupy the highest rank. It can readily be seen how Scheler's concept of the place of man in the cosmos is related to his theory of the hierarchy of values. The participation of man in the various spheres of organic life and his existence as a person determine the needs which have to be satisfied: his vital and intellectual needs, and his spiritual needs directed towards salvation.

Scheler was fully aware that his discovery of the order of the modes of value, which he developed in his ethics, was decisive for his whole philosophical thinking. It motivates his further researches and finds its counterpart in his doctrines of the modes of loving, the forms of knowing, and the relationship between vital forces and the socio-cultural life.

---

* For a discussion of these objections, see the next chapter, p. 154 f.

According to Scheler, love is that movement wherein every concrete individual object which possesses value achieves the highest value compatible with its nature. He criticizes the materialistic theories according to which love arises from impulses that are not only blind intellectually but blind to values as well. The instinctive system of drives is responsible only for the ordering of the selection of values loved, not for the acts of loving themselves. And since all acts can be divided into vital acts of the body, purely mental acts of the self, and spiritual acts of the person, we also have love in three forms: vital or passionate love, mental love of the individual self, and spiritual love of the person. These forms of emotional acts also have an essential reference to particular kinds of values: vital acts to the values of the noble; mental acts to the values of knowledge and beauty (cultural values); and spiritual acts to the value of the holy. Objects whose value is simply that of being pleasant engender a feeling of enjoyment only, but not love. In making this statement Scheler refers to Malbranche's *Recherche de la vérité*.

But to love a fellow-man who is a person means to love him as an autonomous human being who is different from myself. The values attached to the physical, the corporeal, and the mental can always be given to us objectively. The ultimate moral value of the personality, however, is disclosed to us only when we associate ourselves with the other person's own acts of love. As long as we continue to objectify someone on whatever manner, his personality eludes our grasp. We must love what he loves and love it with him. All love evokes a loving response and thereby brings a new moral value into being. And this is the foundation of the principle which Scheler calls the "principle of the solidarity of all moral beings." It implies, that with regard to their respective moral values, each is answerable in principle for all and all for each. Each must share the blame for another's guilt and each is party from the outset to the moral value of everyone else.

Scheler's theory of intersubjectivity is also closely connected with his anthropological view and his personalism. In one of the most brilliant chapters of the *Nature of Sympathy* he refutes both current theories aiming at the explanation of our understanding of other minds, the so-called theory of inference by analogy and that of empathy. We cannot enter here into the details of Scheler's argument.* According to him these theories are the outcome of two time-honored metaphysical assumptions on the relations between mind and body: the theory of the reciprocal influences of two substances and that of psycho-physical parallelism. But both metaphysical assumptions exclude even the possibility of my perceiving the Other's experiences. They confine man to a kind of psychical jail where he has to wait and see what the meta-physical nexus of causality might magically project on its walls. This is so because both theories misinterpret the role of the body as the great selector and analyst of the contents of all our outer and inner perceptions. Scheler's own theory of understanding the Other, which he calls the "perceptional theory of the alter ego" (*Wahrnehmungstheorie des fremden Ich*), refutes the assumption that what we perceive of another man is just his body and its movements. Nor do we perceive merely the Other's Self or his soul. What we perceive are integral wholes whose intuitive content is not immediately resolvable in terms of external or internal per-ceptions. We certainly perceive in the Other's smile his joy, in his tears his suffering, in his blushing his shame, in his joined hands his praying, in the sounds of his words his thoughts. The Other's body and gestures show the structure of a physiognomical unit. The only category of the Other's experience which cannot be caught by direct perception is the Other's experience of his body, its organs, and the sensuous feeling attached to them. And ex-actly these bodily feelings constitute the separation between man and fellow-man. Insofar as man lives only within his bodily feelings he does not find any approach to the life of the alter ego. Only if he elevates himself as a Person above his pure vegetative life does he gain experience of the Other. But, as we have seen, it is one of Scheler's main principles that the Person and its acts can never be objectified. Other persons' acts can, therefore, be seized only by co-performing, pre-performing or re-performing them.

Scheler has supplemented his theory of the order of values by his doctrine of the various kinds of knowledge and their order. Dempf rightly sees in this discovery one of the outstanding achievements of Scheler.

* See "Scheler's Theory of Intersubjectivity and the General Thesis of the Alter Ego," *Collected Papers*, Vol. I.

Man is capable of a threefold knowledge: knowledge for the sake of domination or practical knowledge; of essences or cultural knowledge; knowledge for the sake of salvation or metaphysical knowledge. Each kind serves for the transformation of a region of being: either that of the being of things or that of the culture of man or that of the absolute.

Practical knowledge serves our potential technical power over nature and society. This is the knowledge of the positive sciences; its goal is to find laws in the particular spatio-temporal context of the phenomena. Knowledge of these laws will assure our domination of the world and of ourselves. They are discovered by our observations and measurements, which again are founded upon the exercise of our sensory functions and motivated by our system of needs and drives.

The second form of knowledge is that knowledge which Aristotle has called *prima philosophia*, namely knowledge of the modes of being and the structure of essences of everything that exists. In contradistinction to the first form of knowledge this kind of inquiry methodically disregards the contingent spatio-temporal locations and the contingent qualities of things. It tries to answer questions such as: What is the world? What is an animal? What is the essence of man in its invariant structure? And similarly: What is thinking? What is love? – all this independently of the concrete and therefore contingent stream of consciousness of this or that human being within which these acts actually appear. This kind of knowledge aims at the greatest possible elimination of all drive-determined and need-motivated conduct. Knowledge of essences is not independent of any kind of experience, but it is independent of the quantity of accumulated experiences or so-called induction. Thus, it transcends the very small sector of the real world and refers to being itself as it is for itself and in itself. Whereas practical knowledge is a function of the intellect, knowledge of essence is a function of the reason.

The third form of knowledge should perhaps be better called "meta-anthropology" instead of metaphysics. Surely only from the essence of man as brought into view by philosophical anthropology can the supreme ground of all things, which is God, be revealed by means of a transcendental inference (*transzendentale Schlussweise*). By the very fact that man is a microcosm, in which all regions of being (physical, chemical, living spiritual being) converge, man can also win knowledge of God as the supreme ground of the macrocosm. In other words, the being of man as "microtheos" is also the first access to God.

These three kinds of knowledge are ranked in an objective order which corresponds to the order of values, to the *ordo amoris*, and finally to the structure of human nature. From knowledge for the sake of domination, which serves for the practical changing of the world and our possible performances in it, we ascend to cultural knowledge. By this ascent we enlarge the being and existence of the spiritual person within us to a microcosm, trying to participate with our unique individuality in the totality of the world or at least in its essential structure. And from cultural knowledge we ascend to knowledge for the sake of salvation, by which we try to participate with the innermost core of our person in the supreme ground of being of all things.

Each of these forms of knowledge is represented by a personal type: practical knowledge by the scientist and the technician, cultural by the sage, metaphysical by the *homo religiosus* or the saint. Sometimes in certain great cultures a particular type of knowledge predominates, such as in India knowledge for the sake of salvation, in China and Greece cultural knowledge, in the Occident (since the beginning of the 12th century) knowledge for the sake of domination in the form of the positive sciences.

Yet we find in Scheler's system not only a correspondence between the rank-order of ethical values and that of the forms of knowledge, but also a correspondence of both of these with what he calls the hierarchy of the forces of life (*Lebensmächte*) and therewith of the modes of man's participation in society. This is the starting point of Scheler's remarkable contribution to the foundation of the sociology of knowledge.

There are three basic relations between knowledge and social life: First, the knowledge of the members of any group that they belong together, understand one another and share common values and objectives constitutes the group itself. Second, this knowledge of common values and objectives also determines in various respects the particular form and shape of the particular social group. Third, all kinds of knowledge are determined conversely to a certain extent by the social group and its structure.

It is Scheler's view that neither the content of knowledge nor its validity is sociologically determined but that the selection of the objects of knowledge is co-determined (not exclusively determined) by the social interests prevailing in the particular group. Each particular group shares a stock of insights which are deemed to be given beyond question and which are believed neither to require a justification nor to be capable of any. Scheler calls the sum-total of these insights which are just taken for granted the "relative natural conception of the world" prevailing in this particular group. Its content is a different one from group to group and changes in the course of the historical development within the same group.

The values and objectives shared by the members of the group are manifested in their acts of thinking together, willing together, loving together, etc. These acts may be performed spontaneously or occur in the way of automatic or semi-automatic psycho-physical activities. The anonymous collectivity is the carrier of non-spontaneous manifestations such as myths, folkways, etc. Spontaneous manifestations such as forms of government, laws, arts, philosophy, science, public opinion, require the interference of personal representatives of a small number, of an *élite*.

Scheler rejects all theories of society and all philosophies of history which isolate a single factor as exclusively determining social life as a whole. Society and history are based on human acts, and each human act has a spiritual and a material component. They refer, therefore, to the structure of man, who is the subject of society as well as of history. Hence Scheler's doctrine of *"Realfaktoren"* (factors such as race and kinship, politics, economics) and *"Idealfaktoren"* (such as religion, philosophy, metaphysics, and science). The former constitute the substructure and the latter the superstructure. The *Realfaktoren* are founded upon fundamental impulses of human beings, and Scheler believes that he has discovered a parallelism between the order of the drives in the life-cycle of the individual and the historical phases through which socio-cultural units have to pass in the course of their development. In the former we discover the sexual drives which serve for the maintenance of the species, the drive for power serving for the maintenance of the individual, and finally the urge for food. Correspondingly, in the history of cultures we find three types of integration: first, the domination of blood or kinship-ties; second, the transition to the predominance of political power (predominance of the state); third, the growing predominance of economic factors. The *Realfaktoren* determine which ideas in the spiritual stream might and which might not become effective. They open, as it were, the sluice gates of the stream of ideas, permitting some of them to come to fruition within social reality. They themselves, however, are meaningless, blind, autonomous trends representing in the terms of Comte a *"fatalité modifiable."* The *"Idealfaktoren,"* however, are characterized by potential freedom with autonomy of action, showing, as it were, a *liberté modifiable*. They may guide and direct the blind tendencies of material development.

Thus the forms of life governing society and history have their origin in the needs and the drive-structure of human nature. With Scheler we have to understand under "needs" not only biological but also spiritual needs, including the need for salvation. By the structure of human nature, by man's bodily existence, by his existence with others in the various forms of societal life, and by his capacity of being a person with a relationship to God, the order of human needs has been constituted. Their objective order corresponds to the order of the ethical values, to the order of the forms of knowledge, and to the *ordo amoris*. Even if Scheler acknowledged (in his later period) the predominance of the *Realfaktoren* for the determination of history, he developed his metaphysical anthropology in terms of the spiritual solidarity which makes the realization of all values possible. This is what Dempf calls Scheler's postulate of an integral humanism, which he considers to be at the core of the philosopher's unfortunately unfinished system. The last word of Scheler's metaphysical anthropology is the axiom that the living spirit maintains itself in spite of the primacy of the drive-structure originating in the vital sphere.

MAX SCHELER'S EPISTEMOLOGY AND ETHICS

The work of Max Scheler is not well known to English-speaking readers. It is to be hoped that the excellent translation of one of his major books, *The Nature of Sympathy*, done by Peter Heath, with a valuable introduction by W. Stark,[1] as well as the thirteen-volume German edition of his collected writings, now in process of publication, will call appropriate attention to the stature of this eminent philosopher and sociologist, whose seminal mind has so deeply influenced thinkers such as Ortega y Gasset, Nicolai Hartmann, Alois Dempf, and Paul L. Landsberg.

It is not our ambition to give here a synopsis of Scheler's work and main themes or to follow step by step the various, frequently contradictory, phases of his development. We restrict ourselves to an account of Scheler's theories in the fields of epistemology and ethics.

I. SCHELER'S EPISTEMOLOGY

A. Scheler and Phenomenology

Scheler is generally considered the most original and influential thinker of the phenomenological movement after Husserl. The latter's influence upon him was indeed a decisive one, and Scheler's main work, *Der Formalismus in der Ethik und die materiale Wertethik* appeared in the first two volumes of the *Yearbook for Philosophy and Phenomenological Research*, of which Husserl was the editor. However, what Scheler accepted from Husserl's teaching was mainly the theory of categorial intuition, the eidetic method, and the doctrine of ideal objects. These features,

[1] New Haven, 1954.

interpreted in a rather unorthodox way, became, in Scheler's hands, excellent instruments for the exploration of the realms of emotion and value. But Husserl complained in later years, and not without good reason, that Scheler had failed to grasp the true meaning of his life work.

To Scheler, phenomenology is neither a new science nor a substitute for philosophy, but the name for a particular attitude of spiritual vision by which a realm of "facts" of a special kind, otherwise hidden, is revealed. It is an attitude, and not a method, if we restrict the meaning of the latter term to a technique of knowing employed to attain certain ends in processes of thinking or experimentation. The basic goal of any phenomenological philosophy is to come into immediate contact with the world, "to get at the things themselves," regardless of whether these things are physical or mental, numbers or deities, feelings or values. Phenomenology refuses to identify experience with sensory experience on the one hand and with induction on the other. Only existing things are objects of possible observation and induction. But all forms of intentionality, that is, of "being conscious *of* . . .," such as acts of feeling, of loving and hating, or of religious faith, reveal essential contents which are objects of an aprioristic insight into their pure nature and their order of foundation. This attitude radically distinguishes phenomenology from empiricism in the usual sense. But phenomenology is also distinguished from rationalism; in its attempt to get at the things themselves it refuses to take for granted the validity of any presupposed conceptual schema and even of the findings of any positive science whatever. To presuppose the validity of scientific propositions would block any insight into the essential structure of their subject matter and would, in addition, involve the degradation of philosophy to the role of a handmaiden of the sciences. *A fortiori*, none of the presuppositions involved in the common sense thinking of the natural attitude can be acceptable to a philosophical inquiry aiming at the description of that which is self-given in immediacy. Using another line of argument – and here following Bergson – Scheler defines as self-given that which is given without any interference of symbols of whatever kind: in this sense phenomenological philosophy is a continuous de-symbolization of the world.

Thus, an ontology of the mind as well as of the world has to proceed all epistemological theory; and since, according to Scheler, phenomenology is concerned with the former, it is also at the foundation of the latter. For example, all theories dealing with the question of how we can formulate value judgments or perform evaluations presuppose insights into the essence of the values under scrutiny and their hierarchical order. Phenomenological analysis alone can provide this insight, because phenomenology is concerned exclusively with the structural relations essentially prevailing between the organization of the world and the organization of the mind. It disregards systematically not only the actual performances of the different acts of knowing and the various properties of the organization of the performers of these acts (animals, human beings, God) but also the modes of positing the contents of these acts as reality, appearance, imagination, illusion, objects of belief or disbelief.

B. The Doctrine of the Three Kinds of "Fact."

According to Scheler we have to distinguish three kinds of "facts"; facts given in the common-sense experience of the natural attitude, facts as subject matter of the positive sciences, and finally, phenomenological facts as disclosed by eidetic intuition.

Natural facts refer to the world as experienced in our everyday thinking. It is the world of concrete things and events occurring in the medium within which we carry on the business of living. There, in spite of Copernicus, the sun rises from the sea and sets behind the mountain; it is now red and now white, and the earth is the immovable floor upon which we walk. Physical objects change their size in relation to their distance. Space is articulated as above and below, before and behind, right and left; time as past, present, and future. We take it for granted that things will remain what they are, even if we do not look at them, and that, if we leave the room, we will upon our return find the objects within it substantially unchanged. Moreover, the world of common-sense thinking is a meaningful world of values, of socio-cultural objects, which are taken for granted in a particular socio-cultural surrounding. There are levels of reality and unreality; things come into being and fade away, influence and act upon one another, display forces and faculties of all kinds, are differentiated into living and lifeless things, and into entities such as states and nations which cannot be grasped by sensory perception, but are, nevertheless, elements of the common-sense reality.

The scientific aspect of the world is not a natural but an artificial one. The scientific fact is a construct, derived from natural things by a process Scheler called "scientific reduction." The carriers of scientific facts are symbols, which receive a particular content only by way of a scientific definition. This does not mean that science has to deal with objects and events which cannot be found in the world of natural facts. It merely means that it deals with the same objects or facts in symbolic terms, in different aspects, and in a different arrangement. In his natural attitude man interprets natural facts in accordance with the traditions taken for granted in his socio-cultural environment. The selections, generalizations, and idealizations by means of which scientific facts are abstracted from natural ones are subject to a code of interpretational and procedural rules which are based on conventions and are, as such, not valid for everyone, but merely for all fellow scientists; they have to be communicable and verifiable.

Phenomenological facts are, as to their unity and content, independent of all factors which are not grounded in the things themselves. Particularly, they are independent of all the sensory functions of the percipient. The pure fact, which can be grasped by eidetic intuition, must remain unchanged even if the sensory functions actually vary or are imagined to vary. The pure fact is, moreover, at the foundation of every possible sensory content, and in this relation the former is the independent, the latter the dependent variable. Furthermore, pure facts are independent of all possible symbols by which they might be designated. Scheler considers this theory, that pure phenomenological facts are at the foundation of all sensory perceptions, as one of his most important discoveries. According to him, even Husserl's doctrine of categorial intuition is grounded in sensory contents. Scheler objects that Husserl fails to examine the notion of "sensory intuition," that he identifies incorrectly the prerequisites of any "perception" of the subject matters of categorial intuition with that which is self-given in perception, and that he, thus, does not perform the phenomenological reduction radically enough. These shortcomings lead to the consequence that the order of foundation in which certain acts and their contents are by their very nature interrelated remains unrevealed or is confused with the genetic order in which these acts are produced. According to Scheler, the essential relationships between facts are of a twofold kind: there are first those of a purely logical character, which originate in the nature of all objects in general. The law of contradiction, which is founded upon the incompatibility of the being and non-being of an object at the same time, is an example. There are, second, essential relationships which refer to a particular onto-logical realm of objects, such as the evident connection between color and extension – color is founded upon extension.

Scheler's concept of the order of foundations and its apri-oristic nature requires some additional comment. Like Husserl, he understands by "foundation" the fact that a phenomenon *B* cannot be given if a phenomenon *A* does not precede it in the order of time. Spatiality, motion, change are not, as Kant believed, bestowed upon something pre-given by the so-called faculty of understanding, as forms of the synthesis of its activi-ties. They are phenomena in their own right, requiring careful phenomenological analysis. No thinking or intuiting can produce or form them; they are all found present as data of the intuition itself. This theory leads Scheler to a considerable enlargement of his conception of the *a priori*. All knowledge which refers to the self-givenness of things, all ideal propositions and units of meanings which are discovered by the thinking subject in eidetic intuition have, according to Scheler, the character of an *a priori*. This does not merely refer to the formal *a priori*, that is, to the intuitive, basic facts of logic. In addition, each concrete province of knowledge (such as the theory of numbers, the theory of sets, geometry, mechanics, physics, chemistry, biology, psychology) is founded upon a system of concrete aprioristic propositions. In all these cases the *a priori* in the logical sense is a consequence of the *a priori* of the intuitive facts which constitute the subject matter of the judgments and propositions pertaining to this particular field. Scheler contends that this brand of phenome-nological apriorism differs from the aprioristic theories of most of the current philosophical doctrines, all of which are inter-mingled with idealism, subjectivism, spontaneism, transcen-dentalism, the "Copernican revolution" of Kant, rationalism, and formalism. Scheler sums up his view of the *a priori* with the statement that any kind of knowledge the subject matter of which is pregiven in the order of foundation is aprioristic with respect to the knowledge of objects founded upon the former.

C. The Three Kinds of Knowledge

In the preceding remarks an attempt was made to give a sketch of Scheler's earlier position. During his last years his notion of the role of philosophy and knowledge in general was considerably elaborated and modified. It became connected with one of the central problems in Scheler's thought – the doctrine of the three kinds of human knowledge and their hierarchical order. This idea is at the heart of Scheler's philosophical anthro-pology, and several of the most competent students of his work, such as Alois Dempf and Paul L. Landsberg, consider this theory as Scheler's greatest achievement. In the following we try to state as briefly as possible the main features of his views pertinent to this theory, as developed in his last writings.

What distinguishes the function of human mental and spirit-ual life from that of all other living beings? Scheler thinks that there are three basic features: (1) Man is conscious of the world, in contradistinction to an animal which just *has* a world. The animal is simply determined by its impulses, urges, drives – in brief, by states interior to its organism. Man, however, can transcend this sphere of mere vitality determined by an environ-ment important to the life process. Man is thus the "relative ascetic of life." He can say "No" to his vital drives and impulses; and, quite consistently, the free will of human beings means to Scheler first of all not man's capacity to produce and create, but to check and release drive impulses. In relation to actions, the act of will is always a *"non fiat"* and not a *"fiat."* (2) Man is capable of a love of the world which is detached from all desire and transcends all drive-determined experiences of things within the world. (3) Finally, and this is of particular importance to the problem under scrutiny, man is capable of distinguishing the *"thusness"* (essence) from the *"thatness"* (existence); that is, of obtaining aprioristic eidetic insights which remain valid and true for all contingent objects and specimens pertaining to the same essence.

The same idea is expressed by Scheler in his last essay, "The Place of Man within the Cosmos." [2] There Scheler points out that there are five interrelated levels of psychical existence. Human nature participates in four realms of organic life and in their psychical life: that of emotional impulses without consciousness and even without sensations and perceptions, which is that of the plant; that of instinctive behavior, characteristic of lower animals; that of associative memory, of conditioned reflexes, forming habits and traditions; that of practical intelligence, of spontaneous appropriate action in new situations. But man is also something else. He is not only psyche but spirit (*Geist*). Spirit is not a phenomenon of life and is not derived from evolution; rather, it stands over against life and its manifestations. Spirit includes not only reason but also the power of intuiting essence; it includes in addition certain classes of volitive and emotional acts, such as kindness, love, repentance, etc. The center of activity correlated with the level of mind or spirit is called "Person" and has to be distinguished from the other centers of vitality which Scheler calls "psychical centers."

The realm of the mind is the realm of freedom: freedom from the bondage of impulses, freedom also from the bondage of the environment in which the animal is immersed and whose structure it carries along as the snail its shell. Mind, however, and therefore Person, has the faculty of transforming those environmental centers of resistance into "objects" and the closed "environment" itself into an open "world." The animal sees and hears, but without knowing that it does so; it has consciousness, but not self-consciousness. Man, however, is the only being which is able to place itself not only above the world but even above itself.

To the later Scheler, consciousness (*"con-scientia"*) is merely one form of knowledge in the broad sense in which he uses this term. He rejects the view that knowledge is the function of consciousness. There is also a pre-conscious "ecstatic" kind of

---

[2] Darmstadt, 1928. (See footnote, p. 133.)

knowing which characterizes the way in which animals, children, and primitives "know *of*" the world. Knowing is an ontological relationship: it is the partaking of a being in the Thusness of another being in such a way that no changes occur in the latter. This relationship of being is neither spatial nor temporal nor yet causal. It is rather a relation between the whole and the part. The "known" becomes a "part" of the "knower" without being changed. Mind or spirit is nothing else but the X of the total sum of the acts within the knowing being by which such a partaking becomes possible. In other words, it is that by which the Thusness ("*Sosein*") of a being becomes an *ens intentionale* in contradistinction to its mere Thatness ("*Dasein*," *ens reale*), which remains always and necessarily outside of and beyond the essential relationship. It follows that the Thusness of a being can simultaneously coexist *in mente* and *extra mentem:* the Thatness of a being, however, remains in its contingency always *extra mentem* and is not experienced by intellectual functions (neither by thinking nor by intuition), but merely by encountering the *resistance* of being in acts of striving and in the dynamic factors of attention. Students of Maine de Biran and Dilthey will recognize the influence these philosophers had on this theory of Scheler, which he calls "the voluntative theory of existence." It was his intention to elaborate it in books on Metaphysics and Philosophical Anthropology. His papers of the last period [3] give only scanty hints of his argumentation.

It seems that Scheler rejected critical realism as well as epistemological idealism on the ground that both theories share the wrong presupposition that the Thusness and the Thatness of things are, with respect to the intellectual functions of thinking, perceiving, recollecting, etc., inseparable from one another. Epistemological idealism sees correctly that the Thusness of the things must necessarily be *in mente*, but erroneously concludes from this insight that therefore their Thatness can also be *in mente*. Critical realism, on the other hand, understands correctly that Thatness is always and necessarily *extra mentem*, but believes erroneously that for this reason also the Thusness of things has to be *extra mentem* and only *extra mentem*, so that merely a copy, representation or symbol of their Thusness could be *in mente*.

[3] *Philosophische Weltanschauung*, Bonn, 1929, Bern, 1954.

The neo-Kantian doctrine, according to which "being real" means nothing but a connectedness established by the laws of thinking has to be rejected, if for no other reason than that it confuses the Thatness of things with the givenness of existing objects.

Human knowledge is of three forms: 1. Knowledge for the sake of specific achievements (*Herrschafts-oder Leistungswissen*); 2. Knowledge of essences or knowledge for the sake of personal culture (*Wesens-oder Bildungswissen*); 3. Metaphysical knowledge or knowledge for the sake of salvation (*Heils-oder Erlosungs- wissen*). Each kind of knowledge serves a particular purpose by transforming a particular region of being: the first that of things, the second that of man, the third that of the Absolute, the *ens a se*.

The first form of knowledge is that of the positive sciences. It serves our possible power over nature, society, and history. The experiences, observations, measurements, which are the sources of this knowledge, depend upon sensory functions of the human organism and therewith mediately upon its structure of drives and needs. The supreme goal of this form of knowledge is the ordering of the phenomena around us into certain classes and the establishment of laws of their contact in space and time. This is so because only the recurrence of phenomena in accordance with laws is predictable and only that which can be predicted can be dominated.

The second form of knowledge is that of the "First Philosophy" as Aristotle has called it, that is, the science of the modes of existence and the structure of essences of all kinds of Being. In our time Husserl rediscovered this kind of knowledge by de- veloping the eidetic method. Knowledge of essences methodically disregards the Thatness of things (that is, the contingent location in space and time of everything which happens to be-there in this or that way) and looks for their Thusness, asking: What is the world, what is an outer object, what is an animal, what is a plant, what is man – what are all these in their invariant structure and essential qualities? And in a similar way: What is "think- ing"? What is the experience of love or beauty? It does all this independently of the contingent stream of thought of this or that individual mind within which these experiences actually occur. This type of inquiry is characterized by its attempt to eliminate all motives originating in the drive structure by its abstracting from the real existence of things and by its independence of inductive experience. Knowledge of essences transcends the narrow field of the real world which is accessible to our sensory experience; its insights are those of Reason and not those of Understanding. It has a twofold application: it defines the ultimate presuppositions of the positive sciences (mathematics, physics, biology, psychology, etc.), thus constituting their essential axiomatic systems; and in metaphysics the same eidetic insights are, in Hegel's words, "windows on the Absolute."

Knowledge of the Absolute is the third form of human knowledge. It should perhaps be better called "Meta-anthropology" instead of Metaphysics. Surely only by starting from the essence of man as brought into view by philosophical anthropology can the supreme ground of all things, which is God, be revealed by means of a kind of transcendental inference (*"transzendentale Schlussweise"*). By the very fact that man is a microcosm in which all regions of being (physical, chemical, animate, spiritual) converge, he can win knowledge of God as the supreme ground of the Macrocosm. In other words, man is a *"microtheos."*

The three kinds of knowledge are ranked in an objective order. From knowledge for the sake of domination we ascend to the knowledge of essences. By this ascent we enlarge the being and the existence of the spiritual Person within us to a microcosm, trying to participate with our unique individuality in the totality of the world or at least in its essential structure. And from there we ascend to knowledge for the sake of salvation, by which we try to participate on the supreme ground of the being of all things.

Each of these forms of knowledge is represented by a personal type: practical knowledge by the scientist and the technician, cultural by the sage, metaphysical by the *homo religiosus* or the saint. Sometimes in great cultures a particular type of knowledge predominates, such as in India knowledge for the sake of salvation, in China and Greece cultural knowledge, in the Occident (since the beginning of the twelfth century) knowledge for the sake of domination in the form of the positive sciences.

D. Scheler's Criticism of Kant's Philosophy

The preceding pages outline Scheler's gnosiological position. The basic trend of his thought will become clearer if we turn now to his criticism of Kant's philosophy, which rightly has been considered as one of his most brilliant achievements. We will then be prepared to approach an analysis of Scheler's ethical theories.

It is clear that Scheler's gnosiological position as outlined in the preceding pages is in sharp contradiction to Kant's philosophy. Indeed through all the books of Scheler goes a criticism of Kant which occupies him during his mature years. Scheler recognizes that as a thinker Kant is a giant and that we cannot abandon dialogue with him. But he calls his philosophy one of the closed fist and not one of the open hand. He feels that some of Kant's doctrines, regardless of their inherent greatness, are just echoes of a particular historically determined society. They are deeply rooted in the conception of the state which prevailed in Kant's time in Prussia. Nature is reduced to a kind of enlarged Prussian state, that is, to an artificial architecture purportedly errected by human understanding. The assumption that objectivity (*Gegenständlichkeit*), being, reality, the forms of substance and causality, the intuitive manifolds that are at the foundation of space, time, magnitude, number, relations, values, are products of the human mind is a basic fallacy of his philosophy. It is the presupposition of Kant's epistemology that everything in the things given to our experience, which transcends the content of the "pregiven sensations," must have been produced by an activity of the human mind or even introjected by it into the material. But, on the one hand, the content given to our intuition is much richer than the partial content which would correspond to our pure sensation; and on the other hand, our thinking and knowing are not in the position to produce anything or to form anything except ficta, signs and symbols. Only will and action are capable of producing anything. But these phenomena cannot be understood in their true significance if experiencing and thinking are already supposed to have an inherent creative power. Moreover Kant imputes to human reason an eternal stability when he makes an attempt to describe its functions in the well-known analysis of the transcendental aesthetic and the transcendental analytic. This leads Kant to an erroneous notion of the person and the ego of transcendental apperception. He states that any objective unity of experience and therewith of the object as such – the outer physical, the inner psychical, and even the ideal object – stands under the fundamental condition that the "I think" must be capable of accompanying all other knowledge. To Kant the unity and identity of this "I" is the condition for the unity and identity of the object. "Object" in this sense means to Kant merely that which becomes identifiable to an I. Scheler denies that the identity of the object can be derived from the identity of the I. In addition, such a relationship, even if it existed, would not by any means imply that the objects and the connection among objects would have to conform to the acts of the I and their connections and *a priori* foundations – a theory of Kant's generally known as his Copernican revolution. Scheler speaks in this connection of the specific Kantian fear of "transcendental contingency," his fear that the objects could behave among themselves in a way quite different from that corresponding to the laws of our experiencing, thinking, etc., unless we bind them from the outset by these laws. In general, Kant's attitude toward the world can only be characterized as hostility to and distrust of everything that is "given," as dread of the chaos he considers the external world and internal nature to be: both have to be formed, organized, dominated by understanding and reason and by reason-guided volition in order to make them safe by putting them straight. This attitude is the opposite to love of the world, to trusting it, to surrendering to it in affectionate vision. Expressed by a philosophical genius, it is the way in which modern man faces the world.

In Scheler's interpretation Kant's theory of ethical problems follows the same pattern. It is clearly a continuation of the old Protestant Lutheran and somewhat Calvinistic doctrine of the Fall, according to which, in a manner similar to that of the Gnostic philosophers, sin has its root in the existence of a finite body and its desires, not in the attitude of its finite spiritual personality and its volitions to the drive. Only this view explains the fact that Kant refers the idea of moral perfection to that of the goodness of the will and this goodness of the will to duty. The so-called "infinity of duty" involves the delusion that the essential imperfection of the finite person is equivalent to man's pregiven radical inclination to evil. Only this view explains Kant's contempt for happiness, his failure to make any distinction between the most vulgar sensual pleasures, Greek eudemonia, and Christian blessedness, and his rejecting all of them not only as purposes of actions, but also as guiding aims of the soul. Only this view explains his elimination of love and of all forms of sympathy from the domain of moral forces and the degradation of religion and of the idea of God to an "as if" of the dutiful citizen. Scheler endorses Friedrich Schiller's statement that Kant's ethics takes care of the servants but not of the children of the house.

Scheler sums up the erroneous presuppositions of Kant's ethics, which he believes he has refuted in his main work, in the following manner: Kant erroneously assumes that any material ethics must necessarily be an ethics of purposes, empirically inductive and *a posteriori*, an ethics of success, hedonistic, heteronomous, incapable of determining the moral foundation of action, incapable of furnishing insight into the dignity of the person: moreover such a system of ethics must by necessity refer to the organization of the egoistic drives of human nature as the ground for all ethical valuation. Only a formal ethics, so Kant seems to think, avoids these fallacies.

In his main work *Formalism in Ethics and the Material Ethics of Value* Scheler tries to show that an ethics of concrete values by no means must lead to the consequences outlined by Kant. First, the contrasted pairs "formal-material" and "*a priori – a posteriori*" have nothing to do with each other. Scheler agrees with Kant's rejection of any kind of ethics which tries to derive its propositions from inductive experience. All experience of what is good or evil presupposes an *a priori* knowledge of what might be good or evil. Kant cannot answer the question of how the ethical *a priori* could possibly be known. To state that nothing can be called good without qualification except a will, insofar as this will is determined by the law of reason in regard to the choice of its objects, is to disregard completely the sphere of moral knowledge as the genuine source of the ethical *a priori*. But the willing of the good and the judgment of what is good must be founded upon the knowledge of moral values. The fact of moral insight is, however, entirely unknown to Kant and replaced by the consciousness of duty, which at best might be one of the many possible forms of subjective realization of possible moral insight. That is why Kant substitutes for the nature of the values good and evil the conformity and disconformity of the will to the moral law. According to him, nothing is given to our experience but purposes which are always empirical, conditioned by our senses and, as such morally indifferent. The *a priori* is not situated in the content but only in the function of the will, and these volitional forms are not given to our experience. If we accepted these doctrines of Kant it would be entirely impossible ever to find out whether any action – one's own or another's – was good or evil. It would then be impossible to refer ethics to autonomous knowledge. The dilemma in Kant's ethics is the same as in his epistemology. Instead of asking the question "What is given"? he asks the question "What can be given"? implying that something beyond the sensory function cannot be given to our experience. In his theoretical philosophy he erroneously derives the *a priori* from the function of the judgment instead of from the content of the intuition upon which all judging is formed; and he cannot demonstrate how the *a priori* of the understanding – if such an *a priori* as he assumes exists at all – could ever be disclosed and known, whether by *a priori* or by inductive knowledge. In ethics he derives the *a priori* from the function of the will instead of from the content of moral knowledge. Granted that there is a law of function of the pure will, Kant is unable to show how knowledge of such a law might be obtained and how it might be formulated in the propositions of ethics. Moreover, in his theoretical philosophy Kant assumes that the specific performance of the subjective *a priori* consists in a spontaneous connecting of originally separated given sensations, lacking any form of their own. In ethics he assumes that man's inclinations are in a state of complete chaos, that they are experienced first as a series of events interrelated exclusively in accordance with the principle of mechanistic associations, and that it is only the reasonable will, the practical reason, which bestows some meaningful structure upon this chaotic state. Scheler holds, on the contrary, that man's moral nature is characterized by the fact that even the automatic involuntary inclinations and the concrete values to which they refer are prestructured in an order of preferences, so that the acts of volition refer to a preformed material.

By the same token, Kant's notion of the general validity of judgments is by no means connected with essentiality and has therefore nothing to do with the *a priori*. In ethics he refers all connections of the "ought to be" to the necessity of the ought instead of to *a priori* insights into the context of the values. Yet only that which is good can become the object of a duty, and it can do so because it is good. In Kant's theory the notion of the general validity of morals not only serves as an argument for his view that the moral law is valid for all reasonable beings; it also involves the view, that the maxim which is a content of the moral law is generally valid, since the volition is only good if it is fit to be made the principle of a universal legislation. Kant thus makes the possibility of generalizing a maxim the criterion for the moral justification of its content – even more, for the goodness of its content. He does not say: "Thou shalt will the good and then see to it that other people also will the good," but he says: "That is good regarding which you can will that everyone in your position could will the same." The deeper reason for this view is Kant's subjectivistic interpretation of *a priori* knowledge. If the *a priori* orginates in an activity of the mind primarily in accordance with the law of synthesis and is not recognized as a datum even to intuition, then of course the conclusion is inevitable that any individual can perform this activity only for himself and that the *a priori* is necessarily self-acquired knowledge.

Kant refers to his doctrine frequently as the ethics of intention. He carefully distinguishes purpose and intention and holds that an action does not have its moral value in the purpose which has to be achieved through it but in the intention by which it is determined. The moral principle does not concern the material of the action and its intended result but the form and the principle from which it results. What is essentially good in it consists in the intention, be the result what it may. Moreover, Kant holds that all material ends of action originate in our sensory state of pleasure. Pleasure is the agreement of an object or an action with the condition of life, that is, it is either the result of some action upon the world or the result of the stimulus emanating from the world.

This involves, according to Kant, the view that only a formal ethics can be an ethics of success, which makes the value of the person and his moral conduct dependent upon the practical consequences brought about by his action within the real world. Moreover, one of Kant's most fundamental doctrines is the proposition that any material ethics must also be an eudaemonistic one, which either considers pleasure as the *summum bonum* or at least refers the values of good and evil in one way or another to pleasure or displeasure. Although Scheler agrees that the results of a moral action are entirely irrelevant to the moral values of persons and acts and that intentions and not purposes are the original carriers of good and evil, he contests Kant's thesis that any material ethics must needs be an ethics of success. To Kant, intention is the mere form of the projecting of a purpose (*Form der Setzung einer Absicht*). Scheler, however, maintains that intentions are more than a mere modality or form of striving. Any intention is directed toward well-determined pregiven positive or negative values; it thus determines the material *a priori* scope (*Spielraum*) for the formation of possible purposes and actions. A material specification of intention is possible without replacing the ethics of intention by an ethics of success. Kant denies this possibility because he holds erroneously that everything which transcends intention is subject to the mere mechanism of nature which rules also in the psychological realm. Scheler shares likewise Kant's rejection of eudaemonism, though not his argumentation which is based on unclarified views of the nature of emotional life, of the essence of values, and of their interrelationship. According to Kant, striving is always striving for pleasure without taking the moral law as a yardstick for our volitions. That is why he considers the eudaemonistic postulate, to strive for pleasure, as meaningless; every human being does this by his very nature. Yet Kant fails to distinguish as to quality and depth between sensual pleasure, joy, happiness and bliss. Since he defines as good that which can be commanded and as evil that which can be prohibited, love cannot have moral value because it cannot be commanded. The only feeling which according to Kant is not derived from sensual pleasure is respect for the moral law. It is a spiritual feeling originated by the moral law itself. This is obviously the meaning of his famous postulate of rigorism: that conduct, in order to have moral value, should be performed not only *as* duty requires but also *because* duty requires, that is, out of respect for the moral law. But if Kant means that we have to respect a law just because it is a law, then the question arises: Why does not any natural law have a similar claim to respect? If, however, Kant means that it is the law of the good, namely the law of moral values which has to be respected, then it is impossible to derive the idea of the good from a law and then to demand respect for it. It is only possible to have respect for an imperative if in addition to the judgment relating to the content of the command the value, the realization of which is commanded, is also given to our feeling.

Scheler criticizes seriously Kant's idea of the person and of his autonomy and freedom. Formal ethics first identifies person with reasonable person. It is not initially demonstrated what the essential nature of the person is and what constitutes his particular unity and then shown that reasonable activity belongs to his essence. Kant saves the idea of the person as something which surpasses the X of the reasonable will by identifying this X with the "homo noumenon" and by opposing to him the "homo phenomenon." Yet this homo noumenon is logically nothing else but a term for the absolutely unknowable constant of being called the thing-in-itself as applied to the idea of man. Yet the same unknowable constant also refers, without any other possibility of differentiation, to each plant and each stone. How then could this notion give man a dignity which would differ from the dignity of objects? It could be answered that man is free. But the famous first antimony of the *Critique of Pure Reason* has merely shown the logico-theoretical possibility of freedom for the sphere of the "thing-in-itself." Yet, for example, that not a stone as a thing-in-itself but man is free becomes evident only by the moral law as a categorical : thou shalt, that is, by the postulate that man can do something because he knows that he ought to do it. This is so because man's knowledge of the unconditioned practical starts not from the experience of freedom but from insight into the practical law. We are never permitted first to ask the question "What is within our power?" in order to find out what we should do; on the contrary, we first have to listen to the voice of reason which engages us categorically to an activity, and then only by way of a postulate do we come to the conclusion that we can do what we should. There is thus a basic antinomy in the Kantian notion of freedom: freedom in the positive sense as a postulate coincides with the lawfulness of volition; freedom in the negative sense as a mere possibility is freedom for good as well as for evil; and it is, as such, merely a presupposition for the moral relevancy of any activity whatsoever. Here Kant's doctrine of moral autonomy tries to overcome this dilemma. Man gives the law to himself. But, on the one hand, Kant interprets autonomy of the person, without distinguishing between the autonomy of moral insight into good and evil (as opposed to blind will) and the autonomy of the moral will (as opposed to volitions imposed by heteronomy); and on the other hand, he refers the meaning of good and evil to a normative law given by the reasonable person to himself (the "self-legislation of reason"). To Scheler, fully adequate autonomous insight into the good entails necessarily the autonomous willing of that which had been recognized as good, whereas the autonomous willing of the good does not imply immediate insight into the good intended by this volition. An interpretation of autonomy such as Kant's would exclude any autonomous obedience to the command of another person or of God. All forms of obeying could be of a heteronomous nature. But he who obeys does not will what the other wills because he wills it. Morally valuable obedience might originate in the insight that the other person in his individual being surpasses us in moral excellency. Kant's concept of autonomy would make impossible any moral education and instruction as well as the following of the good example given by the moral genius. Indeed, Kant states occasionally that examples serve merely the purpose of encouragement by demonstrating that the commands of the moral law can be carried out.

As an antithesis to this system Scheler builds his own ethical doctrine and calls his point of view "ethical absolutism and objectivism." In another sense, he states, it might be called emotional intuitivism and material apriorism, and it might finally be interpreted as a newly attempted personalism, since one of his outstanding theses is the subordination of all values to the personal value. We now have to examine in detail Scheler's main doctrines, starting with his theories of values and their order.

II. SCHELER'S ETHICS

A. Values as Intentional Objects of Feelings

Husserl has shown that there are ideal objects of knowledge which are as independent of the knowing subject as real objects are. Scheler accepts this thesis and uses this insight for the disclosure of the realm of values. Values are to him a particular class of ideal objects which are objective, eternal, and immutable. They are given to us as intentional objects of our feelings (*intentionale Gegenstände des Fühlens*), as colors are given to us in and through visual perception. The mode in which values are knowable to us is beyond the grasp of the intellect, which is as blind to them as the ear is to color. The emotional aspects of the mind – feeling, preferring, loving, hating, willing – are not founded upon cognition, but are of an aprioristic character. In our emotional feeling we feel something, namely, this or that particular value-quality. Intentional feeling-functions do not need the intermediary of the so-called objectifying acts of representing, judging, etc., in order to come into immediate contact with their objects.

Values are independent of our subjective emotional states. If I am sad, the sadness I feel may evoke in me various subjective sentiments. I may be heartbroken or composed, defiant, etc. The feeling of sadness remains, while my subjective emotional state changes. Moreover, the causes or motives of a feeling must not be confused with its intentional object. The question: Why am I angry and what makes me angry? is entirely different from the question: What do I feel? Finally, values are also independent of things and relations of all kind which are their carriers, the so-called "goods." For the value-qualities themselves do not change if the goods which are their carriers change. As the color red does not become blue if a red litmus paper turns blue, so the value of friendship remains unchanged if a friend proves to be false and betrays me. Goods are units of value-qualities: through their mediation values become objectified and elements of the real world. This proves the correctness of Kant's view that a philosophical theory of values, such as ethics or aesthetics, must not presuppose goods or things. It also proves, however, that it is possible to discover the realm of concrete values in an aprioristic way and that this knowledge is by no means derived from our experience of goods.

In order to determine the nature of value-feeling Scheler analyzes human conduct and distinguishes between striving (*Streben*), value, purpose (*Zweck*), and end (*Ziel*). The purpose formalistically considered is the "content" of a possible thinking, representing, perceiving, which content is given as something to be realized, regardless of how and by whom. Whatever bears the logical relation of a condition or of a cause of the realization of a purpose is in a formal sense a means for that purpose. Wherever we speak of a volitional purpose we have in view a particular application of the idea of purpose, namely, that a represented particular content should be made a purpose to be realized by our will.

Not every striving is purposeful. There is first the phenomenon that something "soars up" within us without a purpose or even without an end; or our striving is a mere tendency "away from something," but without any direction. Another type or striving is directed toward something, but even this type is not necessarily purposeful: the direction need not be determined by a particular image or meaning-content; nevertheless, it is directed toward a *value* as the end of the striving. We therefore have to distinguish carefully between the *end of a striving* and the *purpose of a volition*. The point is that the end of a striving is experienced by and in the course of the striving itself and is not conditioned by an act of representing, whereas the purpose of a volition is always a represented content to be realized by our will. The end, however, is immanent to our representing. And even in the case of a striving toward an end, an "aiming at," we can clearly distinguish two components: that of the image, and that of the value aimed at, the former being founded upon the latter. It is thus clear that ends, and therewith values, can be given without purposes, but that all purposes are founded upon pre-given ends and their value-components. This is so because all volitional purposes refer to the representation of the content of an end of striving given to us as something which ought to be realized by our will.

The preceding analysis requires two important implementations. First, the fact that any aim of striving contains a value component does not imply that values are experienced merely in acts of striving. On the contrary, we may feel values without aiming at or striving toward them and *a fortiori* without making them the purpose of our volition. This holds especially for acts of loving and hating, which, according to Scheler, are of an aprioristic nature and, even more, are at the foundation of all the other apriorisms – of knowledge as well as of volition.

The clarification of the relationship between drives and inclinations, values aimed at, purposes of volition, and the success of action requires an analysis of the complicated structure called "action." Scheler distinguishes: (1) the "situation" or the world of practical objects, of valuable things or goods, which are elements of the present environment or milieu of the acting subject and become objects of his action; as objects of resistance they determine as such the sphere within which our volitions can be realized; (2) the content realized by the action; (3) the willing of this content on its various levels: from intention through purpose, deliberation, and project, to decision; (4) the willing of the action itself, for example, in the case of outer action, the innervation of the members of the body; (5) the various states of feelings and the sensations connected therewith; (6) the experiencing of the realization of the action, the execution; (7) the state of affairs and the feelings brought about by the content once realized. Whereas the phases (1)–(6) belong to the experiencing of action itself, phase (7) as a causal effect of the action is not experienced in its performing, but merely (anticipatorily or retrospectively) inferred from the assumption that the content of the action has been realized. Thus, the causal consequences of action have to be distinguished from action itself. Only action in all of its phases but never its causal consequences – its success – can be the carrier of moral values.

The analysis of striving and volition, of ends and purpose, of values and action leads to conclusions of fundamental importance with respect to Scheler's theory of ethics: (1) contrary to Kant's position, the rejection of an ethics of purposes does not imply the rejection of concrete values, which are already given in the end of any striving; (2) an ethics of material values does not, as Kant believed, necessarily presuppose empirical knowledge of the image-contents which are determined by the underlying ends of striving and their value components; (3) the Kantian identification of the aprioristic with the rational and of the material with the sensual (and therefore the aposterioristic) is untenable. The dichotomy that a factor of knowledge must be either a sensuous content or something "thought of" is by no means exhaustive. The emotional life also has its original aprioristic content, which is accessible to our eidetic intuition and which makes possible a phenomenology of the emotional life, and thereby a phenomenology of values.

B. The Realm of Values

Scheler's next task is to outline the aprioristic structure of the realm of values. He develops first certain formal principles of a pure axiology valid for all kinds of values, independent of the nature of their carriers. These relations are aprioristic because they are founded in the nature of values as such.

The first essential feature is that all values are either positive or negative (beautiful-ugly, good-evil, etc.). There are, moreover, certain axioms already discovered by Franz Brentano: the existence of a positive value is itself a positive value and so is the non-existence of a negative one. The non-existence of a positive value is itself a negative value and so is the existence of a negative one. Furthermore, there are certain axiological principles of evaluation, such as the impossibility of evaluating the same value simultaneously as both positive and negative. Another group of propositions of pure formal axiology refers to values within the volitional sphere, that is, the aprioristic relations between values and the ought. These will be discussed later on.

Still another group of aprioristic relations, and one of particular importance to Scheler, refers to the hierarchical order of values. It is Scheler's thesis that the whole realm of values is graded in an order of ranks in terms of which the values stand to one another in the relation of "higher" and "lower." According to him this gradation of rank is inseparable from the essence of values; it is self-existent and absolute to the extent that it is immutable and entirely independent of the historically or individually variable notions of the gradation. (The problem of the relativism or perspectivism of human notions of values will be discussed separately below.) Like the values themselves, so also their eternal order is knowable to us in a particular act of feeling, without any interference on the part of the intellect. Scheler assumes, following Pascal, an inborn aprioristic *ordre du cœur* or *logique du cœur* which has its own reasons.

The particular act of feeling by which the height of a value is revealed is the act of preferring. Preferring is an act of the emotional and intentional life on a higher level than the emotional functions by which the values are revealed. It is founded upon these functions of the lower level. Preferring is neither striving nor choosing; it refers to the felt relations among values which may or may not be the end of a striving, whereas choosing is always choosing among goods and as such an act of the will. Nor is preferring an act of judging values; it is an immediate feeling of the relations prevailing among them. It is also not a prerequisite of preferring that a plurality of values is explicitly given to the feeling. The awareness of the existence of a value higher than that given in the feeling might be an element of the act of preferring, although the higher value referred to is not itself felt.

According to Scheler, two different aprioristic orders of rank of values can be ascertained. The first – the formal one – orders the height of values in accordance with their carriers. We refrain from giving an account of Scheler's rather sketchy scheme and quote as examples that personal values have a higher rank than values of which goods are the carriers, and that values of which intentions or actions are the carriers have a higher rank than those measured in terms of success (the latter not being moral values at all). More important by far is the second – the material – aprioristic order, which Scheler calls that of the "modes" of values.

In this order the lower value is founded upon the higher one, that is, the lower can exist only in so far as the higher already exists. In other words, the higher value is the axiological condition of the lower one. This holds good for the gradation of the values belonging to the same mode as well as for the gradation of the order of rank of modes, which, ascending from the lowest to the highest, is as follows:

1. The values revealed by sensory feelings, that is, the agreeable and the disagreeable. They are relative to the sensory nature of an organism, but not necessarily to a particular organizational form thereof, for example, that of human nature. Animals, too, are capable of these feelings.

2. The values revealed by the class of vital feelings: the values of the noble and the vulgar and, connected therewith, the feelings of health and sickness, of vigor and weakness, of age and death; moreover, courage, anxiety, anger, etc. This class of modes can not be reduced to the first one, which irreducibility in itself excludes any hedonistic or utilitarian interpretation.

3. The class of spiritual values, which are completely independent of the sphere of bodily and environmental existence. To these values belong a) the aesthetic ones of beautiful and ugly; b) the juridical ones of just and unjust; c) the value of pure knowledge of the truth as aimed at by philosophy proper. (Truth itself is according to Scheler not a value but an independent idea of a particular type.) The feelings correlated with these values are, for example, spiritual joy and sadness, approval and disapproval, respect and disrespect, contempt and spiritual sympathy.

4. The values of the holy and the unholy, which are distinguished from those of the preceding class by the fact that they refer to "absolute objects," regardless of which things, forces, persons or institutions have been considered by various cultures at different periods as absolute objects. The feelings correlated with this class are those of bliss and despair, of faith and disbelief, of awe, worship, etc. They are objectified in the forms of cults, sacraments, and the manifold symbols related to the Absolute.

Scheler was fully aware that his discovery of the modes of values and their rank was decisive not only for his theory of ethics, but for the whole of his philosophical thinking. It motivates his further researches and finds its counterpart in his doctrines of the forms of knowing (briefly outlined in the first section of this paper), of the *"ordo amoris"* or forms of love, of the structure of human nature, and finally of the relationship between the vital forces of the socio-cultural life. Yet to elaborate upon these relations would go far beyond the frame of the present paper.

C. Moral Values and the Ought

It is striking that the aforementioned four classes of modes of value do not include the moral ones of good and evil. These values are, according to Scheler, indeed situated beyond and outside the four classes of modes. This is so because the values of good and evil refer to the bringing of the other values into existence. Scheler agrees with Kant's thesis that the material content of the will can never be good or evil. The material of any volition is always and necessarily a non-moral value. The moral qualities, as Scheler expresses it, are borne, as it were, on the "back of the deed," but do not appear in the goals it aims at. Nevertheless Scheler maintains, in opposition to Kant, that good and evil are material values and as such are objects of the intentionality of feelings. The will to realize a positive value is good; the will to realize a negative one an evil. Or more precisely: "good" is the will to realize the higher or the supreme value, and "evil" to realize the lower one. The possible moral value of the volition depends, therefore, upon the insight into the values related to choice and upon the insight into the order of preference.

This is one of the reasons why Scheler rejects Kant's doctrine that all moral conduct is based on duty. It is one of Scheler's main theses that any ought-to-be is founded upon a value, and not the other way around. This does not imply that the founding positive value has to be in actual existence. As we have seen, values are to Scheler ideal objects and as such entirely independent of the real existence of their carriers. We have to distinguish the ideal ought-to-be (*ideales Sollen*) from the imperative obligation of the ought-to-be (*Pflichtsollen oder Norm*). The former is founded upon insight into the founding value. The ideal ought-to-be does not create values, but presupposes them. It postulates axiomatically that the existence of the founding positive value ought to be and that the existence of the founding negative value ought not to be. It supposes, thus, the non-existence of the positive value upon which it is founded. The ideal ought-to-be is as such independent of any volition. It generates, however, the ought-to-do, that is, the imperative in any form – such as the command, the advice, the recommendation, the mere suggestion – which refers to a potential volition aiming at the realization of the ideal value content. The normative ought-to-do, like the ideal ought-to-be, not only presupposes the non-existence of a positive value, but in addition presupposes a tendency of the subject to be opposed to this realization. The imperative is first of all directed towards the suppression of this opposing tendency and sometimes even, in addition, to the suppression of an existing negative value. The normative ought-to-do has, thus, a double negative character, which is inherent in any ethics based on duty. Such an ethics misunderstands the irreversible process involved in the fact that knowledge of values generates the ideal ought-to-be and the latter in turn the normative ought-to-do.

D. The Relativity of Experience of Norms

The normative ought-to-do changes from group to group and from one historical period to the other. How is this fact compatible with the assumed objectivity and immutablilty of eternal values and their aprioristic order? Scheler deals at length with this objection. Not the existence of values, but their perceptibility, is relative. The erroneous doctrine of the historical and sociological changeableness of the values themselves originates either in a confusion of the carriers of values (the valuable goods or action units) with the values themselves; or in an erroneous inference from the changes of norms to the changes of values; or in an equally erroneous inference from the lack of generality to a lack of objectivity and intelligibility of the values; or finally, in a confusion of the relativity of value judgments with the absolute existence of values.

This is a special case of a general phenomenon, which Scheler calls the "functionalization of eidetic knowledge." We have to distinguish between eidetic intuition of the essences as such, and the perceiving or judging of contingent matters of fact under the guidance of previously acquired eidetic knowledge. In the latter case, eidetic knowledge is not grasped as such, but functions merely as a selector of those elements of the contingent world of matters of fact which stand to the pregiven eidos and its structure in a relation of fulfillment or confirmation. By this process of functionalization eidetic knowledge becomes a law of mere application of the human understanding, which being directed toward contingent facts, analyzes, interprets, and judges them as "determined in accordance with the eidetic context." Thus the original *a priori* of being turns into a subjective *a priori* in the "transcendental" sense of Kant. His laws of experiencing, which are at the same time also laws of the objects of experience, are, therefore, not originally given, but merely derived. The particular function of this subjective *a priori* is, however, not that of a connector, but of a selector. It does not consist in a synthesizing or constructing but, on the contrary, in a negating, suppressing, or disregarding of all those sectors and aspects of the accessible world of matters of fact which are unrelated to the pregiven eidos.

It is obviously Scheler's view that this selection is conditioned in a twofold manner: first, by the preacquired eidetic knowledge; secondly, by the accessible sector of the empirical, and as such prestructurized world of contingent matters of fact from which certain forms and "Gestalts" are selected. Now, the world of matters of fact is accessible in a different way to various subjects (individuals, peoples, races, cultures, etc.) at various points in their history. And also the order of selecting varies, since it depends upon the possible stock of eidetic knowledge handed down by tradition. Reason itself as the sum-total of these functional laws of selection is in a continuous process of becoming and growing. Thus, the possible knowledge of the realm of essences depends, notwithstanding their apriority and indestructibility, upon the contingent facts of the environmental situation of the subject. It follows, first, that at no time of its historical existence can any individual or group have a total knowledge of the realm of essences; second, that each perspective in which this realm is disclosed to each subject at any moment of its history is unique and irreplaceable; third, that only the cooperation of mankind, as a whole, of all coexisting individuals and groups and also of all succeeding ones which are unified by a common tradition, guarantees the growth of aprioristic eidetic knowledge.

The dimensions of the relativity of value-judgments, especially of ethical judgments, are carefully analyzed by Scheler in his main work. In order to study historically the facts of morals prevailing among various nations or other groups, we have to distinguish first the variations in morals proper, second the varying intellectual insight into the inner and outer causal connections of things and events, and, third, all features of the technique of action peculiar to the compared social groups. Only a reduction of the groups under comparison to the same level of intellectual and technical equipment permits an analysis of their relationship to values. It is quite possible for a highly differentiated intellectual culture to be combined with considerable primitivism of moral feelings, and vice versa. By the removal of these masks which hide the sphere of morals as historically given the problem of the various dimensions of relativity becomes visible. Scheler distinguishes five main levels:

(1) Variations in feelings and therewith in knowledge of values as well as variations in the structure of preferring and of love and hatred. Scheler calls variations of this kind those of the *ethos*.

(2) Variations referring to the acts of judging the values and the order of rank and to the rules governing such judging. These are variations of *ethics* in the broadest sense.

(3) Variations on the types of institutions, goods, and actions which function as factual units because they are founded upon specific units of values. Examples are "marriage," "murder," "theft," etc. Such values are founded upon the existence of a pregiven positive or negative value. Murder, for example, presupposes the destruction of the existence of a person as the carrier of personal values, but not all forms of killing a man are considered uniformly as murder. Variations of this type are those of *morals*.

(4) Variations in the evaluations of the practical conduct of men based on norms pertaining to the order of rank accepted by *them* and corresponding to *their* structure of preferences. The

value of such practical conduct depends entirely upon the prevailing ethos. Variations of this type are those of practical *morality*.

(5) Variations in forms of action and expression within the realm of customs and usage. These are variations of the *mores*.

None of these variations implies, however, a relativity of moral values themselves and their order of rank. The mere experience of the cosmos of values and its adequacy depends upon the perspective at the socio-historical vantage point. Scheler contends that an absolute ethics of material values alone, if correctly understood, postulates the emotional value-perspectivism of historical and sociological units, as well as the essential incompleteness of the ethos on any level of its formation, whereas so-called ethical relativism degrades the ethical values to mere symbols of the historically prevailing value judgments.

E. The Person

Moral values, as we have seen, refer to the realization of the existence of other values and therewith to the performers of the realizing acts, the persons, who are also the addressees of the ought-to-do. Thus, the carriers of the values of good and evil are primarily persons. Moral values are personal values. Only secondarily can the ability of a person to realize higher values be considered as the carrier of moral values. A person experiences his ability to perform what he ought to do as his virtues, and his resistance to it, in spite of his abilities, as his vices. In the third place, the acts of the persons themselves – among them those of volition and action but also acts such as forgiving, commanding, obeying, promising – are carriers of moral values. It is, however, the notion of the Person which stands at the center of ethical theory.

Scheler's main work on ethics has the subtitle "A New Attempt at the Foundation of an Ethical Personalism," and indeed more than one third of its six hundred pages is dedicated to an exhaustive analysis of the notion of the Person. It might be stated that this notion dominates the whole thought of Scheler, his theory of intersubjectivity and the nature of sympathy, his philosophy of religion, and his philosophical anthropology.

Person, it has been said, is the center of activity, correlated to the level of Mind and Spirit, and it must be distinguished from the other centers of vitality. Mind is pure actuality, and Person is nothing else but a self-constituted integration of acts. It is not an empty starting point of acts, but it exists and lives only in the fulfillment of intentional acts. Thus, Person and act belong indissolubly together. The full and adequate essence of any act involves its reference to the unity of these acts, which is the Person. The notion of an isolated act is a psychological abstraction.

In each of its concrete acts the whole Person is involved; it varies as a whole in and by each act, but without coinciding with any of them. Each of these acts is permeated by the individuality of the Person living in it.

According to Scheler, Mind and its correlate, Person, are principally not objectifiable. In the same way in which an act is never given to our outer or inner experience as an object and can only be experienced by performing it, so the Person, as the correlate of different forms and categories of acts, manifests itself exclusively by performing the acts in which it lives and by which it experiences itself. Or, as far as other persons are concerned, they can be experienced by co-performance, re-performance, or pre-performance of the other person's acts, but all this without objectifying the other person.

Scheler distinguishes sharply between the Person and the I. The I – in contradistinction to the Person – is not merely objectifiable but always an object. And again, there has to be a distinction between the I as the correlate of the experiencing – experienced life (*Erlebnis-Ich*) – and the inner awareness of the body as my body (*Leib-Ich*). The inner awareness of the body is neither identical with the outer perception of this body nor with the mere coenesthesis. Scheler distinguishes between the acts which emanate from the Person and mere "functions," such as seeing, hearing, tasting, bodily feelings, all kinds of attention, etc., which belong to the I. The functions presuppose a body, and the correlate of the body is the environment (*Umwelt*). Acts originating in the Person, however, are psychophysically indifferent; they have as their correlate not the environment but the world. Again one must distinguish between the experiences of the stages of the body and the psychological states of the I. There is no continuum with gradual transition from the sensation of hunger to that of colors.

Scheler elaborates the structure of bodily experiences and the phenomena within the sphere of the I in careful analyses. He formulates what he calls the aprioristic material principles of a descriptive psychology. He describes association and dissociation as functions of the body and the sense organs, the interpenetration (*das Ineinander*) of the experiences of the I over against the disconnectedness (*das Auseinander*) of the bodily phenomena, the time structure of the experiences in terms of recollections and anticipations, the experiences of reality and the various forms of causality, of similarity and dissimilarity, the principles of assimilation in their various modes, etc.

Space does not permit the presentation in detail of the wealth of these contributions to a phenomenological psychology of the I. We shall just mention briefly the role which the distinction between Person, I, and body plays in Scheler's theory of love as developed in *The Nature of Sympathy*. All acts, so Scheler points out, can be divided into vital acts of the body, purely mental acts of the I, and spiritual acts of the Person. Correspondingly, we also find love and hatred in three forms: spiritual love of the Person, mental love of the individual self, and vital or passionate love. These forms of emotional acts also have essential reference to particular kinds of values of knowledge and beauty (cultural values); and spiritual acts to the value of the holy. But to love a fellow-man, who is a Person, means to love him as an autonomous human being who is different from myself. The values attached to the physical, the corporeal, and the mental can always be given to us objectively. The ultimate value of the personality, however, is disclosed to us only when we associate ourselves with the other person's own acts of love. We must love what he loves and love it with him.

The same distinction is of basic importance for Scheler's "perceptual theory of other minds." We may have knowledge of other human subjects on the level of vital consciousness, or of the Other's I on the level of the mind, or of the Other's spiritual person. The Person, incapable of being treated as an object, is accessible only by participation or reproduction of his acts in thought, volition, or feeling. In order to perceive the I of the Other in the Other's body, we do not need any process of inference from the perception of the Other's body. Our immediate perceptions of our fellow-men do not relate to their bodies, nor to their I's or souls. What we perceive are integral wholes whose intuitive content is not immediately resolved in terms of internal or external perception. The Other's body and gestures show the structure of a physiognomical unit. The only category of the Other's experience which cannot be caught by direct perception is his experience of his own body, its organs, and the sensory feelings attached to them. It is exactly these bodily feelings that constitute the separation between man and fellow-man. Insofar as man lives only within his bodily feelings, he does not find any approach to the mental life of his fellow-man. Only if he surmounts this and clears his mental life of the ever-present sensory accompaniments, does the mental life of the Other become perceptible to him. And only then, by co-performing, pre-performing, or re-performing the Other's acts, does he participate as a Person in the other Person's spiritual life.

Thus, the Person and its manifestations are not open to perception in the same sense as are the objects of Nature. Nature can not conceal itself, and neither can man insofar as his animate existence belongs to Nature. It is necessarily open to discovery, since animate existence manifests itself – at least in principle – in physiological bodily processes. But it is within the free will of the Person to disclose or conceal its acts, or to keep silent, and this is quite another thing than merely not speaking.

This last statement becomes of particular importance for Scheler's philosophy of religion. God is a Person, and it is inconceivable that there should be objective knowledge of Him. If He chooses to be silent, we can not know Him directly. He remains, then, the *deus absconditus*. Only if He reveals Himself to us, can we know him directly as a Person by the intentionality of the specific religious act, which itself is an act of love characterized by the participation of the religious person in the infinite love of God: to think, to will, to love in God – *amare mundum in deo, amare deum in deo* – this is the co-performance of man of the spiritual acts of God whose supreme manifestation is love. If God is not directly experienced by the religious act, He is not experienced as a Person but merely conceived as the absolute *ens a se* of metaphysics. To be sure, metaphysics and religion are not in contradiction but form together a system of conformity. If God is experienced as a Person, then moral goodness is an essential predicate of His personal quality. The alternative of the Kantian notion of an autonomous moral law (which leads to the logical postulate of the existence of God) and the heteronomous interpretation (according to which the moral will is exclusively determined by fear of punishment and hope of reward) is false. If there is a personal God, then neither autonomy nor heteronomy, but theonomy guarantees the coincidence of the religious and the ethical axiomatic of values. Thus, God and man are related by the same moral principles which originate in the essence of the divine. On the highest level, religiosity and morality are essentially interdependent, although not identical. They become seemingly independent of one another if either morality or religiosity or both are experienced on a level of imperfection.

This relationship between religious and ethical interdependence also becomes manifest in the relationship between the individual and the community. What is of moral value is not an isolated person but the Person which feels itself genuinely related with God and which is in loving solidarity united with the totality of humanity and the spiritual world. At the center of Scheler's ethics is the principle of the solidarity of all moral beings. It implies that, with regard to their respective moral values, each is co-responsible for each and for all. This is so because the ultimate moral value of the personality is disclosed to the individual only if he associates himself with the other person's own acts of love. All love evokes a loving response and thereby brings a new moral value into being. This doctrine of moral solidarity is founded on two eidetic principles: (1) It belongs essentially to the eidos of a Person to stand in community with other Persons. The possible structural units of value and meaning of such a community are aprioristic, that is, independent of the empirical real connection which might prevail among particular persons and their contingent causes. (2) All forms of morally relevant conduct are essentially mutual and of corresponding value. This mutuality is independent of the contingent reality of these acts, the particular persons involved, and the mechanisms underlying such mutuality. It is in the nature of love, esteem, promising, commending to presuppose as ideal correlates the partner's reciprocal attitude.

It is the task of a philosophical sociology to develop a typology of the forms of being-together and living-together characteristic of the constitution of the various social units, and to determine their order of rank. In his ethics Scheler has tried to outline certain principles of such a philosophical sociology. It is obvious, however, that in his later works of mainly sociological content he has rejected or at least considerably modified his earlier theories. We have to reserve the presentation of Scheler's sociology for another occasion. Such a presentation would require also a discussion of the changes which occurred in Scheler's thinking after his religious crisis and which affected both his gnosiological and ethical position. With respect to the former, Scheler developed in outline a new ontology and philosophical anthropology; as to the latter, Scheler transformed his theory of perspectivism of values into a new and highly original approach to a sociology of knowledge.

ALFRED SCHUTZ

COLLECTED PAPERS

Contents of Volume I

THE PROBLEM OF SOCIAL REALITY

Preface by H. L. Van Breda

Editor's Note

Introduction by Maurice Natanson

PART II   / Phenomenology and the Social Sciences

Contents of Volume II

STUDIES IN SOCIAL THEORY

Contents of Volume III

INDEX